BARBED CIRCLES

Barbed Circles

The Perfect Score

A True Story

By

Cornel Vena

iUniverse, Inc.
Bloomington

Barbed Circles
The Perfect Score

All the events described in this book have actually taken place.
However, to protect the identity of some names mentioned, only initials have been used. Any similarity with real names are only coincidental and should be ignored.

iUniverse books may be ordered through booksellers or by contacting:

iUniverse
1663 Liberty Drive
Bloomington, IN 47403
www.iuniverse.com
1-800-Authors (1-800-288-4677)

ISBN: 978-1-4620-3319-5 (sc)
ISBN: 978-1-4620-3321-8 (hc)
ISBN: 978-1-4620-3320-1 (ebk)

Printed in the United States of America

iUniverse rev. date: 09/22/2011

CONTENTS

To my beautiful wife Paula, my gorgeous daughters Christy and Shari, and to my lovely granddaughter Hayley, for allowing me in their lives.

To my beloved Romanian family, my father Marin, my mother Zina and brother Alexandru. Forgive me for abandoning you.

I shall never do that again.

A special thank you to:

Aristide Galimir my fencing coach, Colonel Zidaru my horse riding coach, and to my Head Coach, Captain Ion Muresanu, who has taught me how to work hard, fight, and never to give up.

Cornel Vena 29th August 2010.

"There are but few moments when we can touch for a short instance greatness and feel the presence of the real creator, when we are once again in the realm of miracles;
We shall treasure and guard these seconds to last us for eternity, or until we are graced once again and allowed to touch immortality.

Cornel Vena,
15 May 1999.

WORLD'S LONGEST RECORD IN THE MODERN OLYMPIC GAMES. MELBOURNE 1956 TO LONDON 2012.

1,111 Points obtained by Cornel Vena of ROMANIA in the Fencing event of the MODERN PENTATHLON COMPETITION.

In 1956, Romanian Team of Modern Pentathlon competed for the first time in Melbourne. The Team was made of: Cornel Vena, Victor Teodorescu and Dumitru Tintea with Manciu Viorel as the team reserve.

The team has been formed in late 1953, members been selected through a national Triathlon Competition held in Bucharest, and won by Cornel Vena.

In charge of the team was Captain Ion Muresanu.

Without international competition experience, the Romanian Team finished on the 6th place and individually Cornel Vena finished 14th, Dumitru Tintea 20th, and Victor Teodorescu 30th.

Remarkably, in the fencing event, Cornel Vena won 29 bouts of the 35 matches and was <u>awarded a total of 1,111 competition points</u>.

This result has not been equaled or beaten since 1956 and remains the longest record in the history of the Modern Olympic Games.

MODERN PENTATHLON OLYMPIC FENCING RESULTS 1956-2012

No.	YEAR	PLACE	WINNER	COUNTRY	No. Competitors	Points
XVI	1956	Melbourne	Cornel Vena	ROM	36	1,111
XVII	1960	ROME	Imre Nagy	HUN	58	1,000
XVIII	1964	TOKIO	Ferenk Torok	HUN	37	1,000
XIX	1968	MEXICO	Istvan Molna			
			@Ferenk Torok	HUN	47	1,046
XX	1972	Munich	Boris Onischenko	RUS	59	1,076 (rigged epee)
XXI	1976	Montreal	Paul Ledniev	RUS	46	1,096
XXII	1980	Moscow	Lazlo Horvath	HUN	43	1,052
XXIII	1984	Los Angeles	Achim Bellmann	GER	52	1,066
XXIV	1988	Seoul	Fabian Lazlo	HUN	63	1,051
XXV	1992	Barcelona	Fabian Lazlo	HUN	66	1,034
XXVI	1996	Atlanta	Alexandru Parygoin @Heorny Chymerys	KAZ UKR	24 24	1,000 1,000
XXVII	2000	Sydney	Oliver Clergeau	FRA	32	1,000
XXVIII	2004	Athens	Audrey Moiseev	RUS	32	1,000
XXIX	2008	Beijing	Audrey Moiseev @Znenzna Qian	RUS CHI	32 36	1,000 1,024
XXX	2012	London	?	?	?	?

PROLOGUE

On the 12 of December 1956, the Air India plane was ready to take off from Essendon airport in Melbourne. The Romanian Olympic Team was assembled on the tarmac, apart from four polo players, a journalist and radio announcer, the assistant coach from athletics and myself—Cornel Vena, Romanian Modern Pentathlon champion and captain of the Romanian Pentathlon Team. I had just finished competing in Melbourne in the 1956 Olympic Games.

I was told years later that my head coach, Ion Muresanu, pleaded with "tovarasul" D.S. the minister for sport in Romania in those days, to delay the departure of the huge plane, just in case I was trying to get to the airport but had been delayed . . .

However after some waiting the team was told to board the plane. Moments later the huge plane slowly left the Australian soil on its way to Romania.

This is the story of a chain of events which inexplicably and inescapably changed my life, to a point where even I look back in disbelief. Perhaps this story will help others realize how unpredictable and full of surprises life is, and that nobody can predict what will happen tomorrow, or what is the "right" path to take.

PART ONE

HOW IT ALL STARTED

After I finished High school in Turnu-Magurele, the boredom started to settle in. There I was, 18 years of age, full of ideas and energy, yet I was living in a small sleepy town in the southern part of Muntenia, a region of Romania. Back in those days young people did not have cars, TV, or much money. Even a push-bike was a rarity. Our main entertainment consisted of sport and a lots of outdoors activities. In the winter we did a lot of skiing and during summer we would walk from town through the vineyards and fields of maize, past the old Roman fort until we would suddenly come upon the banks of the river Danube.

It always gave me a real shock to walk through the ordinary fields and then suddenly to see appearing literally out of the ground, this immense body of water, slowly and majestically flowing between the banks of the two neighboring communist countries, Romania and Bulgaria. In those days, although both countries were dominated by the Russians and forced to embrace the communist regime, it was still considered to be a crime to attempt to cross the river to the other country without permission.

Myself, my cousin Cretu and few other members of our adventure-seeking group, took great pleasure in swimming across the Danube, some 800-1000m wide, and then allowing the current to carry us parallel to the Bulgarian river bank. Their border guards would start running trying to keep up with us, simultaneously taking their rifles and aiming at us, pretending that they were ready to shoot.

They did not shoot as long as we stayed at the regulation distance from their shore, about 50 meters away. In the meantime we would shout at the guards and taunt them . . .

"You are too stupid to know where the trigger is" or
"Be careful you may shoot your smelly toe off and smell to death!"
Occasionally the border guards would shoot a warning shot over our heads
just to remind us that they meant business.

After we had had our fun and started to get tired, we would start the
long swim back across the current, aiming to land on the Romanian soil
just below the small port and loading ramp. Usually by the time we were
back, it was already getting dark and we would walk in 3. silence the
dusty country road home. We weren't taught how to swim and my first
lesson consisted of my brother Sandu, picking me up unceremoniously
and throwing me in the water.

Although I felt as though I was fighting for my life and nearly lost
consciousness it was to no avail as Sandu kept telling me calmly to move
my arms and not to panic.

I survived swimming but there were many others who drowned whilst
crossing the Danube or were hit by the boats which navigated the very
busy river route, from Germany down to the Black Sea.

I was interested in flying and being a member of the local aero model
club, I managed to construct few strange looking models which more than
usual, after a short erratic flight ended nose first on the ground in a sad
heap of match sticks and paper. I could not foresee at that stage how my
life was going to be changed by this inoffensive hobby.

My aeromodelling activities came to fruition on the day our instructor
told us that the Romanian Aero-Club was to start a flying course for those
members who had demonstrated an interest in making models. There was
to be a written examination and a medical examination and because of
limited numbers available and the high cost (to be borne by the State),
only 10 students would be selected from our town.

I studied pretty hard, and when the results were posted I was pleased to
find that I had been selected to join the flying school. My parents did not
show great emotion when I told them excitedly that I was going to fly.

My mother, who had always dreamed that one day I would be a
practicing physician, was particularly distressed, and only bent a little
when I told her that this was just something to do whilst waiting for
the autumn university exams in Bucharest. Finally, loaded with food and
clean underwear, and after promising to write at every opportunity, I took

the rickety old train from Turnu-Magurele to Brasov, a beautiful locality in "Muntii Apuseni," in the northern part of Transylvanian region.

The flying school was a few kilometers from the township, surrounded by fields of wheat and corn and hills covered with fruit trees of all kinds.

It felt like an amphitheatre with the school's planes sitting in orderly formation in the middle of this natural stage, ready to commence the performance.

After the initial welcoming speech and introductions, we were divided in groups and allocated an instructor. Most of them were Ex-WW II pilots with many hours of flying over the Russian or German lines, and lots of good stories.

My instructor was Miss Veronica who had been a reconnaissance pilot during the war. She had to fly very low over the enemy lines, to avoid being hit by the ground fire or intercepted by air fighters to deliver messages from headquarters to the front line.

My initial fears about not having a male pilot (to make us work harder) were soon dispelled and she made me appreciate her experience in precision flying, teaching us to respect the machine and to be always one step ahead in a case of emergency.

Although the course only lasted three weeks, we had an excellent grounding in theory and practical flying, so that after 10-12 hours on double command, we were allowed to take off on our first "solo" flight.

I remember the day when Veronica said with a dry smile, "You're just about ready to be on your own"

"No," I heard myself saying, "I mean, do you think so?"

The smile disappeared and she sounded very calm and cool.

"Do you think we can afford to lose a plane worth thousands of lei? Beside you are doing fine and should have no problems . . . these planes almost fly by themselves."

"So it's all set," she continued. "You will go in the normal circuit after Sorin (best flyer in our group), and please concentrate on what you're doing; Don't let me down particularly today when Chief Instructor C.O. is coming to have a look to see how we are progressing.

"In regula? (OK?) "Yes", I said, suddenly not feeling too good.

The fields were asleep and covered with a soft blanket of morning fog, when the mechanics started to tow the planes out of the huge hangar in preparation for daily lessons. They made the required detailed check whilst the refuellers made sure that each plane had enough fuel for the day's flying.

Our group was chattering quietly and occasionally a short burst of laughter would punctuate someone's attempt to brave the tension which we all felt.

Strangely enough I wasn't concerned so much about the complex procedure which involves flying a plane, but more concerned in putting on a good display for our Miss Veronica. She was smartly dressed in long pants and a leather jacket and was talking quietly to our Chief Instructor, a highly decorated ex-war fighter. A few minutes later Veronica walked towards our group and spoke in a quiet voice addressing the group, but seeming to focus on me and Sorin.

"Today I want you all to forget about anything else apart from flying. If you are concentrating hard enough, there's no room for anything else in your mind. Flying is only a matter of following a set routine. If you follow the correct sequence, then everything else works like a Swiss clock, but if you become distracted, then you will start to have problems."

"Today we are going to have Sorin doing his third solo flight, then I will fly double command with Cornel, then he will go on his first solo flight. After that we will go through our normal daily lessons for the rest of the group. Good luck and good flying" she ended.

Then she walked closer to me, smiled, and spoke quietly almost in a whisper:

"Don't be nervous Cornel, just concentrate and do exactly the same as in your double command lessons. I know that you are ready and you will do well."

"Thank you Miss. I will do my best."

So the most anticipated, discussed and analyzed moment had arrived. There was no turning back and there was nobody in the cockpit to swiftly correct a wrong movement. It was entirely up to me. As I was standing on the side of the concrete strip, watching Sorin doing an impeccable take off, I remembered the day my brother Sandu decided that I was ready to ski down the old "jghiab" (funnel) used years ago to send tree trunks down from the top of the mountain, to the old sawmill in the valley.

We were then living in the old medieval city of Bistrita-Nasaud where we went skiing in the winter almost everyday, especially on weekends when we had time to go further afield.

On that particular day, we climbed high through the dense pine forest until we came to a clearing leading nowhere except for a small opening big enough to squeeze through.

"Well Cornel, what do you think? Do you want to go back the same way, which will take us hours, or should we try this way?"

Sandu grinned wickedly as he, pointed to the small opening.

By now we have been skiing for hours, I was tired and very hungry, and the prospect of having to wait for another couple of hours before eating and getting some dry clothes on, did not appeal at all. Of course my brother, who was four years older than me and a much better skier, neglected to tell me that this particular run was a very difficult and dangerous passage and we could finish being plastered against a tree.

This was nothing new, as our relationship was based on a continuous challenge, and I would have rather died than admit to Sandu that I was scared stiff and could not see myself going down that hole, not knowing how steep it was, how fast I was going to go, and in particular, where I was going to finish.

"Come on, make up your mind or it will get too dark to see the run", Sandu called out impatiently, perhaps getting a little edgy himself.

"You go ahead and I will follow you", I said, trying not to stutter. By now I was feeling weak at the knees and found it difficult to stop my heart from jumping out of my chest. Once again we both adjusted our simple, home made leather and rope bindings, and tightened our grip on the rough stocks with a nail stuck at the end.

"See you down there pustiule, (young, inexperienced youth)" and almost immediately Sandu disappeared through the hole and into the narrow channel down the mountain.

I waited for few seconds to have some room in case of a fall, then reluctantly I pushed myself forward with my stocks into the channel. I was expecting a gradual increase in my speed.

The next second I felt my skis sliding ahead from me, leaving me slightly behind. Everything was happening very quickly and I was fighting to keep my balance whilst controlling the direction of my skis, and trying to avoid low branches growing across the pass. The hardest thing was trying to steer and negotiate the turns particularly as there was very little room to move.

There was no room for error in this small "guttering" which was no wider than 900 mm, not unlike those bobsleigh tracks, except that in this situation there were all kinds of branches and old trunks partially exposed. The slope became more acute, my skies were vibrating and my eyes were filled with snow collected from low branches and tears caused by the cold air.

I knew that there was no escape, not enough room to make a plough or to break the speed, there was nothing else to do except stay on the skis and follow the path without hitting the wall of trees on either side of the path. I could see myself in hospital wrapped up in bandages, unable to ski for the rest of the winter. That would have been the worst penalty, skiing being my favorite sport.

Suddenly the tunnel opened up, and next I was flying across this open space covered with fresh snow. Before I had time to slow down I came to the end of this natural platform and became airborne.

Below me I could see young apple trees in orderly rows. Strangely enough I wasn't scared, just curious to see where I was going to land. Although we never measured the distance we jumped, I would be tempted to say that it must have been around 30-35m, which even in those days was a good jump.

I landed with a thud on top of a young tree which cushioned somewhat the initial impact, to be dropped in the deep snow, on top of my brother.

For few seconds there was a complete silence, then we both started to move checking to see if we were still in one piece.

To my relief I found my skis were unbroken, the only damage being a snapped wooden stock.

"I think I am O.K." I heard Sandu saying

"Are you all right"?

I could not answer, as I started to laugh uncontrollably so much so that tears started to pour down my cheeks.

Sandu took a good look at me and then realizing that I hadn't suffered any permanent damage, he started to have a good laugh himself.

After we cleaned ourselves and did some small repairs to our skis, we picked few of the frozen apples left on the trees from last autumn, and started on our way back to the distant town in the valley, where already the evening lights started to flicker and shine on the snow covered streets. In the clear sky above us, we could see beautiful stars and the shining Milky Way.

It felt so good to be alive, to know that I managed to conquer my fears, to know that what I did was better than anything else I have done before, and above all not to be hurt.

I looked at Sandu who was quietly making a path in the deep snow in front of me, leading the way home. I felt for the first time what it felt to have someone that cares about you. He did not challenge me, he showed me the way and helped me to break through my lack of confidence.

"You know" I said, "you could have killed us both".

"Ye" he said, but I didn't did I?"

Years later I finally understood how that frightening descent into the unknown is sometimes forced upon us, how in real life there are moments when we have to take decisions which we do not really like to take. But when we do things we don't think we are capable of, in some strange way, we discover that part of us which otherwise we never have the chance to understand.

Or perhaps we can plan and do things we feel comfortable doing, but only when we have to act outside our set perimeters, do we reach another dimension.

"Cornel, it's your turn to fly. Are you asleep or just dreaming?" said Miss Veronica shaking my shoulder. "Do you want to go on to your solo test today, because if you don't feel ready for it you could do it tomorrow"?

"Don't worry Miss." I said smiling and feeling ready to challenge the world.

"This is nothing, just don't ask me to put my skis on." I could see in her eyes a trace of doubt, perhaps I wasn't ready after all to go on my solo flight "It's alright Miss. just an old joke I use to make with my brother when I was ready to try something I don't fear anymore"

"Good luck Cornel. Don't let me down."

The 10 or so students were assigned to an instructor who then took us one by one in a tour of our school and the fields leading to the nearby village with the old gothic church at its centre. That morning I did the required circuit including the take-off and landing without any mistake, and passed my first solo flying test with top marks.

A few days went by after my solo flying test. Every day at the flying school was full of exciting events, everyone was telling incredible stories of the day's program, of experiencing advanced manoeuvres, of just being able to land without overshooting the landing strip or of a perfect landing when the plane slid over the concrete surface without as much as a bump.

I was enjoying flying so much that I had no time to think of anything else. I was the happiest I have ever been until then . . . flying was in my blood and it felt like I'd always been doing just that. Miss Veronica was happy to sit comfortably in her instructor's seat whilst I was taking off, taking position in our designated practice zone, and going through the various movements as required by our training program. It was only when a new movement had to be learnt that she would take over the dual commands and show me what was to be done.

Miss Veronica was a woman in her late thirties, well groomed and very much in control of her emotions. Many times when I almost hit the trees or forgot to pull the flaps before landing, she would always remain calm and she would coolly call out to me:

"What are the flaps for?" or "This is not a good idea to land directly in the hangar."

But even Miss Veronica had been affected by the time she spent in the war as a reconnaissance pilot. Although she never spoke much about her exploits during the war, I managed to find out from our chief mechanic, L.E., who knew all our instructors and their performance in the war. Apparently one of Miss Veronica's best friends was shot down during a night mission and when he tried to jump from the plane his parachute got caught in the seat, and he burned to death. This perhaps explained why Miss Veronica never wore a parachute in the plane even when we did advanced acrobatics. So every time before sitting down in my seat, I would imitate Miss Veronica and shove my parachute under the seat.

"If you fly your plane well" she would say thoughtfully, "you don't have to jump." Fortunately for the two of us, there was no need to leave the plane at any stage during the flying course, with or without a parachute.

NOT MY TURN

When you are young and lack the experience of life, you tend to listen to your parents and believe that by following their advice you should do well in life. For a long period of time I believed that if I worked wisely and diligently I could influence my future and achieve most things I thought were worthy of my efforts. Now in retrospect I realize how much of our future is already planned for us, and in most cases we end doing things we never intended to do in the first place.

Our training had come to the final stages, and we all had to have some experience in more advanced acrobatics.

Each instructor was keen to show his students his array of movements used for public displays or actions used during the war to escape or to attack enemy planes.

My first experience in low flying was part of our initial introduction to our future instructors. My instructor of the day, N.P., an ex-fighter pilot who apparently downed few Russian MIGs during the German invasion of Russia, moved very quickly, almost nervously, and I instantly felt a little uncomfortable next to this thin and gaunt looking man, who kept smoking near the plane, although we were all told that smoking near a fuelled plane is tantamount to committing suicide.

But I hardly had time to put my parachute and helmet on when he impatiently signaled to the mechanic to turn the propeller. Mind you, this was my first proper solo flying experience, and although I knew in detail all the operations required to take off, from my theory lessons, I was totally unprepared for what was to follow.

Hardly had the motor started to fire when N.P. push the throttle hard and the plane lunged forward, closely missing the poor mechanic who in typical Romanian peasant fashion, crossed himself a few times.

There were a couple of other planes moving slowly ahead of us, much too low for my instructor's taste, who swore quietly whilst deftly passing them with one wheel on the concrete runway and the other on the grass. We didn't quite get to the thick, white starting line where the planes are normally supposed to stop before taking off, when N.P. pushed the throttle lever forward and within seconds with the engine screaming in anger, we took off, making an immediate turn to the left.

The planes used in our school were Czech-made Cessena with dual commands, the pilot always sitting on the right seat, and the student in the left seat. Each seat was surrounded by the full instrumentation required for flying, the stick and the engine throttle. Before the flight, we were all briefed and told that above all, we were not to touch the "manche" (the stick) under any circumstances, the penalty being no flying for two days and peeling potatoes in the kitchen. So there I was, in a sharp left turn, with the tip of the left wing almost touching the ground, enjoying this incredible take off, but somewhat worried about my instructor who seemed determined to break all the rules we all had to learn by heart during our theory lessons. Perhaps I was too young to understand the ego of this man, but deep inside I sensed danger, and watched everything he was doing.

By now we were flying outside the school perimeter, over the lush fields towards the small village in the distance. We were doing a type of flying called "rase-mottes" a French word which describes this type of flying very close to the ground as to almost "shave" the grass. We were no more than five metres above the ground, and N.P. was skillfully trying to follow the exact contour of the old unmade road leading to the village.

Suddenly there it was, directly in front of us, appearing from behind the rise in the road, a peasant wooden cart with big wooden wheels and drawn by two shining oxen, glistening with sweat.

The cart was skillfully loaded with a huge pile of hay tightly compacted in the large tray, and right up on top of it, in typical local fashion, was the owner, sitting comfortably and guiding his beasts with the help of a long leather whip. Just for a split second the whole image became a painting by Nicolaie Grigorescu, the greatest Romanian painter who captured beautifully the country side and the Romanian country people on his paintings. The gentle curves of the hills bordering the lush fields of corn, the distant creek running happily between old willow trees, and a soft blue sky dotted with sleepy clouds I don't know how it is possible to remember all this, but I can clearly see even today after many years gone past, the horrified look on the face of this poor man.

Almost simultaneously with our plane banking sharply to the right, the man half slid, half dropped to the ground, clasping desperately at the straws; In the next second, he hit the ground surrounded by a small cloud of loose hay. I turned my head to see what happened to the poor man, and with great relief a saw him half sitting up supported by his right hand, whilst shaking his whip at our plane.

Unperturbed by the incident, N.P. immediately levelled, lowered the plane, and maintained the low flying position following the dusty road, as if nothing had happened.

By now I started to realize that this so called hero was a bit of a nut and was either mad or trying very hard to impress me.

"Funny isn't it" said my instructor with a chuckle, looking at me whilst the plane was skimming along the ground. "He didn't know what hit him. It will take few minutes before he will stop shaking."

Next the unexpected happened. Whilst N.P. had his head turned to me talking, the plane was heading straight into a group of high tension electrical cables, stretching above the ground. We were racing at 200 Km./ Hour, straight into this deadly trap stretching across our view like a silvery spider's web. I don't know exactly how it happened because everything was like a blur, except that the next second I instinctively grabbed the flying stick in front of me—which we weren't suppose to touch under any circumstance—with my both hands, and pulled it straight back to my stomach. The plane immediately responded by lifting almost vertically with the engine roaring and groaning under the sudden movement, rapidly gaining height. Even so we just managed to clear the wires.

N.P., who was totally unaware of the imminent danger, instinctively grabbed the stick on his side, and started to swear at me whilst levelling the plane.

"What the hell you think you're doing? Have you gone mad or . . ." He stopped short when I pointed down under the plane at the thick tension wires running across the hills.

Although I did not say anything, being still frozen with fear, he understood what went on, and from then on he became very quiet and was concentrating in flying the plane at a safe height above the ground. But it didn't last long, and as soon as we reached the small town, he tried once again to impress me by flying so close to the church's spire, that I only had to reach out of the cockpit to touch it. But I was not in the mood anymore to fly with this maniac.

I realized then for the first time how deadly serious flying was. It was fun and exciting but at the same time did not allow for mistakes or foolish play. This was a serious matter which called for concentration and attention to every detail.

Eventually my instructor decided to turn back to the airport, flying with great skill and control. Perhaps he realized that he wasn't succeeding at showing off his flying skills. When we landed, it was so smooth that I only knew we had landed when I heard the wheels starting to roll.

There was no doubt he was a very skilled flyer, but one with little regard for his own life or his passenger's safety. Fortunately for me, he was allotted another group of students, mainly because one of the students in that group was the nephew of an air force colonel, who apparently insisted on having N.P in charge of his relative.

MY MOTHER'S STAGE PERFORMANCE

Our course was coming to an end. By now, most of the students had completed the required 11 hours of double command flying instruction and the 11 hours of solo flying. We also had to do long distance travel and show knowledge in map reading and orientation. Finally we were instructed in basic aerobics which consisted of doing tight circles, spirals, loops, pendulums and learning how to enter and come out of a flat spin.

Every day each flying group was given a certain zone to practice in, usually at a safe distance from the aerodrome and small villages spread around the area, where each instructor and the student would spend 20-30 minutes going through required routine. The student was usually shown by the instructor how the manoeuvre was to be performed and then he was allowed to have a go at it with the instructor ready at any time to take over the commands if the student got into trouble.

The one movement which everybody hated but had to be done as part of learning, was going purposely into a simulated loss of power by turning the engine off and allowing the plane to fall like a rock to the ground. The cabin of our plane had an extensive amount of clear plexiglass, so that when the plane was pointing to the ground, you were suspended by the harness and only partially touching the seat. It did feel more like a free fall to the ground, like being suspended at the end of your parachute.

The plane would start turning in circles, slowly at first then gradually accelerating and literally throwing itself faster and faster in this deadly spiral. The ground which initially looked like a small painting with many coloured dots, would get closer, and by the time you had counted the required 5-6 rotations, you could hardly restrain yourself from applying the reversing command which stopped almost instantly the spin and returned the plane to a normal flying level.

Although the whole procedure lasted only some 20 seconds, the plane would descend in that short time from an altitude of some 3,000m to about 1500m.

Sunday was usually the rest day, and the huge dormitory was usually empty as most of the students would go for the day to the old and ancient town of Brasov.

That particular Sunday I stayed in and waited for my mother who made the long trip from Turnu-Magurele to the flying school to have a talk about my future and to give the necessary permission to continue my flying career with the Romanian Air Force.

Before the war and the invasion of the Russian army, there were plenty of jobs available in our country, and we didn't have a word for "out of work", or "on the dole" as everybody seemed to have a job.

In most families there was little pressure applied on the children to do well at school, or to study hard and make the necessary grades to enter University Courses. But there was an increasing awareness of the financial benefits resulting from "professional" careers such as medicine, law or architecture.

Perhaps the fact that my grandfather on my father's side, who was a master bricklayer, and had built countless churches in the area of his native town of Alexandria assisted ably by his nine boys, did not offer encouragement for his sons to strive for higher education, and the fact that neither of the nine brothers showed great interest in furthering their education, made my mother more determined that "her" sons, would achieve greater academic results.

The only exception was my father Marin, who from his early schooling showed great ability with figures and eventually went on his own to Bucharest, the capital of Romania, where he managed to enter the Engineering Faculty by open examination, and have all his expenses paid by the state. There was also my uncle Costica who escaped the family circle and went to the mining area of Muntii Apuseni, and become a successful mining engineer.

My mother was of good peasant stock, her family being established in the town of Turnu-Magurele, near the great river Danube where her family owned rich vineyards and vegetable gardens, surrounded by the ruins of an old Roman fort covered with weeds and teeming with snakes, where we used to play and stage grand fights with wooden swords and wooden shields which lasted well in the gentle evenings.

So unfortunately for me, my mother was convinced that I was the brightest thing on this earth, and that I was to elevate the family's name, by becoming at least a doctor. Unfortunately I hated school and I never worked hard like some of my friends who were made by their parents to sit at their desks and finish work, before being allowed to go outside and play.

At that age I was endowed with a very good memory, and I had no trouble in memorizing the lessons taught in the class to the extent that I never had to open a book and study. This in the long run proved to be a disaster especially during my university studies when there was too much to remember, and I had not learned to sit down and study.

The only person in my family who wanted me to work hard and try to become a highly paid professional was my mother. Perhaps she wanted us to have an easier life, but above all I believe now, she wanted her children to be respected and to achieve a social status which would make her very proud. So when she arrived at my school, she was obviously set on changing my mind, and to convince me to give up the idea of becoming a pilot and go and sit for an University examination in the autumn.

As soon as she come into the dormitory, she spread skillfully on my bed a colourful tablecloth, and proceeded to take out of a large basket all my favourite dishes, which somehow she managed to transport in the rickety train, without any spillage. It was a real feast as my mother was an excellent cook. She told me the latest news from home, in particular about my father who hadn't been able to find a job since the Communists had fired him from his position and as a consequence things were getting very tight financially.

We talked about the future, and how we going to manage particularly since my father was being persecuted by the Communists because he refused to join the Party so it seemed there was little hope for him to get another job. As for my brother, he was still studying journalism in Bucharest, and could not take a regular job.

She told me how this injustice was killing my proud father, and that it was affecting the whole family. We had been a happy and prosperous family before the war, but that gradually changed to a life of poverty and misery. I knew how much pain my family had had to go through in the last four years since the end of the war, and although there was little I could have done to help out, I didn't like to cause them any more hardship.

When my mother started to ask me what I intended to do after I finished my flying course and I told her that I had been offered a cadetship in the Romanian Air Force, she started to cry softly. If there was one thing I couldn't stand it was to see my mother crying. She looked very tired, small and frail. I asked her to forgive me but said that I had made up my mind and that flying was the only thing I wanted to do. She stopped for a minute, took a long look at me and then she said: "But what will happen if you get killed in one of those Russian flying coffins?"

(These "coffins" were the new Russian MIG jets which fell from the sky with monotonous regularity almost daily.)

"Have we not suffered enough? She continued.

"Why can't you go to the university like your cousin Cretu? You've always had better marks than him at school."

I kept telling her that I wasn't interested in studying anymore as I already finished my 12th year at the local High School in Turnu-Magurele. Suddenly my mother stopped crying, clutched her left side and slid to the ground looking very pale. She wasn't moving and I wasn't sure if she was still breathing. From my little knowledge of First Aid, I knew that she had to lie down, and I should loosen up some of the tight things around her waist and neck. However she continued to remain motionless and I started to panic. I shook her and shouted to wake her up. Still no movement. "My God" I said to myself, "I think I managed to kill my mother. You selfish bastard" I thought. "Why did I have to be so hard on her? Why don't I care a little about my family and for once forget about myself. "Is flying more important than my mother?"

I felt like my whole life was pointless and there was little that I could do to save my mother. Perhaps this sounds a little stupid and emotional but in those days we were more naïve and less exposed to the hard lessons of today's television and media. I felt tears running down my cheeks, when I heard this little feeble voice saying: "Will you promise your dying mother to stop flying and go to the university?"

I was so relieved to hear her talking and particularly to note that she had slightly opened one eye and was looking quizzically at me, that almost without hesitation I lifted her to my chest, kissed her and said : "I will do anything you want me to do, but please don't die on me again!"

Within seconds she started to get up slowly and although still looking pale, she managed to encourage me to have some more to eat.

"Here have some more, I don't think they feed you here properly. You look more like an "ogar" (greyhound).

Suddenly I started to realize the enormity of what I had just said. In our family we were taught from an early age to keep a promise. I could not have gone back on my promise unless my mother relented and changed her mind.

"I beg you mother to let me fly, I will do anything you want me to do, but don't make me give flying away." I was really sweating now. She looked at me hard and then she said:

"A promise is a promise and I would rather die than let my son kill himself. I will never let you forget your promise.

My darling love. She couldn't have known that in the strange labyrinth of life, by stopping me from flying she had indirectly put me on an escape path out of Romania which would ultimately destroy our family. In retrospect, if I would have been allowed to continue my flying career, I would have probably crashed in one of the experimental Russian jets, like many other young Romanian pilots and that would have been the end of it. But as I was to learn, there was a greater plan in store for me, which would push me on to do things I never dreamt of doing.

But my mother did what her instinct told her to do: Save your child, don't let him fly, that was the immediate need. For the moment everything was safe, and as far as she was concerned I was out of danger, and that was enough for my mother.

The week after my mother left for home, we had to finish all our advanced acrobatics as required by the course. Friday morning, the last day to complete the required aerial actions, my instructor and I left early in the morning for our allotted area. By the time we got there we had gained the regulation height of 3000m. Veronica was as usual, a little uncomfortable, as she wasn't very fond of doing acrobatics, and gladly would hand over the commands to me, to go through the required program. Everything was going smoothly and we were just about to finish when Veronica suddenly pointed to the side of my window to area four.

Do you know who is flying in area four today? There is a plane in that area which has commenced a flat spin."

"That will have to be Mr. N.P." I said trying to get a good look at the plane which was falling rapidly out of the sky.

Veronica was looking very worried when we both heard a muffled explosion.

By the time I turned the plane round to get a better look, a column of smoke and dust had already begun to lift lazily.

"If you don't mind I will take over now and fly the plane back," Veronica said.

We had been told in our theory lessons that the planes we used in our school were very safe except in unusual cases when the plane could enter an uncontrollable spin, called a flat spin, from which was almost impossible to escape.

"When that happens", said our Chief Instructor, jokingly, "remember to keep calm, reverse the commands, and if nothing works start to pray for divine intervention."

There was some polite laughter but we all sensed that this was a serious and dangerous matter; We could only hope that it never happened to the plane we were flying at the time. The fact that even the instructors knew so little about how to deal with this loss of lift under certain conditions didn't give us any confidence. As I was to find out later when the engineers from the factory came to investigate the cause of the fall, the plane—which normally behaves like a bird, using the current of air to give the necessary lift which in turn allows the pilot to use the directional commands for maintaining the altitude or changing direction—suddenly loses its aerodynamic qualities and becomes an inert object which drops to the ground just like a stone.

Imagine that suddenly there is no water under a boat travelling in the ocean and that the bottom of the sea is some 3000 m. below. Without the support of the water the boat would suddenly drop like a rock at ever increasing speed, and crash against the bottom of the sea. This may be construed as a crude explanation of this complex aerodynamics effect, but nevertheless it is very close to what happens to a plane falling from the sky at 260 km/hour. The commands become limp and totally un-responsive, it drops like a stone and hits the ground in a perfectly flat position.

Whilst Veronica was flying the plane with her usual precise control, I was trying to remember who was in the plane with N.P. at that time of the day, hoping that maybe he was on his own, practicing some of his high acrobatics routines, in preparation for the air-show which was put on at the end of each course for the benefit of the guests and members of family.

By the time our plane landed, we could see near the main hangar a large group of students and instructors. It didn't take long before we joined the main group and we were told that N. P. and the Air-Colonel's nephew were the two people killed in the crash. Our Chief Instructor and his assistant were already on their way to the site of the crash to try to gather any immediate information as to the cause of the accident, and to secure the site from unwanted visitors. There wasn't much we could do, except to busy ourselves cleaning the planes, and store them in their bays.

Late that evening after dinner we were assembled in the main hall and our Chief Instructor stood in front of the enormous blackboard used for theory lectures, waiting for a few seconds until everybody was seated and quiet.

"I am sorry to tell you all that we have lost Mr N.P and his student K.D.

"At this stage, he continued, "we don't know exactly what caused the plane to fall, but we will have a better idea of what happened when the aeronautical investigation inspectors from Bucuresti and Prague have done their work. In the meantime, I want you all not to write or talk to your families or local reporters about this accident.

I am deeply sorry for what happened particularly as we had an accident free course until now. However we will continue our program and prepare for the air-show. In the mean time I will personally take over and instruct Tov. N.P.'s group, so that they will not miss out on the final exam."

He stopped for few seconds, then quietly he added:
"Tomorrow I will nominate four of our students, who will have the honour to accompany the body of K.D. to his home village, and form a guard of honour during the burial ceremony. Mr. R.A., my assistant, will be in charge of this group and make all the necessary arrangements. Thank you all for your attendance. Dismissed"

Late in the night we kept talking about what happened, most of us secretly realizing how lucky we were not to be in N.P.'s group.
That night I had a nightmare; I was once again flying with Mr N.P. who was dead and covered with blood, but still holding the flying stick. I kept yelling at him to pull up or we were going to hit the lines.
"Pull up! You are going to kill us both!"
He looked pale and covered with blood and he had a huge gaping hole where his nose should have been. Then we hit the lines and sparks were flying everywhere . . . I woke up covered in sweat being shaken by Sorin, who whispered to me:
"How would you like to go and have a look at the plane? They brought it back last night and it is locked in the small hangar near the canteen"?

We walked in the cool night, trying not to make any noise. When we got near the hangar where our mechanics kept some of their tools, Sorin shone the small torch which he had brought with him through the small window covered with grime. We couldn't see much, which prompted Sorin to suggest we look at the side door. We did find the door unlocked, and quietly walked in the dark space. In the middle of the hangar we could see the broken shape of the plane with its wings touching the ground. It looked like a huge bird with broken wings, fallen to the side. Before we got closer to the plane, I smelt something which raised the hair on my neck. It was a smell of burnt metal, petrol and blood. It felt like being in a huge abattoir filled with the smell of the slaughtered beast who has filled the air with his dying odour.

"I don't think we should be here" I said, starting to feel nauseated, but Sorin was determined to have a good look.

"Here, he said, "you hold the torch and I'll have a look first, then you have a go if you feel like it".

He passed the torch to me, and we both got near the plane. That plane was as badly mangled as if an enormous hand had pushed it down and squashed it against the ground. Every part of the plane was in some way damaged, but the real damage became apparent when we pushed open the right side door of the plane, and we got a clear view of the seats.

In fact, for a moment at least, I thought there was less damage in the cabin than there was outside, until I saw the metal seats in which the instructor and the pupil were usually seated during flying. These seats are usually made of an aluminum alloy highly resistant to stress, and they are very strong and sturdily built. The fall of the plane from 3000m must have increased the weight of their bodies through gravity to 10-12 times their normal weight so that on impact with the ground, the sheer weight of their bodies, managed to push the bottom of these rock solid seats out of shape, enough to partially split the welded seams.

The stick on the student's side was made of metal and had a beautifully hard oak ball on top which made it very comfortable to hold. It was split in half like a piece of cheese!

"The poor bugger" said Sorin he must have hit it (the stick) with his teeth."

"I think we have seen enough," I said, trying not to be sick. "This place is like a morgue. Let's get out of here."

I stepped out into the cool night. It was quiet and peaceful and the sky started to light up in the east with the first beams of light penetrating the dark.

I couldn't believe that everything could be so quiet and beautiful, that everything went on without the smallest sign of disturbance. Two young men had lost their lives without any reason. They had ceased to be part of our school, they were gone forever and they would never be seen again. All of a sudden I felt very fragile and exposed, I wasn't so sure anymore of my ability to be in charge of my plane. I felt that I knew so little about the rules controlling this vast universe and of what the future would hold for me.

For the first time in my life, I started to think about the complexity of our existence, the little that we know of what to expect in life, but in particular how quickly things can change from calm to disaster, from success to failure, and how easily the tide of life can throws us around like little match sticks.

When I got back to the dormitories, I lie in my bed and felt very sad. How would the family of the young pilot feel, who were simple country people and very proud of their son who was to follow in the tradition of his uncle and become a great pilot, an officer in the Romanian Air Force. I felt something running down my cheeks . . . tears? I wiped my face slightly embarrassed, and then I went outside and lit a cigarette.

Then the thought hit me:

It could have been me, not poor K.D. on the first day of my flying course. But why was I spared? I didn't understand then why, but I know now that my life had a different purpose, and that ultimately only God decides what is to take place.

NOWHERE TO GO

When our small group returned from the funeral, we were immediately told to report to the Chief Instructor who thanked us for attending, and also told us our final results in the course, which were announced whilst we were away. As expected Sorin had topped the school, but to my surprise, I finished second. As it was mentioned to us at the start of the course, the first 20 placed flyers were offered a cadet scholarship in the Romanian Air Force. This meant that I had achieved my dream and if all went well, after two years of cadetship I would have been able to join the air force in a permanent position as school instructor. Just to think that I had the opportunity to fly regularly and have at the same time a secure and well paid position.

But in the back of my mind I could not erase the promise I had made to my mother. I couldn't believe that I had been so gullible and given up my opportunity to do what I liked most. However it was too late to go back on my promise now and with a lot of pain in my heart I focused on how to go about refusing the offer made by the school.

On the day of the interview, the twenty students selected for the air force service had to face a special commission made up of Air Force officers, our Chief Instructor, and a representative of the Communist Party. By now I had decided that the only way to get out of the school was to tell them the truth about my father, who was on the black list because of his open rejection of the policies of the Communist Party.

Until that moment I was tortured everyday by the fear of someone finding out about my father's dismissal and his fight with the Communists, which would have resulted in my immediate expulsion from flying school. Yet there I was, standing at ease, in my spotless uniform, in front of a long table behind which were seated the official party, ready to tell them the truth.

"Congratulations tovarase Vena" commenced one of the older officer with an impressive array of service medals pinned on his chest.

"I hear you had no gliding experience yet you managed to finish in the second place" he said with a little smile of approval in the corner of his eyes.

Many of the students in the school had the opportunity to do a gliding course at a school near Brasov, which was a good introduction to actual flying. I missed out because would have cost us too much to travel twice a long distance from my hometown. All the travelling expenses had to be covered by the students.

Thank you very much tovarase Maior(Major), I had a very good instructor."

They turned their heads to our Chief Instructor who started to speak in a quiet and controlled manner which typified this intelligent and capable pilot:

"I recommend strongly this young man for a career in air force. He has good judgment, outstanding flying skills, and the ability to get on with the other students."

Suddenly I was torn inside by the realization that within few seconds I would have to tell them the truth and turn my back on my dream. I heard myself murmuring:

"I am very sorry Sir, but I cannot take your offer, I cannot be an air force pilot."

"What is this nonsense you are talking about" said my Chief Instructor looking totally surprised and bewildered.

From then on it was easy to tell them the whole story. As soon as I told them that my father was dismissed by the new Communist administration, a sudden change of facial expressions occurred, ranging from surprise to sheer horror. The temperature in the room must have dropped considerably as I could feel a chill running down my back.

There was nothing else I needed to add. According to Communist policy, there was no room for me in a government organization even if I was innocent and had nothing to do with my father's opinions. The fact that one member of the family was against the Communists meant that ALL members of the family were guilty. Consequently in my case, I was too much of a risk to be allowed in the Air Force.

There had been a few cases of Romanian Air Force pilots defecting during training flights to Turkey or Greece. They weren't prepared to take any chances even if I was second best in the school. It was an unfair and vicious way of eliminating those people who could oppose in any way the Russian authority. This was also an easy way to place the Communist puppets in positions of influence, and provide faithful servants to the Communist regime, whose main efforts were directed towards diffusing any national movement towards a free Romania.

After the defeat of the German armies, the Russian armies followed the German armies across the border, and invaded Romania in 1945, and in the process pillaged, raped and killed a large number of innocent people, under the pretext of "liberating Romania from the German yoke" and eliminating the "capitalist exploiters". At the end of the war, Romania was left under Russian domination at the mercy of a rapacious and unforgiving regime, which aimed to destroy the national spirit, to exterminate the middle class, and to create hatred between various economical groups, whilst the Russians methodically started to load anything which wasn't bolted to the ground, and send it to the "Soviet Union". I remember even now, the noise of the endless freight trains, which went on through the night for months, loaded to the gills with food, furniture, stock and in particular industrial equipment.

To be a pilot in the Romanian Air Force, apart from having to pass rigorous physical and written tests, one had to have a "clean" socio-economic background, to be able to prove that no member of your family had owned a business or land, or show evidence of some sad story of oppression and exploitation of your family at the hands of the previous royalist regime.

I saluted smartly turned about and left the room. The word got around very quickly that I was kicked out of the school, and all of a sudden I was treated by the other students and instructors as though I had suddenly contracted leprosy.

Veronica sent word that she wanted to talk to me. I met her in her room which was part of the administration building. She was sitting in front of the window overlooking the hangars and part of the concrete strip. For few minutes she continued to look at the familiar view, then she turned and looked at me. Her eyes were hard and steel-like and I felt that she was ready to burst into tears.

"DECE AI FACUT PROSTIA ASTA?" (Why have you done such a stupid thing?) she said and got of the chair.

"You had no reason to tell them the truth about your father; If they ever found out, then they would have kicked you out of the air force, but by then you would have been a fully trained pilot and you could have in time enter the civil aviation"!

Of course she was right but there was no way I was going to tell her about my pact with my mother. That was nothing to do with her or the school. By now she was pacing nervously between me and the window.

"Do you realize that as long as the communists are in power, you will NEVER fly again? You know you would have made an excellent pilot, you have more ability than any other student in this course."

I could see how upset see was, and I felt sorry for her but it was all to no avail; This chapter of my life was closed.

She finally stopped pacing and gradually the anger left her. She set down facing the window once again, looking tired and much older;

"These bastards are ruining our country are destroying us. All these sacrifices for nothing." She did not say the word "Communists", but I knew she was referring to the despotic new regime who was trying to change the old respected traditions passed from generation to generation, to humiliate and to degrade the spirit of the Romanian people.

"Ma scuzi" (forgive me) I said quietly, "but I had no choice but to stop now. There are other reasons why I had to take this decision, but this was the only thing I could have done without hurting my family."

She lifted her head and looked at me in a way which made my heart beat faster:

"You young fool" she said with a gentle smile, "I hope you have learned something and it will help you in the future;

She got up and shook my hand:

"Come on, go and pack up your bags. I will give you a lift to the station. Don't forget to go and say goodbye to the Chief; He was very upset about your decision."

That evening I was once again in the old rickety train, pulled by two enormous steam locomotives which laboured their way through the high mountains towards the valley and the sleepy town of my mother.

Although I received my pilot license, I did not fly again on my own, but I have never lost the desire to be a pilot.

Whenever I have the opportunity to fly for business or holiday reasons, I always welcome the opportunity to be in the waiting lounge, watching the landing or the departures of various aircrafts. I am like a small boy still playing with his toys. Perhaps I will never "grow up" and lose that exciting feeling and trepidation when I see a sleek plane taking off with its jet engines roaring, gradually gaining altitude until it is only a dot in the immense blue sky.

My poor mother never had another "heart attack" and lived to be 83 years old. God rest her in peace. She probably saved my life by not signing the release papers, but I doubt she ever knew or understood the pain and suffering she caused me.

DRINKING IS NOT THE SOLUTION

"This is not the end of the world" said my mother moving around our table, collecting the empty plates. As usual I used to love my mother's cooking, and always managed to leave a clean plate.

Since the flying school episode, she tried to soften the blow by preparing all my old favourites dishes.

My father sat quietly at the head of the table smoking, and my brother Sandu was hurrying trying to finish his plate before he could be allowed to leave the table and go to meet his group of friends.

"I still don't understand" said my father in a controlled voice. "What have you got against flying? There are many young people these days making a good career in the Air Force. Besides they get free uniform, food, accommodation, as well as a good pay. What else can he do these days to get all these advantages?".

My father who came from a large family, was in favour of giving full freedom to the young ones, and allowing them to make a living as soon as they had finished their basic schooling This meant in those days a great release on the family's financial burden. Of the nine brothers in his family, he was the only one who managed to do well at the local high school, consequently gaining a scholarship and completing a Civil engineering course in Bucharest. What impressed everyone about his effort was that he did all that without any financial or moral support from his family who believed that he was just wasting his time . . .

That was how his family functioned. Nobody got anything that they didn't work for. Their father, my grandfather, whom I only met a few times, was a master bricklayer who built numerous churches around the town of Alexandria where all his family lived. They were of Macedonian stock, who migrated back to Romania in the late 1860s and become established in the southern area of Romania called Muntenia.

For reasons I was never told, my father adopted his mother's name of Vena, whilst all his other brothers retained their original name of Filip.

My mother did not think much of my father's family and their lack of interest in higher education, and she made it quite clear on numerous occasions that none of her sons would finish like their uncles. She was determined to send us all to university to embrace a well respected course. There was also a strong dislike for my father's brothers and their "bad example" which resulted in limited trips to the neighbouring town of Alexandria where the whole Filip clan dwelled. A few times we made the trip to Alexandria, where we met our numerous relatives and despite my mother's warnings we had a hell of a good time.

They were all great fighters and used to teach us how to defend ourselves. Locally they were greatly respected and feared for their ability to flatten any kind of opposition. During those visits I found out about my father's exploits as a young man, when he excelled in football (soccer) and gymnastics.

That was in a way a surprise for me because he had never talked about it or offered to teach us any of his skills. My father was a very well built man of a medium height, with wide shoulders and powerful legs. A man of few words, he did not show his emotions, worked hard, and never went to a doctor or to the hospital.

He always made sure that we had all what we needed, and he never imposed upon us to do anything. He gave us complete freedom of action but with that he did not give us any advice regarding life in general which would have helped us a lot later on.

In a way we grew up in a very free climate, the only time we were lectured or punished by his wide leather strap was when my mother complained to him about our pranks.

I realize now how little chance I had to understand my father, how little he let us see about himself. We never got to talk about things or ideas or about his experiences from his youth. To make things even more difficult, he was never able to show his true emotions until just before I left Romania, and by then it was too late for both of us.

The only time I saw a glimpse of his sporting past was on the day when in the afternoon he came back from work still with his suit and tie on, when he came in the yard where I had just finished putting together a rough set of parallel bars which I was trying to get up on.

"Let me have a go" he said and took his coat off.

He grabbed the end of the bars and immediately swung down and forward in a perfect lift between the bars, finishing in a handstand position which he held motionless for a few seconds. He then swung downwards and dismounted laterally with a perfect landing next to the parallel bars.

I just stood there speechless with my mouth open, when he picked up his coat, and said to me with a cheeky grin

"I think that's how it supposed to be done.!"

He looked at me briefly and then walked to the house without saying another word. That was the first and last time he showed me how to do anything.

I got up from the table, and thanked my mother for the food, but I didn't linger on as I didn't want to discuss the matter of my academic education now. I felt rather empty and without my usual desire to do things. I was still annoyed with myself for falling for the great performance by my mother, and I wanted to let her know by not talking too much to her.

"What have you got planned for tonight, Cornel?" asked my mother. "I hear your friends have got into some trouble drinking again. I don't want you to get drunk and get into serious trouble."

"I think I am old enough to take care of myself" I snapped back at her, knowing that she was more lenient with me now, and let me do things which she wouldn't have let me do before.

When I think of those days spent in the sleepy town of Turnu-Magurele, I still wonder how we managed not to die of sheer boredom, as apart from some sport and school, there was very little for a young person to do.

We were all very young and full of energy, with so little excitement in our urban lives. There was the occasional dance at the local Town Hall, but I wasn't much of a dancer, being more interested in outdoor activities. Basically we were very shy despite the bravado we displayed in front of the local girls, and we maintained our courage by bragging about what we had done, but deep down we all knew that it was mostly empty talk, and we were desperate for some excitement.

Amazing isn't it, to see how as we grow older, we forget what we used to be like, and become shocked and critical of young people's behaviour. It is as though there is another person inside us, a person who has forgotten everything that he used to do when young. There is the real danger of passing judgment on the young ones, expecting them to behave rationally and honourably, when we ourselves were real troublemakers in our youth.

Perhaps the most entertaining event took place in the evening, when people of all ages but mostly the young ones, marched up and down the main street, in small or large groups, talking, laughing, calling out to friends and watching the small milk-bars with cane chairs and small tables at the front of the shop, where older people were sitting, drinking small cups of strong Turkish coffee, smoking thick handmade cigars and playing backgammon.

We walked for hours up and down that street, particularly in the summer or autumn when the weather was warm and pleasant. But our main aim was to see the girls, perhaps hoping to find the right one. This, was the only place where young people could meet without being under the disapproving eyes of our teachers or parents. Quite often we would attached ourselves to a group of noisy girls from our High School, and spend the rest of the evening walking together. Eventually if we were lucky enough, and made a good impression, we would be allowed to walk them home.

In those days parents of girls were very strict with their children and did not allow any form of relationship to develop between young people. Romania had a long history of being subjugated by larger nations, and in the process of being controlled and exploited over a period of some 1000 years, had acquired many of the customs of the ruling nations.

We had borrowed many practices from the Ottomans, (the Turks) one of them being the strict supervision of women, and in particular the absolute rule that the woman must be a virgin when she marries. A family's reputation and wellbeing could be ruined if the girl was found not to be a virgin. Consequently parents, and in particular fathers, had the absolute control over their daughters' outings, and more than often they would prohibit their daughters from seeing young men.

But already by 1947, with the horrors of the war, many families were battling to have enough to eat, and the emphasis had shifted from a very strict family life, to a daily struggle to survive, to have enough to eat, and less time was left to supervise the children.

My best friends Gigi and Titi, were both one year older than me, and had already finished the local Commercial High School. When I returned from the flying school, I found Gigi looking for an accounting job, not being interested in further studies, whilst Titi was already preparing for the autumn examinations in Bucharest.

The three of us and my cousin Cretu used to do most things together, and we all enjoyed sports and competing against another schools.

One particular evening I started to feel good again being with my old mates, without any immediate worries, talking, laughing and generally having a good time. I heard the others talking with admiration and envy about my time at the flying school. They wanted to know everything I'd been doing whilst I was away. It appeared to me that they were all bored stiff, and would have given their right arm to have been in my place.

"O.K. that's all I am going to tell you, now you tell me what's been going on while I have been away," I said at last. Nobody seemed keen to answer, and they pretended not to have heard me. "Come on, "I said, "don't tell me you have been doing absolutely nothing all this time?" Gigi (short for George) who was my best friend, who excelled at gymnastics and showed a complete contempt for any form of authority, kicked accurately a small pebble laying on the side of the road and said in rhythm with his next three steps: "NI-MI-CA" (Nothing).

Indeed, since we had finished our studies, all of a sudden we weren't allowed to compete in the numerous school activities or sports which had kept us busy in the summer. There were some local clubs but apart from soccer, they had very little to offer.

I can understand now how young people of today can get into a lot of trouble, simply because they have so much energy to spend and yet there is very little to do unless they have plenty of money. It is even more difficult for young people living in a small rural town. That was one of the reasons why I was attracted to flying, to do something challenging, to test myself to the limit of my abilities. So, once again I was stuck in this forgotten town, and there was the depressing realization that nothing had changed or would ever change, and I was condemned to a life of eternal boredom.

"Hey listen you fellows," said Mihai, another member of our group but a little younger and not very bright.

"My beloved parents are away for the night and I have the keys to the cellar; How about a little party"?

In this town, most people had vineyards and they stored their wines in large cellars built under the house, where the young wine was kept in big wooden barrels, to mature and eventually be sold to the big wine merchants in Bucharest.

Mihai's cellar was renowned for its size, and the high quality of his father's red wine.

We had been there a few times before when his parents were home, and were reluctantly invited by Mihai's father to taste his pride and glory, his red wine. But we never had the opportunity to be in the large cellar without Mihai's father watching over us like a hawk.

Gigi and Titi, who were recovering from another heavy binge the night before, declined the offer, so I decided to go along with Mihai and his two older mates, E.O. and GA, who were well known in town for their drinking ability.

I personally had very little to do with these two, mainly because they were always secretive and nasty; E.O. in particular who was a real bully at school and use to smack and push younger boys, just to show how big he was. The reason why most of us put up with him was because he was in a special class for failed students, and we didn't see much of him except after hours.

However I was happy to be home with my friends again so that I wasn't in the mood to argue with E.O. I just wanted to have a good time and get sloshed in the true local tradition. Besides Mihai was a good friend and an excellent host who tried very hard to please his guests by serving us with sliced cabana, onions, rye bread and large carafes of young red wine.

The night went quickly as Michael kept bringing downstairs loads of food and pickled cucumbers, which we washed down with delicious young wine, drawn in big metal containers from the biggest barrel placed on wooden slippers against the coolest corner of the cellar. E.O. was getting drunker by the minute and was trying to challenge us by calling us little girls.

"Come on man," he said to me," you're not drinking your glass. Didn't they teach you anything at that stupid flying school of yours?"

E.O. and I could never be friends. He was a jealous and revengeful character and he could never forgive me for being better at school, and in particular at sport. His only forte was to remind us with monotonous regularity that he was older and had lots more experience than anybody else.

I will show you how to drink, you little babies."

I had just about enough from this fellow and I staggered towards him, wanting to give him a good smack in the mouth and shut him up, but Mihai managed to apply a rugby tackle on me, and he slithered down to the ground, taking me down with him.

"Don't take any notice of him," Michael said with a loose tongue, and he rested his head on my legs, holding on tight.

Please don't start a fight or you will smash some of the bottles, and my father will kill me." I started to laugh and tried to get him off, but did not have much success as Mihai was rather plump and hung on to my legs like a leech.

In those days, in our town, drinking and getting drunk, was regarded between the adults but more so between young boys as a test of manhood, a test of strength and endurance which determined your place in the group hierarchy. Even between the best of friends there was always an undeclared test to see who could drink the most, and stay sober the longest. To refuse a drink or perhaps to say that you had enough to drink was regarded as a sure sign of weakness.

E.O and G.A. were older than me, and they had to stay at school an extra two years as in those days one had to pass all subjects before being allowed to proceed to the next year. If you failed one subject, you had to do the whole year all over again and not just the subject you've failed.

They were getting a little too old to hang on with our group but more sadly their time was up: Romania had in those days compulsory military service and every able man of 18 years of age had to do two years of military service. The only way to defer it was to start a university course, which allowed you to do a short term of six months of service during the summer holiday, followed by a further six months of service at the completion of your university course. If you failed to pass your university examinations, you would automatically be recalled to serve the full two years of army training. So both R.O. and G.A knew that unless they passed their exams that year, they would have to go into the army for the next two years.

I was getting quite drunk, but stubbornly refused to give in and let E.O tell me how to drink so we all kept tossing glass after glass down the hatch. Suddenly Mihai, who by now was almost paralysed, managed to stand up, staggered towards the door and called out for some quiet:

"Quiet you idiots, I think somebody is coming."

Drank as we were but not totally stupid, we all knew Mihai's father who was renowned for his bad temper, and his long thick leather belt which he did not hesitate to use on Mihai or his friends, particularly if they were found in his beloved cellar, drinking his red wine. We stumbled up the stairs to get out, but it must have been Mihai's mortal fear of his father because we did not see anyone coming to the house.

The fresh air of the night woke me up a little and I decided to go home. E.O and G.A followed me up the road singing out of key and stumbling over the rough cobblestones. There was not a person in sight, and the street was deserted. It was fairly late for anyone to be out in the street, so we were shocked when we noticed a tall girl walking quickly some distance in front of us.

We recognized this girl in front of us to be F.A. who was about 16 years old and went to our school. She was a real amazon, solidly built, attractive, and somewhat defiant. She wasn't what a purist might call a classic beauty but at school we all sensed that she had that kind of animal strength which attracted a lot of attention.

Obviously with such a physique she was good at sport, and when we had inter-school competition, there was always a small gallery of admirers, watching this girl in her short tunic playing volleyball, moving around the court with feline grace, and delighting the spectators with her high leaps in the air, stretching and reaching the ball well above the net.

Perhaps because she was so gorgeous, or because she did not hesitate to tell boring pursuers to get lost if she didn't like them, she started to gain a reputation of "playing hard to get". She would laugh and make irreverent jokes about some of our older teachers, but I think her biggest problem was her tendency to make jokes about people like E.O. and G.A saying things like:

"These two should be given a permanent desk in Room 1 (The room for the first graders.)" or

"If they stay any longer in the school they will be given life membership."

Her remarks must have hurt like hell the "oldies", students who were forced to repeat grades.

The cobbled street was poorly lit, and we were staggering along until we almost caught up with F.A., a slim figure moving quietly in the semi-dark.

"Would you believe that", said E.O. chuckling to himself and slurring his words,

"I think we must be in luck tonight, there is a fantastic chick in front of us. Let's see who it is".

Only then I realized that I was the only one who already knew who the girl was.

We managed to catch up, when F.A turned with a startled look on her face.

"God you gave me such a fright", she said and then she regained her natural cheek and added;

"I nearly wet myself" and then laughed somewhat relived to see some familiar faces.

"Oh I see, you have been drinking haven't you?" Then she laughed again and added:

"I know where you've been and poor Mihai will get killed when his father finds out that you've been drinking his wine."

Suddenly E.O come back to life, perhaps remembering some of the sarcastic remarks made by F.A in the past, because he started to shout at her:

"Shut your big mouth stupid, nobody's asking your opinion. What we do is our business so keep you mouth shut."

We all sobered up a little, but F.A must have realized that she was treading on treacherous ground, and quickly moved ahead of us trying to put some distance between us.

E.O started to whisper in G.A's ear, but not very successfully, because I could hear almost every word he was saying:

"Look mate, she is asking for it, she is nothing but a little whore. This time she's gone too far. What is she doing here, on her own, at this time? I am telling you she is asking for it. Let's go and get her now. I reckon she will enjoy it."

The cool of the night was starting to sober me up, and I was starting to worry about us raping this girl, for the simple reason that she was alone at night? The more I thought about it the less I felt like joining the others, in fact I was getting annoyed just listening to what E.O was whispering to G.A.

There was some talk about her being a little too generous with her favours, but nobody could say this with certainty, besides I could not bear the thought of roughing up this young girl. My family had clear principles about how to treat other people, and in particular we were taught from an early age to respect our mother and to be kind and gentle to the opposite sex. Besides I hated these two bullies, and I could never stand by and see suffering inflicted on people who could not defend themselves.

I was getting more and more annoyed with myself for getting drunk with the likes of these two, and having to be part of an attack on this girl who strictly speaking had never done anything to me. But more than anything I hated the way these two were behaving like jackals ready to rip their victim apart. No, I wasn't going to let them do anything to her, in fact I started to think of spoiling their fun and helping F.A get away.

I suddenly quickened my pace and caught up with her. They were still laughing stupidly, when I grabbed F.A's arm, and started to pull her to the other side of the street.

"Leave me alone" she said trying to wrench her arm from my grip.

E.O. and G.A., who were still on the right side of the street laughing and stumbling over the rough ground when they heard F.A shouting, and thinking that I may need some help, started to run towards us.

"Listen you silly girl" I said, squeezing F.A's arm even harder, "I don't want to rape you, but these two animals will. You understand? Stop fighting with me and keep going."

She stopped trying to wrench her arm from my grip and started to quicken her pace, looking at me in disbelief. I could see the fear in her eyes.

By now my two drinking partners started to realize that far from wanting to be the first to rape F.A., I was trying to get her away from them.

"Hey," called E.O, "slow down will you, I am getting tired of running, wait for us, we'll help you."

By now I was getting sober and I was feeling good about my decision to help F.A. to get away unharmed.

I wanted to look after D.A, to protect her, and then I challenged E.O and G.A.:

"Listen you two," I said turning round and slowing down a little, " I am not going to let you fuck F.A. I am going to walk her home, and if anyone tries to stop me, so help me I will bust his head."

I didn't have any weapons on me so I bent down and picked from the side of the road a good sized rock. My sudden anger and threats must have had some effect because they both stopped and started to talk animatedly between themselves. Whilst they deliberated, I tried to put some distance between our groups.

"You walk in front of me" I said to F.A, "Keep walking fast and whatever happens don't stop. I will walk behind you."

It is hard to say what would have happened if these two had the courage to tackle me, but I knew that they were a lot drunker than I was. Perhaps they were totally surprised of my attitude; I will never know, except that they started to slow down and suddenly disappeared behind us in one of the side streets.

It was early in the morning by the time we got to F.A's home. We stopped and we just looked for few seconds at one another with a big grin on our faces.

"Thank you Cornel, thank you very much."

She looked so young and beautiful.

"What do you want to do?" she said, smiling. "I will do anything you want me to."

"What?" I said, rather taken by surprise.

I took a long look at her, realizing that she was ready to do anything for me. But there was little I could have asked from her. I didn't want anything from her. Whatever I did it wasn't done for a reward, it was something which I did instinctively.

There was no explanation except something inside me feeling very comfortable and happy with myself.

"Look F.A" I said, "I think we had enough excitement for one night. Let's go home." She looked at me smiling:

"I will never forget what you've done for me tonight."

Then she turned abruptly and ran into the house.

I walked back home in the cool of the morning. By then I was sober and started to think what would happen at school when I saw my "two friends." I knew they will not forgive me and probably they would try to get their revenge.

But I didn't feel any fear. Somehow I had gained something very precious that night. I felt much older, stronger, and more confident about myself.

E.O and G.A. continued in their ways, and I didn't have much to do with them anymore.

Some time later, another group of students, some of them well known to me, were involved in another gang rape. This time the local Magistrate sentenced most of them to long terms of imprisonment.

F.A and I continued to be good friends but we never progressed to anything more serious. She eventually left town with her family and we never met again.

MY FATHER'S BIOLOGY BOOK

With the summer almost over I knew that I had to start preparing myself for the autumn exams. I didn't quite know what course I wanted to do but regardless of what I was going to do, I had to revise and improve the five basic subjects required by most universities for their entry examination : Romanian Language, expression and literature, Organic and Inorganic Chemistry, Physics, General Mathematics, and depending on which faculty I wanted to try for, I had to study Biology and Anatomy. Perhaps without the heavy drinking orgy at Mihai's place, I would have continued to waste my time with my friends and finished up staying in Turnu-Magurele, getting a job as an accountant, marrying a local girl, having a family and getting old surrounded by my old drinking friends.

I would have continued to talk about what I could have done if I went to Bucharest to study, but in reality I would have spent the rest of my life regretting not taking the chance to go further.

I started to get the books I needed to prepare myself for the examination. Some were my own, some were my brother's who had finished High

School four years ahead of me and was already studying journalism and media in Bucharest, and one was my father's Biology book which he used his university days.

It was an old book with some pages missing, and without any covers, but the lessons in it were excellent, well presented and of a higher standard than our high school books. I thought it would be to my advantage to know more details about this subject, in particular if I was to sit for the Horticulture Course, so I decided to ignore the few missing pages at the start and use this book for my Biology studies.

The summer was almost over, and the temptation of long swims in the Danube and balmy afternoons with my cousin Cretu at our family vineyards near the ruins was diminished by the thought of the coming examinations. Romanian universities in those days had a quota of places which was usually much lower than the number of applicants. It was quite normal to have 700 students applying for a course which offered only 70 places. To make things more difficult, most courses had a quota of 10 to 15 of the places offered set aside for the sons and daughters of high government officials, or members of Communist Party. But despite all this, thousands of young high school graduates would try to gain entry and to start a career which would guarantee a life time of security and a well paid job.

My initial intention was to try Medicine, but when I found out that in the previous year they had some 2,700 students applying for 70 places, and that out of those, 20 places were "reserved", I realized that my chances were very small and I had better lower my expectations and try for a less ambitious course which would attract a smaller number.

So finally I decided to try Horticulture, which had attracted in past years between 700 and 800 applicants, and had 60 available places.

An added problem was that of accommodation and food whilst studying in Bucharest. Unless I was going to finish in the first 30 places and get a State bursary I could have not survived in Bucharest. My parents could not afford to pay for expenses so for the first time in my scholastic life, I had to settle down to long hours of study, locked up in the house, trying to absorb in a short time all the required information. This was the time when I cursed my lack of regular study during my High School years, when I relied on my natural memory. I found that when it came to a large volume of information, it takes more than just memory, it takes a well organized studying method and perseverance.

When I started on the Biology studies, I was using my father's book which had the first few pages missing. It was the introduction and the lesson on lichens which were missing. As it was a simple topic I decided to leave this chapter for last, and perhaps get a book from the library to gain the necessary information. However I had other subjects much more difficult to learn so that I "reasoned" that I would be extremely unlucky to get such a subject, with so little to talk about when there numerous other topics which were more difficult and likely to be asked by the examiner.

So I continued to put all my efforts in learning and memorizing hundred of pages from this old book, and gradually convinced myself that I would NOT GET THIS SUBJECT IN THE EXAMINATION!

By the time I'd finished my biology book, I was convinced that there was no need to study the lichens;

I couldn't possibly be so unlucky to get that topic in the exams.

UNIVERSITY EXAMS AND LUCK

Whilst waiting to start, I was looked after by my father's cousin Mec, who was employed by the Department of Sport and Recreation and lived in a big sporting complex which had a huge outdoor swimming pool. This was the first time I had a chance to swim in a proper swimming pool with starting blocks and lines.

The Horticulture examination was to consist of two parts: Written and oral.

We sat in a big hall with little desks and I spent the allotted two hours answering questions on Romanian Expression which was rather boring having to deal with grammar and syntax, but when I commenced my section on Romanian Literature which I loved, I started to write with conviction and feeling about what was so dear to me, the struggle of the Romanian people over a long period of time, to survive all kind of disasters and hardship brought about by bigger and stronger nations starting with the Roman invasion of Dacia (old Romania) in 85 A.D. by the newly elected Roman Emperor Trajan, called Optimus Princeps.

I wrote my essay with a feeling of true love and admiration for all those ancestors of ours who never hesitated to give their life in order to remain free. At the end, I wrote a little ode dedicated to the second Dacian King, Decebalus, who fought bravely against the superior armies of the mighty Roman Empire.

In July 105 AD when Trajan finally managed to surround the capital, Sarmizegetusa, and was ready to capture the city, the citizens of the besieged capital decided to set alight the whole town and die with it as free people, rather than surrender to the Romans. Decebalus committed suicide with his own sword, whilst all his generals sat at a round table and took poison.

The Romans took an enormous loot of gold and silver which even in those days must have been of such magnitude that it allowed the Romans to balance the Empire's finances, and build a number of commemorative monuments of which two were of great importance to the Romanian nation.

Of great historical importance for the Kingdom of Dacia and the Romanian people, was in particular the Column of Trajan which was erected in the middle of Rome's Forum in accordance with Trajan's orders;

It is an impressive structure some 40 metres high and circular in shape, overlaid with an uninterrupted marble-sculptured frieze rendering scenes of the two Dacian wars.

It is so real that even today after 2,000 years there is a steady stream of tourists standing, admiring the skills of the artists who managed to capture so vividly the horrors of the war. Another column was also erected at the same time in Dobrogea, the southern part of Romania, in memory of the Roman troops, called Tropaeum Traiani.

I found myself then in the middle of the written examination, looking at my own sentences, and feeling very emotional writing about those courageous ancestors of ours, who fought hard and based their whole life on a free existence.

They were simple people living their lives in a close community, without aiming to dominate other nations, happy to follow their normal lives and customs. Yet when the need arose to defend themselves, to maintain their freedom, they would sacrifice everything—even their lives—in order to remain free.

As I was writing, the very reason I could not stand the new Communist regime dawned on me; They were trying to take our freedom away, to make us forget our past and become another Communist State under the Russian rule. And just like my proud ancestors, I decided then that I rather die than be their slave.

The written examination was over and I had a chance to spend a little time having a look at the old Bucharest, the capital of Romania which used to be called the "little Paris" mainly because before the war it used to have a very colourful night life, with hundreds of little restaurants which served many dishes and good red wine. But of course the most popular were the little portable kitchens which used to appear soon after sundown, and settle at the corner of busy boulevards, and in no time have prepared ready for sale, hot delicious "mititei", little sausages made of lamb's meat seasoned with herbs and plenty of garlic, and hot out of the pot, corn on the cob. The Romanians love their food and they have a large variety of traditional dishes with many of them learned from the Greeks, Turks, Hungarian and German cuisine. My favourite was the hot corn on the cob, which the street seller would have slowly boiling in a big pot over a small coal fire.

Two days before the oral examination, I woke up in the morning with a terrible toothache. It was so painful that I could not see properly, so I decided to go straight away to the University's dentist, and get some relief.

Talk about rough treatment—I had good teeth and I couldn't remember when I had to go to the dentist last. But my lady dentist decided that I had an abscess and it was necessary to drill and open my tooth to allow the puss to come out.

I had no knowledge of pain and drilling, so when she told me that they were out of anesthetic and would I mind if she did the work without it, I said to go ahead.

She did just that except that she never finished the job; As soon as the drill hit the nerve, I gave a yelp and literally jumped out of the chair with the drill still stuck in my tooth.

"You better go home and wait until the abscess subsides then come back." said the dentist, slightly shaken.

I went home and spent a sleepless night, with my head and mouth throbbing like an enraged volcano.

The next morning I started the Biology oral examination, which involved selecting a topic written on a long thin strip of paper. You were allowed to have a look at it and after a few minutes of mental preparation, tell the examiner everything one had learned about that specific topic. At the end, the examiner would ask additional questions if he felt that the student didn't do that well, or if he wanted to see if the student deserved a higher mark.

Finally, one had to skillfully "navigate" between scientific facts and sheer imagination and be able to relate with a perfectly serious face, the most ridiculous claims about the great plans of the Communist regime. One had to lie well and present a plausible, logical explanation of the intentions of our "great leaders", so as to support the answer given to the set topic. Quite often students were failed in various examinations not because they did not know the subject, but because they lacked the "ideological preparation and they didn't use the accepted political jargon."

The biology examination was set to take place in an enormous old badly-lit timber hall used in the pre-Communist era as the university's chapel; It still had the long timber pews in which the prospective students sat looking pale and worried, waiting their turn to be called to the front of the hail to this hideous timber desk which looked more like a pagan barricade.

The questions were there, written on the long strips of paper and laid in an orderly fashion along the edge of the desk. When my name was called I got up and walked to the desk; Behind the desk was an old man, very correctly dressed and looking more like someone ready to go to a burial ceremony.

Professor S.U. was an illustrious scientist who had published many papers on plant physiology, and had an international reputation as a leading researcher in his field. The older students sent word around the faculty to try our hardest when we faced the old professor as apparently he had great influence in the professorial committee, and his word carried a lot of weight when big decisions had to be taken.

We had already been instructed about the oral examination procedure:

Select ONE question only, answer as fully as you can. However the examiner at his discretion may ask for more details if the answer was incomplete or lacked sufficient information. Despite his sombre appearance the professor looked friendly and even had a small smile in the corner of his mouth. I was confident that I would impress him with my knowledge as Botany had been my best subject. Besides, I had gained additional information from my father's old book, or so I thought.

"Please take one subject only, read the question carefully and then you have ten minutes to answer in detail. Please don't hesitate to ask me if you have any problems understanding the question."

Well, I thought, maybe he is not a bad person and he seemed to give the student a fair chance to do his best. After a few seconds of hesitation I picked one strip of paper and opened it up.

Suddenly I cold shiver went down my spine; "THE LICHENS." That was all that was written on that thin strip of paper.

Normally this topic would have been warmly welcomed by any student who had done his work conscientiously and had studied ALL topics prescribed under the Biology curriculum. In fact this topic would have been a real gift, a subject which could have been covered by any reasonably well prepared student in a few minutes.

To me it was bad news, as I didn't know much about this subject and what I heard at lectures would not have been enough for me to get a reasonable exam result. This was so depressing that it felt like a death penalty—a sentence of sudden execution without any likelihood of pardon.

"Have you finished studying your question tovarase Vena? If so please start."

I was in the middle of a bad dream, a nightmare, and I didn't know which way to go when the professor called out to me again:

"Hurry up please, I haven't got the whole day and there are another 60 students to go through the examination."

By now the smile had disappeared from the professor's face and his voice was growing full of impatience.

"Please", the professor said, "could I have a look at your topic?"

I handed my piece of paper over the desk and waited for his reaction.

"I cannot believe this", he said, starting to laugh.

"What seems to be the problem? You have drawn one of the easiest subjects. Even a five year old could manage it."

I leaned forward, trying to get closer to this man guarded by this enormous desk, which at that moment assumed the proportion of a small hill:

"Sir, I know this may sound ridiculous to you, but would it be possible to select another question?"

I must have surprised him because he took a step forward to the edge of the barricade, adjusting his metal-rimmed glasses:

"Ah, I see," he said, trying hard to hide his grin. "You have had the misfortune to find one of the hardest subjects in the course, and you want to take another topic?"

Then he moved away from the desk, straightened his back, adjusted his glasses and in a half serious, half mocking voice, he addressed himself partly to me but more to the back of the hall, to the other students waiting for their turn;

It wasn't much that he had to say, but he spoke with such accuracy and cynicism that would have made a surgeon proud; He was cutting away at the very base of my self-respect, of my belief in myself and the enormous amount of work I'd done in preparation for this exam. There was no pity or place to hide. He made sure that by the time he had finished his tirade, I would feel totally humbled and humiliated.

According to him, we, the new generation of students, had nothing to offer to a university. We were badly prepared, lacking even the most basic elements of scientific preparation, and should not try or even think about a university career. But above all, as far as he was concerned, we were all bad mannered, without any self-respect and yet we had the audacity to sit for an "University Entrance Examination" to this great and noble institution, which had given the Romanian Nation countless scientists and leaders. He made it sound as though I was the main cause of the lowering of the general standards in the University and that I did not deserve to be part of this academic splendour.

Suddenly I called out to him in desperation,

"Look Sir, I know this sounds stupid but I will answer ANY other subject, I will answer the whole book if you want me to. I really have a perfectly logical reason not to attempt this topic." By now I was getting really desperate. I could feel the axe coming down on my neck and unless I could come up with something believable, it was the end of this exam for me.

The professor took an incredulous look at me, obviously concerned about my state of health and then he spoke in a calculated tone:

"Do you understand what I am trying to tell you? There is no second chance for anyone. You either answer your chosen topic or you fail.!"

As a young child I had occasional fits of anger when I was almost out of control and became very aggressive and destructive. I was getting that feeling again and knowing that I wouldn't be able to hold my raging anger much longer, I begged him once again:

"Please don't ask me why, but for a very good reason I would rather take another subject, any subject you like me to do but not the Lichens.

The Professor looked up to the students in the hall and this time he delivered a venomous, sarcastic lecture about how the young generation has not been able to learn to work, to study, and yet expect special favours.

In my heart I knew that he was right, but also I could not tell him the truth, so suddenly I felt something snapping inside my head, and heard myself yelling at the top my voice.

"Shut your mouth you old fool. You think you know everything but you are just a big bully who likes to be treated like God. We've all heard about you, everyone in this hail knows what a dictator you are, but they are too scared to tell you what they realty think about you.

"Well as far as I am concerned you can shove your course and the blasted lichens up your arse. I don't need you or your stupid course."

The Professor stood behind his desk with a took of total amazement, unable to stem my torrent of abuse; The students in the hall, who remained frozen during the exchange, started to move and you could hear isolated, timid laughter.

Feeling that he was losing the respect which he expected from his students, the professor shouted as I was walking away from his desk to the door:

"As long as I am still a Professor in this Faculty, you will never be a student, NEVER.!

I will make sure that you will be expelled from this course, even if you have the highest notes in the other subjects."

I was out in the autumn sun, and I could still hear his words and somehow I knew that this was the end of my horticulture studies. But strangely enough, I felt rather pleased with myself, to stand up to this person who thought he had the right to treat me like dirt. In those days it was suicidal to express any views, but to openly insult a leader, a representative of the hierarchy, meant an immediate and swift application of the harshest possible penalty, which in my case meant expulsion from the examination.

But the hell with this place, it felt good to say exactly what I felt.

Unfortunately, despite all my work and good results in the other subjects, I managed to ruin my chances by taking on the most important person in the examination committee. My future in this Faculty was finished for ever and I had to re-asses my priorities. At the end of the exams I was called to the Registrar's office where I was told to see the Assistant Registrar, who I found out, knew my parents.

"I cannot believe that anyone in his right mind could pick a fight with Mr. N," he said.

"I have never seen him so furious. At the professorial meeting, the professor stood up and told the meeting that under no circumstance should this Vena student be allowed to join the Faculty, even if he has the highest marks!

Why did you do that, or are out of your mind?" he said, slightly amused, then he continued after taking a quick look around:

"I tell you I think the old wizard deserved it. Just that this is the first time anyone has had the courage to tell him off."

I didn't know whether to feel good about what he was saying, but he must have sensed my disappointment because he added:

"You know you are very unlucky not to make the entry in the course as you were equal second after the written examinations, and you had excellent marks in all the oral subjects except for Biology, where professor. S.U. gave you the lowest possible mark, **"2."**

He continued:

"The University regulations state that the mark of 2 is given in extreme cases of insubordination and is used more as a disciplinary measure; Even if you had top marks in all the subjects, you could not have been admitted to the course."

I left the office feeling very dejected, realizing that I had ruined a very good chance to start an university career, and I had no alternative but to go back home and look for a job.

That evening I spoke to my cousin (Mec)who calmed me down and made me feel a little more confident.

"All right Cornel, you've lost your place in Horticulture, but you weren't given the chance to explain, or to show that you have prepared yourself for this exam. The Professor should have listened to you or given you another subject. After all you did very well in all other subjects and in particular in the written examinations which are supposed to be the hardest."

I was trying not to show my gratitude for having someone be so kind to me after all the battering I'd had lately, but deep down I knew that I'd lost my control and that I deserved all the punishment dished out to me by the professor.

"But I didn't have to insult him like that, did I?" I tried to sound very mature and righteous.

"Look Cornel" said Mec, "there are a few more faculties holding exams late in the autumn. Perhaps you can go back to Turnu-Magurele and prepare yourself for the next round"?.

It was during this conversation that Mec convinced me to try for the Physical Education examination to be held late in September. I had good general preparation for the Horticulture exam, so that with a little more study of Anatomy and Physiology I should be able to do reasonably well in this exam.

I felt much better after Mec's encouragement, and I could see myself with a good chance to stay in Bucharest and not have to go home and explain to everybody how I managed to fail.

I asked Mec if I could stay with his family for the next three weeks and prepare myself for the exam here in Bucharest, which was no problem for Mec and his wife.

TRY AGAIN OR GO HOME

I stayed in Bucharest for the next few weeks, and in the autumn I passed the entry examination for the Institute of Physical Education and Sport.

To my surprise, I finished in 35th place out of 700 candidates, which entitled me to enter the course and receive free accommodation, food and tuition for the four years duration of the course.

In particular I was happy to get a full bursary which meant three meals a day in the Institute's canteen, full accommodation and some equipment and books. All I had to do was to maintain 75 per cent passes in all subjects and watch myself and not start to show my deep resentment towards the Communist Party. So once again destiny took my life in a direction I never consciously intended to follow, particularly as until then I did sport only for recreation and had never contemplated the idea of becoming a performance athlete or a sport teacher. In the period that followed, I had to do sport not for recreation or enjoyment, but solely as a means of survival.

After the examinations I went home for few weeks. My parents were partially pleased with my results. They would have liked me to do a medicine or law course, which they thought would lead to much better paid and respected jobs, however the fact that I had a place in the Institute, and didn't require any financial assistance was convincing enough for the time being.

Even my mother agreed that this was at least a move in the right direction, and in time I could undertake an additional degree in another faculty.

HUNGER THE BEST STIMULANT

In the spring of 1952 I packed my few belongings and headed for Bucharest, to start my course. The first few month of the Physical Education course went very quickly.

I was very busy keeping up with the lectures, practical work and studying.

Many days went by without any chance to do anything else. There were times when I felt like a prisoner in a cell, without the time or freedom to meet people or to do things that most people enjoy doing.

But gradually I organized my work better and started to have more time for myself—meeting people, going to some parties—this felt more like the life I imagined, to cope with the demands of studies, yet have a little free time as well.

After the war, Romania and in particular Bucharest, the capital city, went through a gradual deterioration, due mainly to a great shortage of food and basic goods. The shops which before the war were full of products of all kinds, were now almost empty and only few state-owned stores had some items for sale, which were of poor quality and could only be bought on ration tickets. The war was over yet people had to continue to wait long hours in queues to secure basic items such as flour, sugar or if they were lucky, some lard.

It didn't take long for the people at large to realize that the new Communist regime was a puppet of the Soviet Union, and far from being interested in improving the living standards of the Romanian people, was robbing the country bare of anything of any value. It was during this period that we Romanians started to experience what it meant to be dominated by the Russians, through their faithful servant the Romanian Communist Party, which was even more rapacious and corrupt than their commissars from Moscow.

For any person who has never had the misfortune to live under a communist regime, it is very hard to comprehend or to understand how they operate.

Initially they move quietly, they sneak in almost undetected, and in a short time they have control over all aspects of the country's economy.

This whole process of taking over a fallen country by replacing the old regime with a new communist regime was well rehearsed by the Russians, commencing in 1918 with their own "proletariat" revolution which brutally brought down the Tsar and its Imperial Monarchy, replacing it with a Communist regime.

The theory behind the communist regime is based on the principle of treating everybody equally and ensuring that everybody has the basic requirements for a decent life.

It also proclaims the removal of class differences, abolition of economic exploitation and the provision of a high standard of living for all citizens. Great aims indeed, but as time progressed, these great statements remain empty words, an open and shameless lie used with nauseating regularity by the political leaders and the state controlled media.

The idea of fairness and equality of all citizens of a country has been analyzed by many thinkers and philosophers, but unfortunately none of these schemes have ever come to fruition. The main fault of all these admirable theories lies at the very core of human nature, which is basically greedy and selfish, and invariably tends to abuse power and take advantage of those who cannot defend themselves.

In ridding the country of the Tsarist regime, the Russian Revolution claimed the establishment of a new free society, but they never mention that in the process, millions of innocent people were killed or deported to Siberia never to be heard of again, their properties confiscated by the State.

As time went by the "old" Imperialist society was replaced by a new exploiting class—the select members of the Communist Party. Whilst the majority of workers found it harder to live and have enough to eat, the selected members of the powerful Communist Party took over the properties owned by the previous owners, lived in luxury, drove expensive foreign cars and went on vacation to their private villas on the Black Sea. So much for the promised equality and a better deal for the working class.

So in the end the Russian people continued to starve and work under appalling conditions, stripped of all their human rights—freedom of speech, an independent press, democratic elections, freedom to travel outside the country, and freedom to stage any protests against the working conditions or the political regime.

When the Russians took over Romania in 1946, they immediately proceeded to introduce a system of domination and brain-washing similar to the one that had been so successful in their own country, but even harsher, as they had almost a free hand to treat Romanians as war prisoners, even though Hitler forced the reigning king, King Carol, to send troops to Russia, despite the expressed desire of the Romanian people to remain neutral.

My most vivid memories of those war days, are centered on the lack of food, intense hunger, and how people changed as they were literally starved to death. I don't think anyone can explain what it means to be hungry day after day, to wake up and to go to bed hungry. Food becomes a main obsession everything else is subservient to the ever-growling stomach.

My parents, like all their neighbours and friends, had to start selling items of furniture and clothing to buy food.

By the time I managed to enter the university, things at home were getting desperate without any hope of improvement. I knew that I had to do very well with my studies and could not afford to fail; If I did fail this time, that would have been the end of me. I had to succeed.

UNIVERSITY LIFE IN BUCHAREST

University life as it goes means involvement in a multitude of activities, but one has to keep the main aim in view or risk becoming sidetracked and finish failing exams.

I become involved in many new things, but managed quite well with my studies.

It took a little time to make some friends but fortunately in the same course was my old friend Tudor Bompa, whom I knew from my old High School in Bistrita, a delightful old city with many historical buildings situated in the region of Moldavia.

It is interesting to note how the Russians, who after the war were given the Eastern region of Romania called Basarabia, managed to change its name to Moldavia. Any person with basic knowledge of geography will note that Moldova, the region still belonging to Romania, is the same region as the one before the 2nd WW.

How then can the Russians claim "another" Moldavia?

Obviously they had in mind, in time, to take over the region correctly called Moldova, and so to finish with a much larger portion of traditional Romanian land.

My friend Tudor came from an old family of boundary guards who were held in great respect for their courage and tenacity. They had special rights and properties bestowed on them by the King dating hundred of years ago. It was good to be with Tudor after we left Bistrita, as he was a very good and sincere friend.

Our days usually consisted of getting ready early in the morning, then walking the 6 kilometres to the university canteen, where we had our first meal of the day. Then we had to rush to the lecture room before the huge oak doors closed promptly at 9.00 am.

Once when we arrived one minute too late, we found the doors locked and missed our lecture. The very same day we were both called to the Secretary of the University Communists Party who gave us a stern warning:

"You come late once more and you will lose your canteen ticket"

We tried to explain that it wasn't our fault, but he had no time to argue with us.

"You do as I tell you or you will be kicked out of the University."

There was no room for argument as the Secretary always had the final word.

Learning was strictly a matter of memorizing a swag of political jargons, which basically was a litany of empty words praising the wonderful Communist regime and its creators, Lenin and Stalin.

During compulsory tutorials, we were expected to regurgitate well rehearsed, nauseating and idiotic political lies. We all knew what "real" life meant under Communism, as we were living it, yet we had to pretend that we lived in a true "communist paradise".

If any of the students would ever have had the courage to utter the smallest criticism directed at the regime, they would have been immediately asked to pack their bags and leave the Institute.

Every person in Romania had a personal secret file which contained every possible detail about parents, relatives, personal records of studies and in particular it had a complete record of one's attitude towards the Communist regime. It didn't matter where you went, within a matter of few days the local Communist Secretary assisted by the local police would have a complete record of your movements.

A new system operating soon after the establishment of the C.P. (Communist Party), prohibited ordinary citizens from leaving their village or town without having a police issued permit. A person intending to go to Bucharest for instance, had to report to the local police in Turnu Magurele before departing, and give a good reason why they were travelling to the capital and how long they intended to stay away. They would be told to report on arrival to the nearest police station in Bucharest and present the official permit which had issued by the local police.

Before returning, the person had to report once again to the local police in Bucharest, and have the permit stamped, and finally on arrival back home, report once again to the local police station to have the whole document verified.

If you did not comply with this ridiculous procedure, you were fined or not permitted to leave town for long periods of time. This procedure ensured that everybody was accountable to the police state, and that the Police or the Secret Service could find any person they wanted anywhere in Romania within a matter of days.

Our country under the new Communist regime become a huge jail, a monstrous enclosure. It didn't matter where one lived, the feeling of being trapped, watched and manipulated, stayed with all of us, day and night. There was no escape, there was no freedom, there was no future.

WHY ROWING?

Our university already had a fairly successful rowing team and the necessary facilities, but was lacking a top coach. This changed in 1952 with the arrival of I.D., a fresh graduate of the Leningrad Sport Science Institute, where he did a post-graduate course in advanced methods of training for rowers and studied the latest methods for intensive training.

I had never done any rowing before coming to the Institute but I was assured by my friend Tudor that there was nothing to it and that we could both become members of the University Eights in no time.

"Why do you think they are asking for new members?" Tudor asked with his usual confidence.

"They haven't done very well in the inter-University games, and they need some fresh blood in their team. Some real power."

We were in the University dormitories and being a Sunday there was very little to do apart from studying.

"Come on Cornel," Tudor persisted, "Let's join the Rowing Club. I hear that if we make the "A" boat, they are going to give us extra food and tickets, plus in the summer we will be training at lake Snagow and perhaps we will have a shot at the National Titles? What do you think?"

The prospect of not having to go back to Turnu in the summer during the University break, plus the opportunity to go to the beautiful location of Snagov, a natural lake surrounded by dense forests—the ex-playground of rich Bucharest society during the days of King Carol—made me decide to listen to Tudor.

"All right, let's do it" I said.

"That's my boy," Tudor said, and promptly started to pound the ground with few steps of Caluseri, a vigorous Romanian dance, which is performed by young men in the villages to express their youth and strength.

The next day we went to see the new coach and find out what we had to do.

My first impression of people is always the best one as I seem to sense what they are like even before they start to speak.

I guess I inherited this quality from my great grandmother on my mother's side, who I was told had some Spanish blood. She apparently could read the cards and tell the future very accurately. Some jealous people said that she had some gypsy blood, but nothing official. It made it sound more interesting, as Romanians regard the gypsies as people with great healing powers, able to cure many diseases, and in particular able to tell the future.

A shiver went along my spine when I saw this thin man with his watery blue eyes and narrow white lips. His hair was blond and lifeless, and he looked very tired and in need of a blood transfusion.

"Have you boys done any rowing before?" he asked. His voice was more of a whisper, and he seemed to use a lot of energy to open his mouth.

"I did some at school in Bistrita," Tudor said slowly, "and Cornel rowed boats on the Danube".

He looked at us with a face devoid of expression. Then after a long silence he told us that it would be hard work but the rewards would be there for those who could keep up with the training.

"I want to build a real University Eight, a strong boat so that by next year we will be in contention for the National Titles and will challenge Dinamo and CCA."

Suddenly he was coming to life, and I could see that he was excited about this prospect. But I thought we must be dealing with a dreamer of the worst kind. How could anyone expect a young team of inexperienced rowers to face in direct competition the two strongest and and most successful rowing Clubs in Bucharest?

"I can tell you that this is your chance to do some real training, something that hasn't been tried before. It will take guts and willpower—I can tell you that much."

I.D., as we were to learn later, had the ability to bring out the best in his charges simply by appealing to their sense of worth: How good are you, or perhaps you are not what you would like to think you are?

The coach smiled wryly then looked at his assistant and whispered a few words.

"All right then boys, you can have your endurance test now, and see how you go. The test is done in the practice tank and will take between 15 and 20 minutes.

"You decide who goes first."

I decided to go first and entered the room under the soccer stadium where the training pool was built. This was where the rowers trained, particularly in the winter. In the middle of this concrete pool floated an ordinary competition single skiff anchored to the side of the pool by steel cables ending in rubber cords.

To commence the test you sat in the sleek and narrow boat, which fortunately was kept in balance by the steel cables, and started to row. It was very realistic and felt like the real thing, however it was much easier to keep your balance. The water moved by the oars, traveled around the concrete pool and under the boat, giving the sensation of actually rowing, totally unattached.

The assistant told me what I had to do, and that I had to keep up with a mechanical pacer, commencing at 30 strokes per minute and gradually accelerating to 42 strokes a minute, keeping this pace for about three minutes.

As a young kid I had experienced the effects of prolonged effort which basically meant enduring a lot of pain for long periods of time. Swimming in the Danube for hours was always difficult and demanding, but more painful were the long cross-country skiing competitions, over distances varying from 10 to 25 kilometres. So I did have some idea about endurance effort and pain, but rowing was different from all other experiences of the past: Because you are enclosed by the confines of the boat, which is pretty narrow, it does not permit the rower to move about too much, so that the intensity of the effort is felt more precisely, more localized.

I started to row on the signal and for the next few minutes I had no problem keeping up with the pacemaker. The coach was sitting opposite me with a log book in which he kept making notes as the time went by. His assistant would occasionally call out to me to put the oar deeper in the water, or to keep my upper body upright.

In rowing one is seated on a small trolley seat which allows the rower to move forward when catching the water and then slides back when pulling the oars. Rowing involves all the big groups of muscles in the body, which demand large amounts of oxygen and places great stress on the lungs and heart.

By now I started to feel the muscles of my forearms contracting, and the back muscles started to ache a little.

"We are going to increase the pace now," said the assistant.

"Keep up with the pace and don't stop until I tell you to do so."

I was wondering how long one had to keep going before they would be satisfied with your effort, but I was determined not to stop before the signal. The rest of the test became a distorted sequence of effort and pain, and an incredible desire to stop, to rest my arms. Now and then I could see I.D's face.

He was watching me intently and kept taking notes. It hurt a lot, more than I expected, but I managed to keep it up, not because I was that strong, but because I felt something stronger inside, telling me that this was my test of survival, and no matter what I must not stop.

A few days went by before Tudor and I got over the blisters and the sore backs, but we both were told that we had passed the test, and would shortly start our autumn preparation. This experience, painful as it was, it shaped my future actions and attitude to life.

Perhaps it's not too late to acknowledge the importance of having I.D as a coach, but I doubt that he was interested in my psychological quest, as he was obviously only interested in results, regardless of what it took to achieve his plans.

WRESTLING WITH TUDOR

Before the Second World War, there was little knowledge of organized sport in Romania, and there was a great need for physical education teachers and experienced coaches.

The Communist Regime was aware that they could use sport to their advantage and create a good international image extolling the virtues of the new regime.

The formation of a Central Sport Committee was aimed at creating a body which had the purpose of developing superior programmes and methods for promoting quality and to obtain the best possible results in international competition, in particular, the Olympic Games. For the first time in Romania there was an organized effort, a plan aimed at preparing its athletes for high level competition. There was a great rush to produce qualified coaches and to get the maximum support from the higher Sport Institutes. Sport medicine started to play an ever-increasing role in discovering the best scientific methods for preparing athletes.

New sports such as Modern Pentathlon were introduced, and older traditional sports such as Fencing and Gymnastics were given full financial support. For the first time elite sport became fully funded by the State, which covered all the expenses for coaching and travelling.

My Institute for Physical Education and Sport (I.C.F.) was given the specific purpose of producing highly specialized coaches in all of the Olympic Games events. The four year full-time course covered some 32 units such as anatomy, physiology, chemistry, physics and body mechanics (Kinesiology) among others. In addition they introduced compulsory study of Marxism-Leninism, as well as the study of the Russian language. No other language was taught. All subjects were compulsory and had to be passed before a student was allowed to proceed to the next level. Bursary holders had to get marks above 75% in every subject or the bursary was terminated.

Prior to joining the university I had a try at most sports and managed to compete in a few big regional competitions. I was also interested in athletics, in particular in javelin and discus but until then I had done sport more as recreation and had not taken it too seriously. For the first time I had to learn the correct techniques in various sports.

To my surprise I started to improve. In particular I was starting to get some promising results in Javelin throwing with throws in the 50 metre range. But once again destiny took over my newly found prowess, and decided that I wasn't to become involved in athletics, as there were others things in store for me.

As part of our practical activities we were required to study and practice Greco-Roman wrestling. Our lecturer was an ex-national champion, still solid and powerful, with a short thick neck and cauliflower ears, but he wasn't trained as a teacher so he had little understanding of graded exercises so students could gain the necessary skills without major accidents. Perhaps there wasn't enough time allocated for his area, however we had to progress very rapidly from simple grappling techniques to complex movements which required years of preparation.

This particular morning, we were shown the "souple", a movement which involved turning your opponent over by arching your back whilst holding him, then land on top of your head, forming a bridge and tossing your opponent over. This is a difficult movement as the attacker has to have a strong neck, able to withstand the combined weight of the two participants at the moment of the impact.

Usually at the end of the practice session we had short wrestling bouts with a selected partner. On this particular day I had Tudor as my opponent, as we were both about the same weight. The match was pretty even, but Tudor was able to foil my attempts to bring him down. Finally I decided to try the newly learned movement, so I took a good hold round his waist, lifted him off the ground, and then tried to arch backward.

All went well until I was halfway down to the ground, when Tudor swung his weight to the left, making me land on my right shoulder instead of landing on the top of my head as planned.

As soon as I landed on my shoulder I heard a nasty crack and then I felt an excruciating pain. They took me to the infirmary where I was told after a short examination that I had dislocated my shoulder badly and torn all the ligaments. What was more worrying was hearing the doctor tell me that my javelin throwing days were over and I had to try something else.

Because the rowing action does not involve lifting of the arm above the shoulder level, and did not cause any pain, it was obvious that I had no choice but stay in the university rowing squad. It became necessary for me to specialize in rowing and not athletics as initially planned.

The second stage of my road to Modern Pentathlon and the Olympic Games was already set.

SUMMER CAMP AT LAKE SNAGOV

My first year at ICF went very quickly and before I realized it, we had been doing a lot of preparation for the upcoming summer camp at the beautiful lake Snagov where most rowing clubs had their boat houses and all necessary facilities for training and accommodation. Towards the start of summer in July, we were ready to start the intensive month of training at the lake under the supervision of our rowing coach. Up to this moment, although we were starting to feel the intensity of training in the "dry dock", we had no idea what was in store for us.

One morning we were taken by bus to the lake, where we were quickly allocated to our cabins, which were comfortable and set between beautiful tall trees near the edge of the water.

Our program started early at around 5am with an "easy" 5 km. run through the wild untouched woods surrounding the lake, on tracks covered with leaves and small fallen branches. The air was heavy with the fresh smell of the forest vegetation, and we were experiencing the thrill of being young and fit.

After the run we usually had the first session of upper body strengthening, which consisted of hundreds of push-ups, sit-ups, jumps and climbing ropes suspended from a high wooden frame some 6 m. above the ground. I had done similar exercises in the past and I was capable of doing quite a bit of work but this time things were different because of the training's intensity, volume and the very short periods of rest.

Our new rowing coach, who has just returned from an advanced course for coaches in Moscow, and was pushing us to do things that it was hard to believe were within the range of our physical abilities. Before this camp I thought that my level of fitness was quite good and I took pride in being able to do some 30 correct push-ups, 10 to 14 chin-ups, and around 40 sit-ups. But I was soon to find out that these numbers were far from satisfactory in the eyes of our coach.

For a start he introduced us to the "pleasures" of a system of body conditioning called Circuit Training, a system totally new to us, which involved 10-12 exercises, each addressing a different part of the body and to be performed in the shortest possible time.

Initially you have a test to determine the maximum number of movements which you can perform over a period of 60 seconds. This constitutes the "maximum number" you are capable of performing at this stage. All 12 exercises are tested in a similar manner, then to find out your maximum numbers, you divide these numbers by 2, which then gives you the "working numbers". When you start you circuit training you have to go through all 12 exercises without stopping, using the working numbers, in the shorter possible time. Then you have to go through the same exercises for the second and the third time. At the end you record the total time taken to complete the circuit.

After a number of sessions one is able to complete the whole routine in a shorter time. When you can do the whole circuit in half the initial time taken during the maximum test, you are ready to be tested again, and set new targets which inevitably will be higher and harder to complete. This system is extremely successful, but it is very demanding physically but in particular mentally. One has to push himself to the limit, and try to go beyond the pain and fatigue.

This was when I started to realize what "supreme physical effort" meant. It wasn't just a word, it was very real and at times frightening experience, which placed excessive demands on your body, to the point where you felt that you would collapse if you had to take one more step. But somehow I managed not to give up, to push myself beyond what I thought was my absolute limit, and survive this brutal introductory training program.

It was a true do or die effort.

OUR COACH IS A MADMAN

At the end of our first week of intensive training we were all dead tired and every bone and muscle in our body was asking for mercy. This was when I.D. decided to increase our effort and started to put us through two sessions of rowing a day, plus the morning run and the fitness session. I initially thought of rowing as being an interesting, pleasant sport, being in contact with the beautiful surroundings of a river or lake, and whilst rowing gently becoming one with the tranquil scenery. But competitive rowing doesn't allow for any pleasure or enjoyment unless you are a masochist. Perhaps the only pleasure is the moment you stop the effort and you can rest your protesting body; In any case I had never experienced such pain and discomfort in all the sports I had practiced until then.

Normally the distance covered in a race is about 2000 metres, which has to be covered at a pace of 37-39 strokes a minute.

The first two or three minutes of the race goes fairly quickly but soon after that, the whole body starts to tire due to the large oxygen demand placed on the lungs and heart by the intense effort of the major muscles of the arms, trunk and legs.

Shortly your mouth gets very dry, you start to gasp for air, and your heart gallops at a furious pace; Your arm muscles start to cramp and it becomes very difficult to hold the oar; Every stroke hurts and you want to stop, to end the inhuman pain, but you know that there is no escape, that you cannot let your mates down and stop, so you keep on rowing with the last ounce of energy left.

When the ordeal is over and the boat crosses the finishing line, the inside of the narrow boat looks like a battle field covered with wounded bodies. Some cry in pain, others lean over the side and dry reach, and everyone seems to be affected in some way regardless of how strong or fit they were before the race.

Fortunately the rowers tend to recover within four to five minutes after the race, particularly if they had trained correctly and were used to high intensity effort.

So in order to be able to withstand the full 2000 metre race, one has to gradually become used to the continuous effort, lack of sufficient oxygen, intense pain and partial cramping of the arms or other parts of the body, and experience what we call "second "and even "third wind".

Our coach believed that the only way our boat of eight was going to do well in the coming Autumn National Championships, was to do twice as much work as our main opponents, Dynamo and C.C.A. Consequently he convinced us that rowing 25 kilometres twice a day at a medium pace was absolutely necessary in order to improve our balance and team work. As well as that, we had to complete between 8 and 10 500 metre short sprints when we had to learn how to start fast and establish an early lead.

The resting periods between the sprints were kept to a minimum, just enough time to recover partially from the intense effort.

If anyone of us appeared to slow down or not give one hundred per cent effort, we were immediately detected by I.D. who seemed to have an extra sensory perception. Nobody could get away with it. The penalty for not trying hard enough was applied swiftly and without exception:

"One for all and all for one". We all had to do extra sprints until everybody was totally exhausted and had given their last ounce of energy. Enough to say that by the time we struggled back to the camp and lifted the big boat out of the water, quite often one of the crew would collapse on the wooden pontoon. We were that tired that many times in the evening we would not go to have our evening meal, and instead collapse in our beds.

If the first week was hard on all of us, the second week become even harder because of the extra rowing session. We were starting to count how many days before the camp was over and we would return to Bucharest.

The summer days were getting hotter and the only pleasure left was to take a long swim in the cool waters of the lake in the evenings. However to our surprise, we started to feel much better by the third week and most of us seemed to cope a little better with the volume of work imposed.

This was when our coach decided to introduce us to his "special" spirit cruncher.

As it happens, we don't have in the Romanian language the equivalent of the English expression: "This will separate boys from men". Our coach wanted to show us how hard the Russian rowers were training but in particular I believe he wanted to find out how many of us had what it took to be top competitors as well as experimenting with stress exercise and its effects on the various individuals. This test was aimed not so much at the physical qualities required by a good rower such as speed, strength endurance, but kind of a TOTAL test of the will to survive, of the ability to block the intense pain caused by excessive effort and the ability to continue to row despite intense pain verging on torture.

I had never experienced anything even closely resembling the test that was to follow, although I.D had given us some idea of what was involved in high performance training.

This particular morning, after the usual 6 km. run, we were assembled on the basketball court and told that we were to be tested to find out the level of fitness and endurance we had achieved during the training camp. Additionally he told us that only those rowers who performed well in all the tests would be allowed to continue training with the University Eight. There were four levels we could try for, and we were advised not to hold anything back as this would jeopardize our selection in the top eight.

The exercises selected were push-ups, sit-ups, chin-ups, up-jumps and climbing the rope. From the explanatory sheet given to us at the start, one could work out what was required to do to obtain a pass or a better mark. We were fit, but even so we realized that it was going to be hard to get a pass and almost impossible to get above the pass level.

Tudor was scratching his chin and for once I could see that he was a little worried despite his enormous natural strength:

"He is a mad bastard," Tudor said, poking his finger at the instructions:

"He doesn't want to see how fit we are, he wants to show us that we are not strong enough to pass his test . . . he wants to humiliate us!"

I didn't feel too confident, particularly as I could not see myself passing even the lower level: It was well above what I have been doing in practice and I had to use all my will-power just to finish the tests.

"Are there any questions or is anything too difficult for you to understand?" I.D. said, with a sarcastic grin on his face.

"Well then, take your position and decide who is going through the test first. Oh, and by the way fellows," he said, "Good luck in particular with your rope climbing".

He was making some strange chuckling sounds, almost like someone about to have a good meal. We all froze when we heard that. The climbing test was performed on a thin rope of about 6 m. long which we had to climb at the end of every physical fitness session.

It had to be done with the hands only and no support from the feet.

One had to go up to the top and down without touching the ground, then climb once more to the top and down; A pass was considered to be three times up and down the rope. Many of us had failed in the past to go up the rope more than twice, and more often than not we would slide out of control, unable to hold the rope, and slide to the ground, burning the skin of our hands. That meant rowing with very sore and inflamed hands, but this was never allowed as an excuse, and we had to row just the same.

These were the standards set by our coach:

1.	Push-ups:	Fail=120	Pass =135	Good= 140	V.Good=150
2.	Sit-ups:	" 100	" 120	" 130	" 140
3.	Chin-ups:	" 30	" 45	" 50	" 55
4.	Up-Jumps	" 80	" 90	" 110	" 120
5.	Rope climb	" 1	" 3	" 4	" 5

I would imagine that most people are familiar with the first three exercises from their P.E. classes at school so I won't explain how they are done.

However the Up-jumps are not as common ; These are jumps performed on the spot, by jumping and trying to bring the knees high and to touch the upper chest; If the knees did not touch the chest, the movement wasn't counted.

Additionally one was not allowed to take two small jumps between the knee lifting as this meant a longer rest between the jumps.

So we had to do a large number of physically difficult movements under any conditions, but the catch was that we had to do it in a given time, which makes all the more difficult. Additionally we were told that if we failed any one of the four tests, we will be considered as having failed the whole test.

There was also the matter of rest : There was to be only 60 sec. rest between the exercises, so that there was little time to recover from the previous test;

The next hour was like the inside of a Mediaeval torture chamber, with young bodies sweating profusely, groans of pain and relentless agony from which there was no escape. Some of us could not finish the test and collapsed on the floor covered with sweat, others were started to throw up.

When my turn came, I could see from the corner of my eye a cynical smile on our coach's face. He was enjoying himself witnessing this spectacle of pain, justified in his belief that his coaching methods would show to all concerned how well prepared and tough he was:

He would no doubt in future land some secure and well paid coaching position with some of the bigger clubs, or perhaps be put in charge of the Olympic Rowing Team.

Tudor was my partner and he had to do the counting for me.

He looked at me hard, before I was to start, and then he said in a quiet tone:

"Don't give this bastard the satisfaction of showing you are in pain, or you are out of the team. You can do it if you really put your mind to it, I will help you, I will be with you all the way."

Quite often we tend to exaggerate the magnitude of an event which is going to take place in the future. I worried a lot before this physical test, mainly because I did not want to lose the advantages I was receiving for the first time in my life: good accommodation, good nourishing food and the prospect of travelling nationally, and if performance was exceptional, even the Olympic Games was a possibility.

But as I went through the test, I was totally surprised to see how much I had improved, doing a lot better than I would have believed myself capable of only few month ago.

My results varied between pass and good, and on the rope test I climbed 3 times which was far better than I had done previously.

When Tudor's turn came, as expected he managed to get the best results of the whole group. His 5 climbs on the rope established an unofficial record for the camp. His humour was infectious as he kept humming bright Romanian country songs and performing little swift dancing steps between tests, steps of the "Caluseri", a country dance for young men, best known for its dynamic and vigorous movements;

Tudor normally was a quiet young man who hated to show openly his emotions. This was why we couldn't understand what came over him as soon as he started his tests. When he started his turn most of us were dead tired and to a certain extent too tired to be in the mood for fun. I.D. had us all in great pain and discomfort, enjoying our struggle to cope with the difficult tests while Tudor was doing all that was required of him physically without any sign of pain and then he was able to show our coach complete contempt for his "difficult" tests.

Gradually his comic performance, done with great spirit, started to lift the performance of all the other participants. The grunts and the groans were gradually replaced by small chatter and even laughter. We all felt great pleasure from seeing how I.D.'s face stopped grinning and started to look annoyed, but he could not do anything to stop Tudor who was making a mockery out of the most difficult tasks.

I wished I had a video-camera to take a picture of our coach's face. His moment of glory had been dissolved by this unexpected source of energy, a true demonstration of the invincibility of human nature under most difficult conditions. The strength of the human spirit was right there in front of all of us to see.

We didn't feel the pain anymore, we were enjoying doing things thought impossible by any normal person, and yet it was more than that. We felt taller and stronger, invincible and defiant; We were able to tell this Russian-trained coach that the spirit of the Romanian people was greater and stronger than anything he had learned in Russia. We were the winners and he knew that. He left the field before the end of the test.

Tudor and I made the final eight, and we competed in our first rowing club event championship in the autumn in Bucharest where we finished in the third place.

Shortly after that, Tudor and I were to move in different directions and once again I was pushed towards my unknown destiny by an irresistible force.

PART TWO

Our rowing training camp ended in August, and after the Nationals we had a short holiday before the start of the new university year. I had time to think about what happened during the rowing camp and to try to understand a little more about myself.

There was no argument as to which method of training produced high results:

I.D. proved to us all, that his Russian-learned method was working better than the previous methods used. Hard work and repetitions gave the best results.

Perhaps he lacked a deeper understanding of human nature, but he definitely has learned how to push his charges beyond what was considered impossible.

He was taught to ignore emotions when working with potential competitors, to push them to the very limit of their physical and mental make-up even if this meant losing any personal contact, any attempt to understand some of the beliefs and aspirations of his athletes. In the end he was working AGAINST the very people he set himself to make champions. He succeeded to make us his greatest enemies, his most fierce critics, yet without his strict regime, we would have never achieved great results.

We did not win to prove what a great coach he was, we won because we hated him with all our might: "Will we show him".

So in the end, a coach cannot be a "great coach" even if he trains Olympic medallists, unless he goes a little further and learns to understand his athletes, to teach by example, to motivate, to inspire and to give confidence to his pupils.

Then he truly can say that he has fulfilled his dream and become a better person, a great coach of people. In time I thanked Mr I.D. but he will never know that. I thanked him because I learned how to treat my athletes, and not to make the same mistake he did.

So what makes a great coach?

Teach your charges the best techniques, make them reach deep into their mind and body, show them what their bodies and mind can do, push them beyond their wildest physical and spiritual experiences, but never forget to show them your respect and support whilst they go through these difficult experiences.

Ultimately, I.D. was relaying in his results to keep his position. Unfortunately we became his greatest problem: If he didn't win the national titles in couple of years, he would have been replaced. He had to be hard and show no sympathy for our personal problems.

Despite having less time to study and spending all my free time in training sessions, I was pleasantly surprised to see good results in my first year of studies.

Tudor and I were still involved with the rowing team, although we had somewhat lost our enthusiasm and respect for our coach. I must admit that at times I had nightmares in which I had to climb ropes which led to the top of Eiffel Tower whilst I was chased by ferocious dogs.

We decided to wait for the time being, and continue training with the rowing team, mainly because as members of the rowing team, we were given special conditions such as extra food and sport equipment. However we were never given any form of payment and the situation at home was getting more hopeless. I had to learn to live without any luxuries and be satisfied with the little I was getting from sport. There was no room for self-pity or complaining as most of us were in a similar situation.

So I was directing my efforts at succeeding and dreaming of a time in the future when I would have enough money to buy myself a push-bike, and not have to rely on public transport.

The autumn season in Romania used to be a happy time, with most of the crops ready to be harvested. With the acute shortage of food and basic essentials, Bucharest was still struggling to return to normal after the destruction caused by the World War II and the ferocious plundering by the Russians.

By the end of September the balmy weather started to give way to the first cold winds coming from the north, and people started to store firewood for the harsh winter which would normally start in November and bring heavy snow and blizzards for the next few months.

I can't remember the exact day but it was either a Wednesday or a Thursday when we had to attend a lecture in the basketball hall, and because we were running late I suggested to Tudor to take a short cut through this dark, smelly alley running between the main building and the basketball stadium. Normally we would have avoided to go this way because this alley was used quite often by male students to relieve themselves, particularly if they were late for lectures and didn't have the time to go to the main toilets.

"Aleia pisatului",(the piss alley,) as it was called by students, was as usual, dark, wet and smelly. We both stopped and relieved ourselves on the brick wall, when I noticed a small note on the wall;

"Who is the idiot who posts notices in this place" I said trying to avoid the bad smell by not breathing too often.

It's probably someone having a laugh at our "beloved "Communists leaders" said Tudor closing his fly.

SELECTION TRIALS

"This is an invitation to compete in the first National TRIATHLON CHAMPIONSHIP for male students. Events to be contested are:

1)   4,000 m. Cross-Country,
2)   l00m. Swim. (any style)
3)   Rifle shooting, (5 shots at 50 m.)

Those interested get in touch with Mr Muresanu at the Sports Committee.

The competition will take place between 10th and 12th November, 1953.

Signed. Captain Ion Muresanu
Co-ordinator.

"Do you know anything about triathlon ?" Tudor asked as we rushed to the hall.

"No, I've never heard of such a sport. Maybe it's an army sport or one of the newly introduced sports in the Olympic Games?"

"Anyhow, I can swim and run pretty well," I said, slightly interested.

"The only event I don't now much about is rifle shooting."

Tudor listened to me while scratching his chin in his usual manner when he was not sure of what to do next, then he said:

"I could manage the run and the shoot but I will sink to the bottom of the pool like an axe. I don't even know if I can swim 100m. without drowning."

"Listen Tudor," I said rather seriously, " we have to try something different or we will have to put up with mad Dumitrescu next summer. I hear he is already bragging about winning the National Titles next year even if he has to kill us."

"I for one I have had enough of his circuit training, and I don't want to work with him again if I can help it," I said.

Tudor looked at me and realized that I was ready to give rowing away, even if he wanted to continue:

"In regula" (the Romanian equivalent of O.K) Tudor said, "let's give it a try and see what comes out of it."

NEW SPORT

A triathlon competition was organized by the Central Committee of Romanian Sport as a selection trial to establish a training squad from which to select a team who could represent Romania in the sport of Modern Pentathlon, in the 1956 Olympic Games in Melbourne, Australia.

Olympic Sports were strongly supported by the Romanian Communist Regime. The Communist leaders were aware of the positive repercussions in the international scene of success in the sports arena and in particular in those sports included in the Olympic Games program. Romania did not have a great tradition in Olympic sports, mainly because the previous regime did not encourage sport, which was more the scene of the very rich people who had the means to train and travel overseas for competitions.

So the time was ripe in 1952 to start a well planned program, to prepare and to enter the world arena in the hope of attracting attention and respect from the developed countries, and indirectly to attract positive comments about the Communist regime, and to prove to the rest of the world that the Communist system was superior not only in the socio-economic arena, but also in sporting endeavour. In reality, sport in communist countries was nothing but a well disguised exercise to cover-up the shocking state of the economy, the blatant social injustice, the inhuman treatment of those who dared to contradict the regime, and in particular the ever increasing poverty of the working class, whilst the communist leaders lived a life of luxury.

Because in the past Romania did not have a great tradition in sports like gymnastics, water-polo or fencing, or they did not take part at all in sports like Modern Pentathlon, the Communist leaders commenced a program aimed at creating a strong base of expert coaches, based on sound scientific research. University doctors, physiotherapists and psychologists were involved and directed to study and produce the best possible information leading to scientific training of athletes.

In addition, national centres were opened in various cities where young promising athletes were trained under the guidance of leading coaches. For the first time in Romania, sport became a respected occupation and a method of escapism from the reality of the Communist regime.

As we learned later, countries such as Eastern Germany, Hungary, Bulgaria, Poland and Czechoslovakia, through their state controlled programmes, gained an impressive advantage against traditionally strong sporting countries such as the USA, England and Sweden which were still using obsolete methods of training and conducted their performance sport strictly on an amateur basis. As a result, Romanian sport, for the first time in its history of international participation, experienced a tremendous improvement and literally overnight began to accumulate high results and unprecedented success in sports considered to be traditionally the domain of long established cultures and schools, such as fencing and gymnastics.

Without our knowledge, our triathlon selection was to be the start of the first Romanian Modern Pentathlon Team, trained and prepared to represent Romania in the Olympic event of Modern Pentathlon in the 1956 Melbourne Olympics.

WOULD CORNEL VENA STAND UP

I had almost forgotten about the notice on the wall for the triathlon competition, when early in November 1953, Tudor and I received an official invitation to attend the triathlon trials which were to be held on the weekend of 10-12 of November.

By then winter had almost taken over Bucharest, with very cold mornings, and cold winds. The ground was frozen and hard like concrete.

The first event, the 100 swim, was held at the new sports centre at Herastrau.

The water in the pool was very warm and inviting. My swimming was pretty rough as I was using then a style called trudgeon, which is a mixture of side leg kick and one arm only going over the water. This was an old style used more in rescue technique and long distance swimming. I taught myself this particular style when I was swimming across the Danube, and it was quite effective, but not fast enough for speed events. Fortunately for me, most of the other competitors were poor swimmers and did not go very fast. Tudor had a real struggle to finish, as he managed to swallow gallons of water. At the end he looked rather pale and tired.

The next event we had to compete in was totally new to me. We had to shoot with a .22 rifle at a target 50 m. away. We were given 5 shots and a short introduction to target shooting after which we had to aim to get as many 10s as possible. We were shooting in a laying position, which made it easier to hold the rifle steadily and hit the target.

After finishing my 5 shots, I wanted to know how I had gone, but I was told by the range officer that the results would be given to us when everybody else had finished.

As it turned out, we never found out our shooting results.

The last event, the cross-country run, was run on the last day, on a course around the Institute. It was very cold and the ground was hard like a rock. My fitness was good due to the severe fitness program. at the rowing camp, and my youth experience in cross-country runs. I knew that I could do well in this event and I was confident of a good result. We were given the start as a group, so that some 35 young athletes surged shoving and pushing to the front. From my previous experience I knew that it was better to start slowly, keeping fairly close to the leading bunch for most of the race, and sprint only towards the end, when most of the athletes were getting tired. It worked pretty much as I planned, and I managed to finish second. Tudor, who was basically a sprinter, did a fairly good run, but he finished well back in the field.

A few more weeks went by and we were busy trying to catch up with our studies, when we were called to the University's main office and informed that we were to attend a special meeting at the Central Sports Committee, and that under no circumstance were we to miss this meeting. It was rather uncommon by CSC standards to make such a big fuss about a meeting, when most of the students would go through the whole duration of the course without ever seeing or having any contact with the C.SC.

Neither Tudor nor I had any idea of how we'd performed and we didn't think we'd done that well. This was the time when I started to learn about the importance of not placing your opponents on a high pedestal, or to think that you are not the best or that the other competitors are much better. In reality the difference between the champion and the others is usually very small, and there are other factors more important than the physical performance that determines the outcome.

We hear a lot more these days about "believing in yourself", which in retrospect I realize now, has great bearing on any physical performance. This valuable attitude allows athletes to compete without fear, with complete confidence in themselves and to gain the full reward for their efforts. This is a valuable lesson which should be taught by all coaches to their young charges from the start, namely to believe in yourself, and not to regard your opponents as unbeatable. This could make a big difference to their final results.

Of course there are some individuals who are "born" with that sense of being better than their opponents, and they exude that special air of confidence. These people are very hard to defeat for the very reason that they do not doubt themselves and they can perform at their best regardless of the level of competition. Fortunately for us average people, there are not many such people, or it would be a lot harder to win at anything.

The Romanian Communist regime had established a well structured body to be responsible for the development of sport and recreation in Romania called the Central Committee for Sport and Recreation. They were given a large building in the business quarters in Bucharest which housed most of the Olympic Federations and other sports.

When Tudor and I arrived at the meeting, we were directed to a small room filled to capacity with young people. I recognized most of them from the triathlon competition.

We waited for few minutes until everybody was seated, when a group of officials entered the room. The captain, whom I recognized as the one in charge of the trials, stood up behind the wooden desk, and began to address us.

"First of all I would like to congratulate you for finishing in the top group," he said.

Allow me to introduce myself, I am Captain Ion Muresanu, and I have been appointed by the CCS to select and organize a group of young athletes who will form the nucleus of our future Romanian Modern Pentathlon Team.

"Hopefully if we improve enough and be good enough to compete against the major teams, we could have the opportunity to represent Romania in the 1956 Olympic Games in Melbourne, Australia. This will be the first time for a Romanian Pentathlon Team to compete in the Olympic Games."

You could have heard a pin drop in the room whilst Muresanu spoke, but when he mentioned the word Olympics, we all started to move excitedly.

"Please let me finish," Muresanu said, trying to gather our attention once more, then he continued:

"I know this is very exciting news for you but I must caution you not to get too carried away . . . there is a long way to go, many things have to be learned and perfected and above all it is going to be extremely hard work, and many of you may not be able to cope"

The tone of his voice was cold and calculating, perhaps even slightly threatening. We all sensed the hidden power this man had.

"But let's start by reading the results and announcing the winner and those selected in the squad to commence training for Modern Pentathlon in the near future."

It was a lot for us to digest—the possibility of representing Romania in the Olympic Games was a dream every athlete cherished. There we were, entering what we thought was a minor competition, and then being told by this fellow about the possibility of representing our country in the next Olympics. It was very exciting.

Just when Tudor started to whisper something, Muresanu called out:

"Quiet please. " I am going to read the results of the competition in REVERSED order. The last 15 names to be read, will automatically be selected in the future Olympicl Modern Pentathlon Squad. The other competitors will be kept in our records and called to the national squad to replace any athlete who cannot cope with the training code, becomes sick, or in our opinion, does not make sufficient progress."

So they weren't going to go easy, I thought. They will keep in the squad only those who can put up with the training load. At least Tudor and I had a very good grounding in the rowing camp, and I was pretty sure that nothing could be harder than what " mad Dumitrescu" put us through . . . but of course I was wrong as I found later.

Muresanu started to read names and one by one would stand up. They were then told in what position they have finished. "When you hear you name and place, could you stand up.?"

The room was getting very hot and sweaty, as we all were waiting with great anticipation to hear our results. The list was going on and by the time Muresanu started to announce the last remaining places, I started to think that there had been a mistake,

Perhaps they called me by mixing my name with somebody else. I shouldn't have been there. Tudor was trying to show very little concern, and whispered to me that if it comes to the worst we still had our rowing.

"And in 9th place is Tudor Bompa," Muresanu said, looking to see where Tudor was.

"A very good result, but you will need to improve a lot your swimming style" Muresanu said, smiling slightly.

Tudor sat down, swearing softly.

"I am not a bloody fish," he said morosely when I realized that Muresanu had stopped reading the list and was looking around the room. Somebody behind me, touched my shoulder and said:

"I think he's asked for you to stand up"

"What?" I said, taken totally by surprise, not realizing that Muresanu had called out my name as I was talking to Tudor.

Muresanu called out again:

"Would Cornel Vena stand up please."

I got up and my knees were shaking when Muresanu said smiling widely,

" Congratulations, you are our first National Triathlon Champion."

I was hearing what he was saying, but I could not believe he was talking about me. It was a mistake. There I was, only few seconds ago, thinking that I must have been called to the meeting by mistake and then to be told that I had won? It was like a dream, I felt like I was floating on a cloud. Tudor took my hand and shook it with great force.

"You bastard you never told me you were good at this"

"Yes, you are right," I said, pushing his hand away. "I didn't know myself".

I still don't know how all my childhood experiences led precisely to getting me ready for this sport. Cynics would say that it was just a coincidence but I know now that nothing so complex can be stumbled upon just by coincidence. As the great Mahikari teacher Sukinushisama said:

> *"Nothing in this world happens by coincidence, everything happens in a pre-arranged order and sequence."*

So for the first time in my life I experienced the incredible joy of being a winner, being the best. It was a real surprise to me, and it took a little time to sink in.

I was to learn in the months to come, that when you are good at something, when you have that natural ability for a given activity, things just happen.

Soon after the meeting, we were given the necessary equipment and commenced our training for the five sports required for Modern Pentathlon. We had to learn very quickly how to ride horses and jump fences, fence with the sword, pistol shoot at moving targets, and try to improve our performance in cross-country running and particularly in swimming.

We had to fit in a minimum of three training sessions a day, and somewhere along the line, those of us who were students were expected to squeeze in our normal university attendance. Our day started at 4.30 a.m. with a running session, then we would hurry to the university lectures followed in the afternoon by fencing and riding lessons. In the evening we had to prepare our assignments for university and finally would go to bed, totally exhausted by 10.00p.m. Time was our main enemy and gradually Modern Pentathlon started to completely take over our lives.

I knew that this was something special, something which may never happen again, and that I had to try harder than ever. I was more determined than ever before and I knew that this was my best opportunity to achieve the impossible, to represent my country in the Olympic Games and the best opportunity to get out of this cursed country with its abominable regime. I had to do it no matter what. A dream, or perhaps something I was meant to do? Only the future would have been able to give the answer to that question.

HANG IN THERE OR STARVE

If I thought that training for rowing was hard and painful, perhaps I should have waited until I started to train for Pentathlon.

The Modern Pentathlon was introduced in the 1912 Stockholm Olympic Games by the founder of the Olympic Games, the Baron of

Coubertin, who wanted to have a sport in the games to resemble the Pankration of the Ancient Olympic Games held in Greece between 776 BC and 393 AD.

Unfortunately there was nothing even distantly related to the ancient pentathlon that could be introduced in the modern games. However a Swedish delegate to the Olympic Committee spoke to the Baron of a sport taught in the Swedish Army Academy, which was considered the ultimate training for future Swedish officers.

It consisted of five disciplines—horse riding over fixed cross-country obstacles, fencing, duel style with epee for one hit, pistol shooting at a turning target at 25 m., a 300 metre swim and a cross-country run over a 4000 m. course.

The results of the five events were translated into points, added together with the highest total of points deciding the winner.

There is a quaint history behind this unusual combination which says that during a war between Sweden and Russia, a Swedish officer was sent to Headquarters to deliver an important message to his superiors. He left on his own, riding a horse and armed with his service sword as well as a pistol. Soon after that, as he was crossing enemy lines, he was ambushed by two enemy soldiers who opened fire and killed his horse. He managed to wound one of his assailants with his pistol and chased the other soldier with his sword. The officer then continued on foot towards his target, swam across a small creek, and covered the remaining distance by running. The message was delivered and his action was commended in one of the dispatches after the war.

I don't know how much of this story is true or pure fiction, enough to say that it impressed the Baron who then suggested this type of event be introduced in the 1912 Olympic Games in Stockholm. In time civilians started to participate in the competitions and by the time our Romanian team competed in the Melbourne Games in 1956, there were some 16 teams involved.

It is a most difficult sport to learn as the five required disciplines are totally different and additionally it required a great amount of time and energy to be split between five the disciplines. As well, most of the initial members of our squad were students, who had to squeeze lectures and assignments between training sessions. But the luxury of three regular meals a day in the special restaurant reserved for members of the Romanian Olympic Team and the thought that maybe one day I would be able to get out of the prison I was living in, made me more determined to keep up and do what was asked of me.

BROTHERLY LOVE

In 1953 the winter in Bucharest was one of the worst on record.

I had to travel long distances between university lodgings and training venues which were spread all over the place. The snow was deep and reached the window sills, but we had to be punctual and attend our scheduled training or our coaches would penalize us.

It was our responsibility to get to the respective venue on time, even if the outside temperature was—16°C and the public transport had stopped.

As I was broke most of the time, I had to travel quite often without a ticket on the trams, hanging to the rail with one hand and trying to keep my balance on the boarding platform, ready to jump if a tram inspector was in sight. In the summer it was pleasant to travel in this fashion but in the winter, after a longer trip, I was totally frozen.

One morning I woke up with a splitting headache and feeling very sick. My head felt like a football which with any movement I made would drop off. I got in touch with my brother Sandu, who at that stage lived by himself in a miniscule apartment. He immediately came to see me and took care of me. I refused to go to a doctor, fearing dismissal from the squad.

So for the next few days I went through intense agony, feeling very ill and nauseated. Sandu stayed with me most of the time and took care of food and whatever I needed. Eventually I started to feel better and then I realized that perhaps I had been working too hard and expecting to improve too quickly.

As soon as I felt better, I went back to training with renewed vigor and tried to make up for time lost. My fencing master, Aristide Galimir, was a small plumpish man with gray hair who did not look like an ex-World Champion, although we found out later that he was an exceptional epeist who had won many international competitions in Europe.

He was of Jewish origin, a man of sophistication, who between other things could speak French, Italian, German and Yiddish. He taught us the classic epee, and although pressed by Muresanu, our head coach, to teach us quickly, Galimir was a perfectionist of the old school who believed that a good fencer above all must have perfect footwork and hand techniques.

He told us from the beginning that apart from the lessons we were to receive from him three times a week, we had to practice assiduously after the formal lesson on our own.

I took his advice very seriously and began to practice every free moment I had, in the train, lecture room or in the dormitory, using my index finger as my epee. This drew many startled looks from the passengers and the students at the university. Quite often, in the evening sitting on the edge of my bed in the dormitory, I would practice for hours, going through the whole gamut of parry ripostes, disengagements and other movements learned during the lessons.

The other students were initially intrigued and asked me what I was doing and then they left me alone, but there was one individual, I cannot remember his name, who thought I was just making it up, and he felt I was just trying to impress everyone, when in fact I didn't know much about this " epee fencing".

"If you are that good why don't you bring you sword here one day and show us how good you are?" this fellow said to me.

So one evening, I took two epees back to the dormitories and showed the students what the epee looked like. As usual, when most people see swords they have an uncontrollable urge to take hold of the weapon and go through some form of duelling movements.

"Is this how you do it, Zoro?" this individual said, laughing and clowning.

"No this is not what we do, what you see in films is a different matter," I riposted. I was starting to lose my patience with this simpleton.

"Besides, one has to have the proper protective uniform and a mask if you want to fence. It is too dangerous to practice or fight without a mask."

This fellow must have thought that this was his chance to show the other students how good he was so he decided to challenge me.

"Well how about you give me a chance to show you how it's done or are you really scared of being hurt?"

I had been taught by my Master not to fence without a mask under any circumstance but somehow I couldn't let this big mouth get away with it. So I agreed to fence providing that we both direct our epee points to the any part of the body except the head.

Epee was the type of weapon used in duelling in the old times, thrusting and cutting movements were possible, however the modern epee can only be used as a thrusting weapon. We cleared the middle of the dormitory and the other students sat round this circular ring. I took on-guard and I called out to the other fellow to start.

Suddenly he became quiet as did the rest of the spectators. It was something which didn't need be explained as everyone felt the tension.

Normally a fencing bout takes place along a "piste" which is a length of carpet or metal mesh, 12 m. in length, which allows each competitor to move forwards or backwards.

But, like in the old times, we were forced to fence in a circular space and we were moving more like boxers in a circular ring.

After few minutes of moving around, he made his first thrust which I easily parried.

I realized almost instantly that he was very slow by what I have learned in lessons, and that he was totally exposed to my parry-ripostes. It was a matter of hitting him when I wanted, not when he made a mistake. It gave me an incredible sense of superiority when I realized how easily I could have hit this novice.

By now my opponent was sweating trying to hit me, moving awkwardly and making great attempts to reach me, whilst I was deftly moving out of his range. It was so easy to avoid his cumbersome attacks it was more like playing with a child. Suddenly I had had enough so I launched a simple direct attack to his chest which hit him whilst he was attempting a ridiculous wide, circular parry.

We stopped for few seconds, then he said he wanted to have another go. So we went on again, him trying and getting more frustrated by the minute, whilst I had a good practice hitting him with parry-ripostes, stop hits and some simple indirect attacks.

But after a while I got tired so I started to hit this fellow in his sensitive areas.

It didn't take long before he stopped accusing me of using unfair tactics. He tried to save face in front of the others, but after I took my weapons away, one of the students told him to shut up and stop making a fool of himself.

After this incident I wasn't challenged again and I felt that the other students respected my sport. It felt so good to be in control, to know what to do and how to do it; My training with Mr Galimir had not been wasted; I had learned my lesson well.

ONLY TRAITORS WANT TO LEARN ENGLISH

Back in those days in Bucharest we students loved to hear and learn other languages, in particular English. We had to study Russian as a compulsory language and it was prohibited to try to learn English which was classed as a decadent language. The only place one could learn English was the English embassy in Bucharest. So one day I went to the embassy to see if I could enroll myself. They told me that they would be delighted to teach me but asked if I was aware of the dangers involved.

"What dangers?" you may say. How could anyone consider learning English as being a danger to the Communist society? Well, you may not realize but in the eyes of the Communists learning English was akin to committing a treason against the State. The next day I was called to the University Communist Youth Bureau where I was asked to explain what I was doing at the English embassy the day before.

"I was just having a look around to see what these "Imperialists "were doing," I answered.

"You mean to say you just had a look and nothing else"? said the young bespectacled secretary.

"That was the only reason why I went there" I lied, looking straight into his eyes.
"Well, that's alright, but don't you ever go near that place again or you will be in real trouble."

"I understand and I apologize," I said, trying to sound apologetic,
"I will never go near that place again."

FIRST TRAINING CAMP AT SIBIU

I was born in an old medieval town situated in the northern part of Romania. It was a lovely place with beautiful old buildings, an ancient city with its old quarters of the German settlers. So when I found out that our first pentathlon training camp would take place in Sibiu, I could not hide my delight.

Our head coach, Muresanu, who was a good organizer, secured accommodation for our squad in an old hotel which had seen better times. The rooms were enormous and had high ceilings. I had a room to myself whilst the others were placed two to a room. In the morning we had our breakfast in an old dining room with wooden paneling and silver crockery. We felt like barons of the old empire treated with great respect by the servants who laid in front of us delicious food.

The training routine consisted of a morning run of 5 kilometres followed by breakfast and a short rest, after which we walked to the local outdoor pool where we did some work, and then we had our lunch. In the afternoon we would practice on the shooting range and finally finished with a riding session or a fencing class in the gymnasium of a local school.

I must admit that this routine was much easier to take, not having to hang off the trams or travel great distances. Everything in Sibiu was close to our hotel, and it was a great pleasure in particular to run through the beautiful park dotted with old oak trees.

We were told that in this park hundreds of Hitler youth members committed suicide rather than be taken by the Russian soldiers who were renowned for their insatiable desire for watches and young women.

I was trying to imagine as I was running under the majestic trees, how those beautiful blond German girls placed the noose around their necks, and then jumped . . . what a terrible waste.

Muresanu was a self-taught trainer who had a great ability to persuade people to train his way. He introduced us to repetition sprints, where we had to sprint for 200 metres and then walk back to the start and do it all over again. This went on for 12-14 sprints and it was quite exhausting. I didn't know how to pace myself, so I gave 100 per cent effort to the point where I would finish totally exhausted, whilst other members of the team like Viorel or Dumitru would finish quite fresh.

I don't know why, but in those days the only way for me to train was for me to push myself to the point where I would exhaust all my energy and feel totally drained. I had to try hard, I felt that unless I gave my outmost all the time, I would not become a top athlete and I knew that I would not get another chance like that to be a champion. It took some time before I felt that I was getting better, but in time my efforts started to be rewarded with improved times both in running and swimming. The only person who in the end could leave me behind in running was Victor Teodorescu who was a cross-country specialist. He was an excellent athlete with the smoothest action I had ever seen in running, with the exception of Herb Elliott. This fellow did not run, he glided over the ground with a smooth and even pace. There was no effort for him, just a perfectly relaxed movement which made him advance effortlessly over the terrain.

Learning to ride was a great experience, particularly as we had a great teacher by the name of Colonel Zidaru. He was a tall thin man, a chain smoker, who sat slightly hunched on his horse whilst calling out instructions to his students. He was extremely patient, and persevered calmly with us, ignoring our complaints about our old hags or when we parted company with our horses and hit the ground with great force. He did not lose his temper or raise his voice, he just continued to tell us to get back in the saddle and have another try.

As we got to know more about our coaches, we were told that Colonel Zidaru, in his youth, held at one time the European Puissance High Jump Event and had cleared 2.65 m.

A man of few words, he never spoke about his achievements.

He would take us on the trail through the hills surrounding Sibiu, crossing creeks, jumping over old tree trunks and usually finishing with a short spirited gallop. We had already gone through the basic riding exercises in Bucharest in the old dressage building belonging to the Romanian Cavalry Regiment. I cannot remember during that introduction period, how many times I fell from my horse whilst trying to canter or trot without stirrups. But the Colonel never let us feel sorry for ourselves. He would immediately call to us to get off the ground, catch our horse and re-mount. There was not the slightest suggestion of pity or feeling sorry for our sore backsides.

"What do you think you are waiting for?" he would say.

"Get back on that horse immediately and let him know who is the boss."

Admittedly we were lucky not to have any serious accidents, but that could have been because of the type of horses we had, old hags which were to go to the abattoir, but were reprieved and assigned to Colonel Zidaru's crowd, the Modern Pentathlon Squad.

I had done little riding before this camp, and I must admit I was enjoying myself, particularly during the jumping sessions when we had to work very hard in order to get our old hags over obstacles. One day after trying for a long time to get my horse over a small tree trunk lying on the ground, I called out to the Colonel:

"Ma scuzi Mr Zidaru, but this horse does not jump, he will never jump no matter what I do!"

The Colonel looked at me, still puffing on his eternal cigarette, and then he calmly told me that I wasn't really trying.

"Look Sir," I said rather heatedly, "I have tried everything but this bag of bones cannot jump. Nobody can make him jump."

The whole group stopped, listening to my complaint. As a matter of fact, we had never seen the Colonel jumping a horse, as he usually just sat motionless on his horse, giving instructions and smoking his cigarette. In a way, perhaps without realizing, I had challenged him, or maybe he just felt that it was time to show us how it was done. It was time to teach us about more than just sitting on a horse, he perhaps wanted to show us how to use our will, how to influence and make these tired old horses do things they had never done before.

In Pentathlon you do not compete on your own horse. You have to draw a number out of a hat which determines which horse you are going to ride. Then you have to take your horse to the mounting yard where you have to saddle it, put the bridle on, and then you have 20 minutes to get used to your horse in the warm-up area, do a few jumps and then start on a 5 km. course, which takes you through rough terrain; across creeks, through narrow paths in the forest, and additionally you have to jump some 15 fixed obstacles placed in the most difficult positions.

Many good pentathletes have been eliminated and finished up in hospital as a result of their inability to understand their horse, and as the riding event used to be the first of the five events, quite often these unfortunate athletes, who spent many hours training, could not go on and finish the event, being hospitalized with injuries or remaining scoreless. So it was imperative that we learned to deal with ANY type of horse, and be able to jump even the most difficult type.

Then our Colonel did something which surprised us all: He actually dismounted and asked me to hold his horse. Then he took hold of my horse, calmly adjusted the stirrups and checked the girth. Then he placed his foot in the stirrup and mounted the horse with a quick and smooth action. I will never forget what happened next. He took the rains short, sat straight in the saddle and made good contact with the horse's flanks. This was nothing new as we all had learned the proper procedure, but it was the transformation that took place in the way the horse changed his posture—it was truly amazing.

This was an old white horse, thin and bony, tired and ready to collapse with fatigue, which did not even have the energy to trot and was always the last horse to get back to the camp. It was a horse who kept his head down most of the time and looked like dropping dead in the next few seconds. I felt quite sorry for this old horse and I was convinced that he just could not do anything strenuous, and that if I pushed him too much he would drop dead under me. But I was to find out that not all things are as we see them and that there was still plenty of life left in this old fellow.

Suddenly this horse lifted his head and stood much taller. Can you imagine a horse which looked one moment like dying and in the next second lifts his head and arches his neck, starts trotting and then when pushed towards the obstacle takes off and flies over without any effort?

We all sat there speechless, watching our coach collecting and literally transforming this old horse into a beautiful creature which moved with the grace of a young and well educated horse.

He brought the horse back to me and simply said.:

"There is nothing wrong with this horse. It is you who cannot jump."

He was right. As time went by, I learned how to ride and get my horse over any obstacle, regardless of what he looked like in the mounting yard. The colonel was right when he told us that to make your horse jump, you must first throw your heart over the obstacle facing you and then your horse will jump anything.

NO TIME FOR TEARS

The horses we were allowed to ride were the property of the Romanian Regiment of Cavalry stationed in the town of Sibiu. We did not have to look after our horses, just turn up in the morning and have the horse saddled and ready to go.

Each horse had a minder, a soldier who had some experience from his civil life in looking after horses. They were there to look after any need we had, and they took particular pride in getting the horses ready for their daily lessons looking their best.

Initially I thought that a horse was just that, an animal who you try to stay on and if you are doing the right thing it will eventually respond to your commands. Wrong.

Horses are like people. Each one has a personality of its own, likes and dislikes of its own. But they are also very suspicious and cautious and have an excellent ability to remember the things they enjoy, but more so, the things that hurt or upset them.

We had the opportunity to watch and learn from our individual minders how to prepare the horse for the ride, and in the process they would also give us hints about what the horse was like and what to watch for during the ride. Most of our horses were old and semi-retired from service, with the exception of a few horses who were beautiful creatures much sought after by all the team members. Colonel Zidaru made sure that each one of us had a different horse almost every lesson so that we would learn to handle different horses, as would be the case in competition.

Our favourite was a beautiful stallion called Satan who was a muscular horse with a beautiful black coat and a lovely head, powerful and game to jump anything. We also had a nasty mare called Tismana with a long history of sudden and frightening bouts of kicking and biting, and an extremely stubborn horse to ride.

One day we were returning from a very good lesson when we had ridden across the hills, through deep descents, jumping the occasional fallen tree, and generally having to apply the things we had learned in the last few weeks about riding and competing in a cross-country riding event. I had Satan for the day and he did everything better than any other horse. He seemed to really enjoy this variety of terrain and he was at his best. Finally our Colonel signalled the end of the lesson and motioned for us to line up in indian file. He asked me to go last with Satan and to bring up the rear. In front of me was Tismana who had been behaving erratically the whole day and kept trying to rear up and get rid of her rider.

We were getting near town, riding along a small creek bed which had high banks on either side and allowed only for riding in single file. Normally we had to keep a minimum distance of two horse lengths between the horse in front to avoid being kicked.

Normally I had no problem keeping my horse away from the horse in front, but Tismana did not behave normally, stopping and starting and being very difficult. Suddenly the Colonel gave the signal for us to start galloping, and we all changed from walking to trotting and then started to canter. All but Tismana who was trying unsuccessfully to mount the bank on the side whilst her rider was hanging on for dear life. Finally she started to canter so that my horse had room to start his canter. I kept yelling to Tismana's rider to push her along, and to give her a good kick when suddenly she partially stopped and lashed out with a low and vicious kick which caught Satan below his right knee. He tried to avoid it but he wasn't fast enough: I heard a crack like when a heavy branch of a tree is broken, at the same time he gave a short neigh of pain.

My heart shrunk with a numbing fear. Although I had little experience with horses, I knew instantly that this magnificent animal was badly hurt. He kept cantering ignoring my attempts to slow him, to bring him to a stop, to prevent further injury. By now the whole group had stopped and the Colonel called out to take care and keep our distance.

It was the saddest experience having to ride this horse back, to see how he was still trying to do his best for me and not to stop.

I dismounted and slowly led Satan back to the stables my eyes filled with tears.

The Colonel came that night in the dining hall carrying a big parcel of newspaper and left it in the corner next to the door. Then without looking at us or saying anything he left the room;

Finally we all got up and I opened the parcel; It contained one huge bone with a deep crack just below the knee. The vet, we were told the next day, had to put Satan down as there was no way they could save his leg.

Tismana went on terrifying our riders, and the last we heard about her was that she was finally sent away when she managed to push a young soldier into the corner of her stall and almost killed him.

Fortunately for me, although I continued to ride for many years after this incident, I never again had the misfortune to see a horse I was riding being hurt.

THE RUSSIANS ARE COMING

We returned to Bucharest at the end of August and started to prepare for the final for our first international competition against the Russian Team. By now we had some 6 months to learn to fence, ride, shoot as well as becoming better runners and swimmers.

I didn't think we were ready but this was 1953 and we only had a couple more years before having to compete in the Olympic Games in Melbourne in 1956.

The Russians brought to Bucharest their top team who had already been training for some years and had competed in the 1952 Olympic Games in Helsinki.

Their National Champion was Igor Novikov who finished 4th in the Individual Event of the Modern Pentathlon in the 1952 Games in Helsinki, whilst their team was placed 5th overall. So here we were, our young inexperienced Romanian Team, with the bare minimum of skills necessary to compete in this demanding event which normally takes years of practice before one is ready to start competing. I can only say that our coaches must have been petrified at the thought of testing us against the might of the Russian team, and probably just hoped that we would somehow come through this trial without being totally discouraged by the whole experience.

The Russians were experienced competitors, well prepared and keen to make a good impression on their selectors. But although we were very green and lacking experience, there were two things in our favour: pride and hatred.

I for one, like many other Romanians, hated the Communists and indirectly the Russians because we blamed them for bringing this detestable system to our country after defeating the Germans. So well before the competition started I was planning my revenge, looking forward to beating these Russians, to pay back some of the suffering inflicted on our country.

So the competition began and our team managed to show that we hadn't wasted our time, and that our coaches had been doing a great job and teaching us well.

Fencing in the Pentathlon is probably the only time when you meet your opponent face to face, when literally you have to fight with all your strength and knowledge, to defeat your opponent. You are, as someone put it, the general, the captain and the foot soldier.

In those days in a fight or bout as it called in fencing terminology, we had 6 minutes of fencing;

There was only one hit necessary to win, more like a real duel, and any part of the body from the head to the toes is the target and can be hit, unlike foil or sabre fencing. In foil you are restricted to hitting just the chest and in sabre the target area is the chest, head and arms. In conventional fencing even if you lose the first hit, you can recover and still beat your opponent because you are fighting for 5 hits or more.

Pentathlon fencing requires a great deal of concentration, the imperative is to watch your opponent for the whole duration of the bout, and be able through immaculate and faultless defense, to avoid being hit by a lightening-like attack which can be launched at any time without warning by your opponent. Additionally one has to try to score because if nobody scores, at the end of the 6 minutes, both fencers receive zero points. So you may have the satisfaction of not being hit by your opponent but it will not contribute to your overall score, and in pentathlon only a few points can decide the fate of the first placing.

I won't go through the whole five events, because it was pretty ordinary, and we performed close to the results we had obtained in our own trials. The event which proved to be most exciting and challenging was the fencing event, where we as the beginners had nothing to lose and we could challenge the Russians who were not totally aware of what competition fencing involved.

Well, we were in for a big surprise from the start; The Russians were very fast and every time we got near them they would manage to get away only to launch a counter-riposte which caught us floundering. Bout after bout we returned to our corner, dragging the epee and the mask behind us, only to be glared at by our head coach Captain Muresanu, intimating that we hadn't tried hard enough. Our dear Mr Galimir, our fencing coach who was a real gentleman, tried hard to tell us what to do, how to deal with a particular style, but to no avail. We lost almost every bout and started to feel very dejected.

After I lost my initial bouts, Mr Galimir told me to try and make every bout go to the limit:

"This is the time for you to learn. Forget about winning—that will come later, but now try and do everything possible not to be hit in the first few seconds".

So I changed my initial plan, and postponed my desire to "kill" the Russians. I started to move around more and frustrate the Russians' attempts to hit me. My last bout was against the smallest of the Russians, who was very fast and moved like a rabbit, making it almost impossible to hit him. So I started copying his method and kept moving so that he did not have a steady target to hit. This is when I learned another lesson about pentathlon fencing: You don't become careless and lose your concentration.

In the next move he stepped forward, threatening my face with his point, which made me instinctively take a short step back and do a high parry called a "quinte"(the 5th parry). The Russian immediately lunged low under my parry and hit my right foot which was moving a fraction too slowly out of his range.

I had to shake hands and then I went to our corner swearing and cursing at myself for being so stupid and falling for his trap. Muresanu looked at me and tried very hard not to say anything, whilst Mr Galimir smiled and said quietly:
"You have done well, much better than anybody here understands."
A few weeks went by and we were back at training, more aware of what was expected from us in international competition, but still somewhat proud of our efforts, realizing that we had made good progress in the short time we had been learning about pentathlon. I had good comments from all our coaches with the exception of Muresanu who looked very grim and quiet.

The autumn weather started to close in and I had to rush to the special restaurant reserved for the Romanian Olympic Team, where I would have my breakfast before rushing to the Institute for the first morning lecture. One morning, I was met at the restaurant door by Muresanu who asked me how I was and if I had received my meal ticket for the month.

This meal ticket we received every month had one ticket for every day of that month, and every ticket had three detachable portions for breakfast, lunch and dinner.

In the restaurant one had to detach the appropriate section and give it to the waitress; If one ticket was missing you would miss out on that meal, similarly if the date on the ticket said the day before, you could not use it. No ticket-no meal.

"Can I have a look at your meal book" Muresanu said, innocently enough.

I looked at him, suddenly sensing danger:
"Why do you want my book?.
"Nothing, I just want to see if they have got it right and have the dates in the correct order."

In the past we had had some problems with the tickets, and were refused our meals. It was a reasonable request so I handed in my book to Muresanu. He opened it and started counting the first 6 or 7 tickets, then he tore out the breakfast sections and returned the rest of the book to me.

"Why did you do that? " I said, regaining my voice. I could not believe he had done that, after all, it was my meal ticket book and he had no right to take it away.

He started to talk to me in a voice we call in Romanian "mieroasa", (honey like)

"Remember when you let the little Russian hit you in the foot? Well I didn't say much then did I? You let the whole team down, you did not try hard enough and that is why I think that you don't deserve to eat breakfast until you learn to fight to win."

I went back to the Institute and for the next few days I went hungry in the morning. I promised myself that one day I would show him who was the best fencer.

PART THREE

MY FATHER IS WATCHING

On our return from the camp I had to make a desperate effort to catch up with my studies, which I had been neglecting due to an ever-increasing demand for longer and more severe training sessions. Gradually I found that there was little time for anything else except training for pentathlon; I even neglected to write to my parents and just managed to see my brother Sandu who was doing his second year of journalism and media.

But one thing became evident to myself and to the team: The hard work was starting to pay off, and we were breaking our personal best results with almost monotonous regularity. In the autumn it was cold and wet in Bucharest and we avoided competing in outdoor sports and concentrated on improving our swimming (which was our worst event), shooting and fencing. To increase the standards and raise the competitive level in all sports, every aspiring person attempting to reach a higher level had to compete in regular club and regional competitions, and aim at obtaining better results and to be promoted to a higher class.

The categories were set in such a way that almost any person with a little training could achieve the required standard and get his certificate and a brightly coloured medallion for the category "D". But the standards became progressively higher and became harder to achieve for the "C" and the "B" standards, and became almost impossible to reach by the time one attempted the "A" grade. For those who reached International level, there was the Master of Sport Award, which was most the respected and sought after award.

In our sport of Modern Pentathlon there were no set standards, being a new sport, so we were entered in competitions controlled by our "next door" Federations of Swimming Fencing, Riding and Shooting.

We were entered in the epee event of the Bucharest Open Championship for fencing. This was different from the usual pentathlon fencing where you have to fence all the other competitors for one hit. In ordinary fencing you have to fence in a pool of 4-6 fencers, graded according to their class, for five hits. To qualify for the next round a fencer has to win a minimum of bouts, which means those with a lesser number of victories are eliminated.

The Bucharest Open Event was a popular annual competition as it allowed higher award fencers to prove their skill against new comers. The competition started early in the morning in an old high school gymnasium which was already full of people by the time we got there.

Up to this point neither of my parents had a chance to see me doing any of the new sports, additionally they lived some 70 km out of Bucharest and they didn't have the necessary transport. My brother was there doing a project for his course, but apart from a few words of encouragement, I didn't see him again until the end of the competition.

The hall itself was set up in such a way that all the fencing strips were set across the hall and the spectators were sitting either near the fencing strips or up above in a narrow balcony. Our team was divided in individual pools, and I found myself on strip (piste) four which was one of the eight strips.

Fencing for five hits was different from what we were taught and although I lost the first few hits, it didn't take me long to see what my opponent's weak points were, and I started to score hits on his mistakes and won the first bout. From then on I understood how important it was to watch my opponent fencing another person so that I could pick up his favourite movements as well as noting his weaknesses.

Our Master, Mr Galimir, was running around us like a proud hen looking after her chickens; adjusting our equipment, giving advice and thoroughly enjoying himself.

During one of the short stops, something made me look up to the gallery and there, just for a short moment I saw my father's face. He looked rather embarrassed and tried to disappear behind the crowd onlookers. It was rather unusual for my father to show any signs of affection or interest in what we did; He was brought up in the old tradition of not being allowed to show emotions or to get too close to your family. That's why I was surprised but at the same time pleased to see him up there, watching me for the first time competing.

Most of the bouts were finished for the morning session, except for those on the middle strip where I was fencing my last bout of the round against a tall, blond fencer, who moved very smoothly and started by scoring the first point against me. But I had the chance to note what his favourite preparations were and saw his tendency not to cover and protect against attacks directed to his underarm.

I was concentrating very hard and I wasn't interested in anything else except trying not to give my opponent the opportunity to launch one of his long lunges and catch me napping. The official scorer would call out the score from time to time, and at one point I heard her saying something like "Four love in Vena's favour"?

This was good news as it meant I only had to score one more point to win the bout; The other fencer looked rather annoyed and become more aggressive, trying to hit me without much success as I kept moving away and would parry-riposte any of his attacks.

The man in charge of the bout, known as the president, stopped the bout at the request of my opponent who pretended to have some problems with his epee. I took the opportunity to take my mask off, to get some fresh air, when I heard a voice in the nearby crowd asking :

"Who is this skinny fellow belting the lights out of our national champion.?"
Another voice answered, not without a note of derision
"I don't know who it is but he is killing P.R."

It didn't occur to me that they were talking about me and my opponent until I was waiting to be put back on-guard and finish our bout. I looked round and realized that we were the only pair still fencing, and all the other strips were empty. Next I panicked to the point where I could not stop my knees from shaking, realizing that I was beating P.R., the Romanian epee champion, a fencer whom I'd never met but one who had been mentioned often by our Mr Galimir, who thought that his style of fencing based on the French style, was the one to be followed by other competitors with a few little modifications such as a tighter defense position and more extended arm.

My fencing changed immediately. I became tentative and could not gather the courage to launch a direct, strong attack or perhaps a running attack(fleche) and risk a double hit which would have given me the point I needed to win the bout.

P.R. sensed his opportunity and started to launch smooth feint—disengage attacks and in a short time he had won the bout at 5-4. As it is customary in fencing, at the end of the bout we took our masks off and shook hands.

"Who is your Master?" he asked condescendingly as we moved away from the metal piste.

"We have been trained by Master Aristide Galimir," I said, still fuming with myself for letting this fellow of the hook.

"Not bad for a beginner", he said smiling slightly. Then he added "Give my regards to the Old Master, I had the honour to have few lessons with him years ago when I started fencing."

I walked back slowly to our small group where I was congratulated by the other members of the team. Master Galimir, who had a smile from ear to ear, came and squeezed my hand.

"You got him, you showed him how it is done. He was lucky not to lose his bout, but it doesn't matter. Next time you meet him you will beat him easily".

I was embarrassed by his praise and felt I didn't deserve it:
"But I could have won the bout easily if I had tried a little harder".

Then he said something to me which was to become my guiding thought and pushed me along to undreamed heights:

"The day when you will be able to take five hits from me without letting me win a single point, that day you will be ready to beat everybody!"

We used to have short bouts with our Master at the end of a lesson, when he would encourage us to try to hit him with one of the movements we had just learned in the lesson. None of us could him at that stage and I thought that I may never beat him 5-0 in a bout, so felt he had just been trying to encourage me after that dismal loss to S.U.

That first competition against real fencers taught me—apart from fencing with more care and imagination—that nobody is unbeatable, and everyone has a weakness which can be used to your advantage. But even more importantly I learned that one must not place his opponent on a pedestal or treat him with too much awe, or you would be placed at a disadvantage.

Although we had only six month of fencing, three of our team managed to pass the required standard for "B" Grade fencing, and I got the "A" Grade for epee fencing.

My brother Sandu and I had lunch with our father, who was looking very tired and had aged a lot in the last few months, and perhaps for the first time in my life he actually told me how impressed he was with my fencing. It was rather late, but I started to feel closer to my father, regretting that it had taken so long to understand him.

THE RUSSIANS ARE COMING AGAIN

Our performance in the fencing tournament did not pass unnoticed and soon after this event, we were told by Muresanu that we had been given permission to compete in 1954 in the World Modern Pentathlon Championships in Budapest, Hungary.

This was to be our first real test against the rest of the world, and it would show our leaders that we were capable of representing Romania in the Olympic Games. It was a matter of do or die, and no excuses could ever change our future participation in the international events.

We were put to a rigorous pre-season fitness program during the winter, and some of the initial members of the squad decided to quit the sport and try something easier, particularly after one of our members had a heart attack and had to stop any form of physical activity. I was lucky to have experienced the rigours of rowing training, and able to take a lot of physical pain. Tudor decided to give up this sport, and go back to rowing mainly because he could not improve his swimming. I kept plodding along and gained the reputation of being able to work harder than anybody:

"The horse"(calu) became my nickname as I practiced long after everyone else had stopped. I started to understand, particularly in fencing and riding, what was required of me to be proficient. I understood that my improvement was directly affected by the correct execution of that particular technique, plus repetition of that movement until it became almost unconscious and consequently much faster than the normal actions, which are guided by our conscious thought.

Muresanu was an extremely strong person who did not allow any excuse for missing planned sessions, and he pushed us along with an almost inhumane urgency to the point where we were left totally exhausted at the end of a training session.

Strangely enough, until now I had never had the desire to put so much work into sport, but this was different, I knew it was a chance I could not miss.

When the Russians arrived I quickly found out that their team had almost the same members, and that the little fellow who had beaten me the year before in fencing was also present. Fortunately for me I discovered that I had a good recollection of various movements my adversary and I had both performed during a bout. I had the ability to visualize the actual movement used months or years ago to defeat or to score a good point.

I could clearly remember the sudden attack and being hit on the big toe of my right foot by the Russian, and I had learned the correct evasive action called "rassemblement", which is performed by retreating the front leg, whilst doing an arrete stop-hit to the head of the attacker.

As usual the competition started with the riding event which took place near Bucharest on the site of an old open sand and gravel mine. The Russian pentathletes were mediocre to poor riders, and they had a lot of problems navigating the course which involved 15 fixed obstacles and lots of turns in a terrain full of holes and rocks.

The next day we had the fencing event when once again our team had to meet all the Russians in direct bouts for one hit. Muresanu told us to do whatever we could, but to show the Russians what we made of.

"Of course they are our dear friends, but we must not let them beat us again or some people in our squad may have to go without breakfast again.!"

Muresanu gave a quick look in my direction. I knew he was referring to my previous effort, and that he wouldn't let me forget losing against the little Russian. Fortunately for all of us, we were fencing much better and even started to take some points away from the Russians.

My long awaited bout with the little Russian (I cannot remember his name) took place just before the lunch break.

I could see his eyes smiling with the anticipation of an easy hit, and obviously he thought I would be an easy target. Wrong. He commenced by being very aggressive, pushing me back with impunity, treating me like the beginner he thought I still was. I played the role, and pretended to be scared of him, moving back nervously, performing large and coarse movements and generally exhibiting a total lack of confidence or skill.

The trap I was setting was too much for the Russian who became greedy and decided to totally embarrass me once again by hitting my foot with a direct attack as he did in the bout the previous year. But he didn't realize until it was too late that I was waiting for him, and as he tried to slide under my high parry, I extended my arm, pointing at his mask whilst doing a perfect "rassemblement".

A split second before my point hit his mask, he instinctively tried to protect his face and turned his head to the side presenting the temple. Masks are designed to offer maximum protection to the front of the head, having a heavier gauge wire, however in those days the manufacturer used a thinner wire for the side of the mask, which under normal circumstances would have been sufficient. The combination of the speed of the Russian's lunge and my strong and fully extended stop-hit found the weak spot in his mask and my point broke through the mesh, digging deep into his temple.

The next few seconds went almost like an old black and white film, the fear on his face, blood pouring out of his head, the officials and the first aid officers rushing in trying to help; I took my mask off and stepped forward wanting to apologize to this poor bleeding wretch, when I realized that the point had not penetrated his skull and was just a flesh wound.

When I started back to my team, I could see the spectators' faces, slightly pale but with a look of satisfied wonder; It was very seldom that we the " Romanian slaves" could stand up to this invading people. But strangely enough I was feeling sorry for the Russian yet anger and desire for retribution mounting with every step towards Muresanu. As I got near our group he come forward and tried to shake my hand.

Before he had a chance to say anything I stopped and looked straight into his eyes, remembering the way he had treated me only few months ago, not wanting to be congratulated by him.

"Is this enough for you, or would you rather have me kill him Captain.?"

He stopped with a totally surprised look on his face, and then after few seconds of glaring at one another, I left him standing on his own, whilst I went to my chair and sat down, feeling that I had become another person, a fierce competitor.

The competition ended with the Russians winning once again all the major positions, but it became clear to all concerned that our team was far from being disgraced, particularly in the technical events of fencing and riding where we were ahead of the Russians, who beat us convincingly in running and swimming.

Our team got the green light to compete in the World Championship in Budapest, in autumn, so we started to train with a sense of pride and confidence in our ability.

As for Muresanu, although he never forgave my challenge, he never dared to insult me, or take my meal tickets away again.

WOROS CHILAG, 1954 WORLD MODERN PENTATHLON CHAMPIONSHIPS

The news that we were going to participate in the individual and team events of the 1954 World Championships was hard to believe, and although it was only a short train trip to Hungary, which was also a Communist controlled country, it filled us with great excitement.

It was after all very unusual for any normal Romanian to travel even inside our own country, but to have official permission to travel outside Romania was only the avenue of High Communist officials or scientists on specific duties to attend international conferences.

It was announced that our team would consist of four competitors plus Muresanu and Master Galimir. We were slightly disappointed not to have our riding coach, Colonel Zidaru, who had the experience of numerous international competitions in his day.

But we were told that there were only limited funds, and it was either us or the coach. As the time approached to leave Bucharest, we were asked to fill in numerous forms and declarations, and we were issued with a complete set of competition equipment as well as smart uniforms for the official opening and other important events.

The day of departure arrived sooner than expected and we said goodbye to our families and friends, who kept waving and calling to us long after the train left Bucharest station. For most of us this was the first time that we had the opportunity to travel outside Romania, and to see our neighbour and most fierce sporting opponent, the Hungarians.

There had been always a certain amount of friction between Hungarians and Romanians, a situation which goes back many years into the history of these two countries.

In a way we have many qualities in common, but over the years people have made little effort to become more tolerant towards one another, to try to live together in peace.

Even as a young child I remember how we were told of the great injustice committed by the Austro-Hungarian regime, and how they tried to destroy the spirit of the Romanian people. It was inevitable that our team would try their utmost not to be shamed by the Hungarian team, regardless of the fact that they had a long and brilliant record in Modern Pentathlon. So right from the start we were looking for a confrontation of some kind, but to our surprise we got excellent treatment and we were looked after in the best possible way.

They were very attentive and tried to give all the competitors the best chance to obtain good results. It took me personally many years to rid myself of the misguided hostility I had felt since my childhood, and to realize how damaging and poisonous early teachings about race and differences between people can be. However that hostility, fortunately for us, was expressed only in heated and well fought contests, which eventually led to better performances for all our competitors.

HOW DO YOU BEAT AN OLYMPIC CHAMPION?

The competition started with the riding event. After we drew numbers from a hat, we were allowed to inspect and get used to our horses. Like most Romanians I spoke a little Hungarian, which helped me to find out from the horse's strapper what the horse was like.

He told me that he was an excellent horse, and as long as I put him straight to the obstacle he would jump anything.

He was a slender dark horse, lightly built but full of energy. Hungarian horses are renowned for their stamina and high spirits. Additionally these horses would have received the best preparation for the difficult and demanding cross-country course.

As it turned out, apart from a little rearing at the start, thanks to our Colonel's instructions, I leaned forward on his neck and held tight on his neck but avoided pulling on the reins.

When the starter lowered his flag and allowed me to go, my horse moved smartly and confidently towards the first obstacle. Just before engaging in his jump he tried to move slightly to the left, when I lowered myself deep in the saddle, and started to push him towards the middle of the obstacle.

He was an intelligent horse with a beautiful soft mouth, easy to guide and as soon as he understood my aids, he responded by doing everything I asked of him. A good horse feels the rider through his back and in an inexplicable way the horse can sense almost instantly if the rider is confident and knows how to lead the horse, or if the rider is scared and doesn't know how to communicate, or how to "ask" the horse what to do.

It takes long hours of riding at sitting trot, without stirrups to learn how to keep contact with the horse yet maintain perfect balance and not interfere with his movements.

When we finished the course, I dismounted smartly, kissed my horse and rewarded him by stroking his neck, glistening with perspiration. The handler shook my hand and said in Hungarian "Nogyon yo", Very good. Obviously he was pleased to see that no harm had come to his horse and that we had both finished the course in a good time.

All our work with Colonel Zidaru had given all of us in the team a strong foundation in the basics of horse riding and jumping fixed obstacles, allowing us all to compete in numerous competitions without sustaining serious accidents.

My time of 9.30.6 gave me 1,002.5 competition points, whilst the other two team members, Victor and Dumitru, scored respectively 857 and 255 points. The standard of the horses was evident by the fact that some 19 out of 34 competitors scored over 1,000 points, and only five riders failed to score any points, one of them being Mannonen from Finland, who later in Melbourne in 1956, won the Silver Medal in the Individual event.

Everybody in our team was happy, delighted to have finished the riding event without injuring ourselves. Quite often competitors would have a nasty fall and they would withdraw from any further competition, which meant that the rest of the team was also eliminated from the team event. We were told in Romania to try not to finish last, and anything else for a start, could be regarded as satisfactory.

Living in Hungary in 1954 was obviously no different to our country. We found the signs of acute shortage of all the basic essentials of life. One evening, on our way back to our hotel after we had finished training, the taxi driver who spoke a little of many languages, told us how he and his family were starving and just managing to live from day to day.

It was the same story of rapacious, predatory actions, the dispossession and appropriation of anything of use by the Russians, leaving the country reduced to unheard poverty and misery. And if this blatant and open plundering wasn't sufficient to demoralize and destroy the spirit of the people, they shamelessly, through nauseating propaganda, tried to convince everybody of the advantages of the "Communist Paradise", the new society free of exploitation by the capitalists.

That night at a dinner table loaded with delicious food of all sorts, I felt guilty of taking the food from the table of that poor taxi driver. It became evident how much I was repulsed by the Communists, and how much I hated their hypocrisy and lies.

The fencing event was, as expected, very exciting and lasted the whole of the second day of competition. For the first time we had a chance to experience fencing against other countries such as Sweden, Switzerland, Austria, England, France, Czechoslovakia, the USSR and Hungary.

There were 10 countries competing and 33 competitors after the American, Brinker, withdrew from competition after riding.

Our team was the most inexperienced entry in the fencing event, and despite the guidance and encouragement by our Master, Mr Galimir, we could not beat the experience of these seasoned fencers, who literally played with us. I tried everything I had learned in my fencing lessons at home, only to find that although my defense was good, I could not hit my opponents when the opportunity arose. I simply could not commit myself and attack without holding back.

Apart from timing and precision, fencing requires determination and courage to attack at the right time, without hesitation, although fully aware that if your point misses your opponent's target, you have little chance to get back on-guard without being hit by a quick parry-riposte. It was even harder for us in pentathlon, where there is only one touch to be gained and if you miss your opponent you won't see him again until the next competition. Every touch was worth some 60-70 points, which was very important in the overall scoring, and quite often the fencing event decided the position in the final classification.

During a short break in the competition, whilst changing pistes for a new match, Mr Galimir spoke to each one of us, giving individual advice and urging us to fence with courage and to use movements learned in our lessons, even if we lost points.

"The only one to fear is yourself, your opponent is only as good as you let him be."

He spoke as usual with conviction, accentuating words with short thrusts of his hands, aiming at invisible opponents:

"You have already gone half way through the competition. What is that, eleven, twelve bouts, and you should have won at least 25 per cent of them."

He looked at Victor Teodorescu, the oldest in our team and an accountant by profession

"What's that Victor? You are good with figures."
"Approximately 6.6 bouts, if we don't consider the experience factor," Victor replied. He was smiling when he said that, which was just as well because Mr Galimir wasn't in a happy mood and immediately launched an indirect attack at Victor's soft spot:

"I am glad you feel like making smart remarks Victor, as it reminds me of someone back home who felt confident enough to beat even the Hungarians, but all I have got from you has been just talk and no action."

He paused to get his breath back, then perhaps he realized that he was doing a "Muresanu", he was getting personal rather than coming up with a workable solution. In his position he was very much at the mercy of our performance as his position as the Fencing Master of the team relied on getting results and getting them quickly or he would be replaced by a younger coach.

I respected my Master for his fencing ability, for his intelligent approach to training young people, and above all, despite all the injustice heaped upon him by the Sport Committee, he managed to keep calm and in control. I decided then not to let him down, to try even harder and to start to attack.

At that stage I think we had accumulated between the three of us some 12 victories which was less than the planned 20 per cent which would have been between 18 and 20 victories. Next we were against the Hungarian Team, the Olympic Champions in 1952 in Helsinki, a team of the highest repute in the Modern Pentathlon world and in particular in the fencing event. The team's standard in fencing was high enough to place them in the top ten epee fencers in Hungary. Their captain, Gabor Benedeck, had the highest standard, and he was asked a number of times if he wanted to represent Hungary as a member of the National Epee Team. However he refused, stating that he wanted to defend the title won in 1952.

My first bout against Szondy was much better than the previous ones, and although I lost, Mr Galimir praised me for attacking and being more aggressive.

Victor won one bout and we all got some confidence back, then I lost another bout and Dumitru lost his bout against the second Hungarian.

At this stage something went wrong with the electrical circuit supplying the judging box, and the President told us that we would have a 10 minute break. I went into a corner away from everybody, covered my head with a blanket and started to sob with anger and choking frustration.

What was the point of all my hard work if I didn't have the courage to attack? Why was I such a coward, not doing what I had planned? I was jeopardizing my position in the team and indirectly I could be responsible for the dismissal of my favourite coach.

I felt so hopeless and miserable, alone and defeated; What was the point of it all? I felt I didn't have what it takes and they had made a mistake to include me in the National Team. Looking back I realize now how narrow the margin is between failure and success, and how easily a person can feel completely hopeless and give up, to abandon what he or she has worked for. But I was lucky to have someone who cared, someone who understood what I was going through. A hand touched my shoulder and Mr Galimir spoke to me in a quiet voice:

"I know I told you to do this and that, and I also I wish I could be in your place and win the bout for you, but there are things in life that you have to do yourself. There is the right timing for everything that happens in this universe, and everything has to be done at the right time, or it can never be done again."

"But I've done everything you taught me to do and still it doesn't work," I blurted.

"This may be so Cornel, but as long as you keep holding back, as long as you are not prepared to take the risk, you are only practicing. Don't you understand that this is not a practice. This is the real thing."

"Thank you Master," I said. "I think I know what you mean. I will do it, I know I can do it."

It was an amazing thing. I felt relieved, with a clear purpose in my head. I understood for the first time how important it was to think competitively, to feel that there was nothing else for me except to win—no doubts, no pity, no niceties; I was there to prove that the Romanian Team was capable of beating the Russians or Hungarians or any other team. No more placing my opponents on a pedestal, admiring them for what they might have done, but today, now, recognizing that it was my time.

When the equipment was ready, I was called on the strip to face the Hungarian champion, Gabor Benedeck. As usual when Gabor fenced, a crowd immediately formed, eager to learn from the best epeeist.

We commenced on the command "Aller" (fencing uses french commands), "Go", and for the next few minutes Gabor and I moved around without making any definite attempt to hit. He was aware of my inexperience but because in fencing you must treat everyone as an expert until you find his weak spot, so Gabor was going through the ordinary preparatory movements, beating my blade, extending and feinting to the arm, doing an occasional prise de fer, (taking my blade), and now and then a short lunge to the arm;

I knew that it was only a matter of time before he would launch a deep, penetrating attack to my chest, possibly preceded by a beat feint or a direct disengage. There was little I could do except wait and lose once again; At least nobody would laugh at me for being beaten by Gabor. Suddenly I remembered Master Galimir talking to us about the element of surprise and how in the old days of the open duels, many renowned duelists were killed by relative unknown and inexperienced fencers by this method.

"The reason why these experienced people were killed was because their opponents did unorthodox movements, a movement which wasn't normally taught in the Salle D'Arme," Galimir explained. Then he told us about what to do in dangerous situations which demanded survival and the death of your opponent. It was a "secret" movement:

"First you must push your opponent back by beating and feinting to his body, then you stop briefly and give the impression that you don't intend to pursue this form of aggression . . . and then," he stopped momentarily and had us all hanging on his words, "Then," he said, "you roar like an angry lion, you straighten your arm, close your eyes and run with all your speed, aiming straight for his Adam's apple."

"But surely you would miss your target if your eyes are closed?", one of the boys in the group said with a smile of doubt on his face.

"Of course you will miss if you think about it. You don't think and you don't aim;
There is no time for that. You other hit him or he gets such a fright that you will get him as soon as the bout is re-started."

This was what I was going to do; If I was going to lose at least I would give him something to remember. It was almost as if I was watching somebody else doing all the preparation for the kill . . . push him back, beat his blade noisily, make him retreat.

The rest was almost too easy to be true. I heard myself making this furious bellow, extended my blade and simultaneously started to run, (Fleche attack) aiming at his neck.

I did close my eyes and I just kept running. Suddenly I heard a scream and I felt someone holding the end of my epee; When I opened my eyes I saw poor Gabor, trying to stop my epee penetrating his neck just between the lower part of the mask and the fencing vest.

The President called us to stop, checking to see if my opponent was all right. So here I was, facing this champion, who probably for the first time in his career didn't know what had happened, facing this Romanian maniac who for all intents and purposes had almost killed him.

At that stage I knew that I had him, and that I would eat him no matter what.

I WAS IN CONTROL

No sooner had the President asked us to recommence, when once again I attacked Gabor with exactly the same movement, except this time I kept my eyes open and hit him smack in the throat!

This bout changed my whole attitude to competitive sport and I learned that there is no place in this kind of event for kind people; If I wanted to better my life in Romania I had to win to survive, and to have all the advantages of being a top sportsman.

Our team finished in the 8th place overall ahead of the Czech and French teams, whilst in the individual event Victor finished 20th with 3,612 points. I finished 23rd with 3,360 points and Dumitru came in 30th place with 2,481 points, mainly because he scored very poorly in the riding event. In fencing we all managed to win 9 bouts each, which was slightly better than the planned result.

Our coaches were assured of continued employment and we were given $US25 to buy some presents.

Back home at the Bucharest railway station, we were received by a large group of supporters, and it was great to see all my family smiling proudly and congratulating us for our unexpected success.

All of a sudden we had become public property, and people started to ask about our sport, this mad combination of five different activities.

It didn't matter. We had proven to our critics that we could learn this difficult sport and achieve results of an international standard. But there was little time to rest, and we had two more years to get ready for the biggest competition of them all: The Olympic Games.

LEARNING TO COPE

After our return from Budapest I found that I had a different attitude towards my training sessions. I became interested in getting better and stopped complaining about the rigours of training. It's amazing how much we can be motivated by good results, knowing that your hard work is being rewarded. It was quite evident that those members of the squad who did not put heart and soul into their training were starting to be left by the wayside and become disheartened. Just the same, apart from improving at sport, I continued to have a difficult time trying to keep up with my university assignments and lectures, travelling by public transport across Bucharest to attend various training sessions, and finding enough energy to do all the things required of me to do.

Sandu found cheap accommodation in an area fairly close to the city centre.

It was a small room at the back of the landlord's residence, with some furniture given to us, but without a fridge or any form of heating. So in the summer it was unbearably hot, and in the winter we froze.

The winter of 1954 was one of the most severe in memory. We had to go to bed keeping our track-suits on, covered with two blankets, and yet we still felt the cold. One night I forgot to empty the glass water jug. In the morning the water was frozen solid and the glass broken. We decided to take turns and empty the carafe before going to bed. It worked for a while until the night when I brought home my new girl friend, U.A.

The first time I saw her, she was training with the University Diving Club.

U.A, was a very attractive second year student and I was immediately impressed by her athletic body. As I got to know her better, we found that we had a lot in common and gradually became very close. One of the problems in those days was to find a quiet spot where you could be alone with your girl. Fortunately my brother agreed to go to one of his friend's place if I needed the room.

I were finally alone in this tiny room of ours, when Sandu started to knock on the door:

"Open up! I am freezing out here in the snow."

I put my hand on her warm mouth and we tried very hard not to start laughing.

"All right, I know you are there. I'll go to Bebe's place for the night Cornel, I will see you tomorrow".

He finally left, and by then we started to undress one another. She had a great body and beautiful silky skin but her chest was something any man would love to hold and caress;

We were both very young and inexperienced but full of energy so that our love making turned into a spirited wrestling match, which steamed the window and made us forget completely about the cold.

When I finally entered her, she arched her powerful back and squeeze me tight with her muscular legs. It was only then that we discovered how good it was to hold one another tight, to move strongly, to feel every part of our bodies; We made love for a long time and finally we dropped to sleep.

The next morning, she left before me for an early lecture at the Institute.t, Sandu arrived shortly and rather angrily demanded to let him know in future of my amorous exploits:

"I am glad somebody had a good time last night" he said trying to make me feel sorry for keeping him out in the cold.

"Look brother, I said, we have both agreed on this arrangement so don't start" and I went to the small basin where we kept our water jug.

"No, not again, I didn't empty the jug last night and it is broken again," I uttered, feeling slightly embarrassed. Sandu, who was much calmer than me, reassured me that no harm had been done.

"Look at it this way; we just got some money from home, we can by a metal container that will not break. You can pay your share".

At the end of winter we were told by Muresanu that sometime in March in 1955 all those athletes selected to compete in the 1956 Melbourne Olympics would be housed in a top city hotel where everything would be provided for our comfort, and paid for by the Sport Committee. I shared a room on the fifth floor with my good friend Wilhelm Roman, and finally we had everything we needed for proper training. We were given preferential treatment reserved only for top sportsmen. The food we were given was of top quality and plentiful. For the first time, from every meal I was able to save food for my brother, who like the majority of students in Bucharest, was starving.

It is not hard to understand how our Communist Leaders could demand almost anything from the Romanian people, or how leading athletes were totally dependent on the generosity of our leaders. When you are hungry, you start to lose your ideals, your will—power and ultimately your resistance against injustice. Like a wild animal you try to stay alive, to survive and to do anything you are asked to do without question.

YOU ARE WITH US OR AGAINST US?

Through my ICF studies which led towards a Degree in Physical Education and Sport, I gained a very detailed and sound grounding in the correct application and methods used for physical performance. Many of our lecturers at the Institute were doctors or professors with international reputations and numerous publications in their field of expertise to their credit. Wilhelm and I started to realize that with the exception of Mr Galimir and Colonel Zidaru, the other coaches didn't have a proper scientific grounding in sport physiology, and their methods were based on some personal experience at a lower level.

The two events we managed to improve just marginally were swimming and pistol shooting. The reason was becoming obvious. Swimming lessons were not supervised, and we were asked to work from a hand written program. Additionally there was no coach available at the pool to correct our style or the make sure we were doing the right exercise. Apparently our swimming coach who was in charge of the swimming squad, did not have the time to train us, although he was given this particular responsibility, because the swimming squad took priority.

Our pistol shooting coach was a little man who always gave the impression of being frightened by his own shadow. He was always late for training and lacked the energy to impart his knowledge.

I had a talk with Willy (Wilhelm) and decided to talk to Muresanu and see if he would see fit to introduce some changes in our training. But we did not realize how stubborn and proud this man was. He became extremely agitated and told us that we didn't know anything about training and that he was a true innovator in the sport of modern pentathlon.

"How dare you tell me what is the right approach. You've done a few lectures and now you think you know it all. What you know is just theory! I teach the real thing, so I suggest you go away and do your studies and I will do the training."

He marched out of the hall furiously and left the two of us completely baffled:

"Why do you think he is so bloody angry?" asked Willy, who was a nice and very calm young man.

"I personally think that he is scared we will find how little he actually knows, and to admit that we are right would literally put him out of his job."

It was the wrong thing to do, and he never forgave the two of us but in particular me, because he knew that I could see through him. From then on I was the "bad guy", and could not do anything right. He was openly unfair to me and in many occasions I was on the verge of punching him, except that I would have been sent packing the next day. So I had to learn to hide my feelings and just do my training, although I started to practice those things I felt we were deficient in.

The relationship between Muresanu and I worsened almost to breaking point, so that I started to rebel against his methods and disobey some of the strict dictatorial rules he enforced on us all. This was the time when I started to resent more deeply the type of life we were forced to live. Perhaps I was getting exhausted with the long hours of training, with the unrelenting pressure to improve and the added worry of attending university and studying.

I had never been a quitter and I fought hard to finish what I had started, but this relentless combination of hard physical work and studies were starting to take their toll.

The situation at home was another worry which I could not solve or escape. My father could not get another job and things were getting very difficult for my parents, particularly as they were too young to even have a pension.

In those days there was little talk or understanding of the word stress, although we were made aware of the damaging effects of over-training and becoming physically exhausted. Muresanu pretended not to see that we were displaying the classic symptoms of chronic fatigue syndrome, and pushed along relentlessly with harder and longer training sessions.

We started to hate him, his secrecy and lack of communication, his total lack of understanding of our needs. Repeatedly we confronted him and asked him to give us some free time, but to no avail.

During one of the shooting practices at the range, I had a big argument with him and told him that he was going the wrong way and that he would destroy us all unless he changed his attitude and methods. As usual, Muresanu did not want to listen to anybody. "Either you do what I tell you or you can leave the squad right now!" Muresanu said, trying to end the discussion.

But I had had just about enough of this heartless, insensitive individual so I told him how we felt about him, and how we had come to hate his methods and lack of understanding.

"This has nothing to do with training, we all know that you are a good coach, but you don't understand anything else. You see us just like some kind of robots, you press the button and we all start moving, you press the button again and we stop. You have no interest in what we do or how we feel. To you we are only some instruments you use to achieve your aims."

He listened without saying a word, just glaring at me with a hateful stare, then after a short pause he looked around to make sure that nobody could hear him and then he started talking, carefully choosing his words:

"You have given me a lot of trouble lately and I don't know what is the real reason. Whatever that is, you are not helping. I expected you to be an example to the others but instead you are making things more difficult for me. When are you and the others going to understand that it is not my choice? We have to produce the results or we are out of the Olympic Squad. If I make your sessions easier, if I give you more free time, do you honestly believe that you are going to improve?"

He stopped for few seconds and then he continued with a resigned look:

"I am not going to tell you again Cornel, you are my best athlete and you are improving all the time, but unless you stop trying to tell me how to run MY program., I am going to kick you out of the squad. That goes for Willy or any other member of the squad who doesn't like my methods."

I walked away totally deflated, realizing that I had wasted my time. He would never change or try to see my point of view. Perhaps deep down in his heart he knew we were right but he had to defend his own job by getting the results at any cost.

When the evening came, and we had to take our bus back to the city, I decided to walk and told Willy not to wait for me. The pistol range was some 20 kilometres from Bucharest, in the middle of a lovely forest. I started walking along the road when the bus caught up with me, and the driver, who was a friendly man, slowed down and signaled me to get in the bus.

"No thanks, you go ahead. I will walk back, I need some extra training."

The bus gained speed and I was at last alone, surrounded by lovely green vegetation and tall trees. As I walked along in the cool, fresh air, I started to feel very sad and dejected with my life. I could not see any solution to my hopeless situation, with the lack of freedom, unable to cope with the demands of our present system, being deprived of any freedom; it wasn't just Muresanu and his neurotic obsession with intense training, it was the realization that I COULD NOT LIVE WITHOUT FREEDOM.

Suddenly the thought of escaping this system, this prison-like country, entered my mind. I started to consider and weigh the arguments for and against defecting to a non-communist country, where I could start a new life. But my family, how could I leave my parents and my brother without my support, knowing that if I defected during one of our oversees competitions, the Communist Regime would come down very heavily on my family? I could not come to a decision and I continued to walk in the night without being able to see a solution to my situation.

A FRIEND FROM THE PAST

My relation with U.A was suffering as I was too busy to be with her, and often did not finish training until late at night. We were working feverishly to complete our preparation for the coming World Championships in Switzerland in the autumn of 1955.

Muresanu decided to increase our experience by entering us in various local and regional competitions which were held mainly on Sundays. That was a little too much for U.A. who told me to choose between her and pentathlon. There was no choice to be made, so I had to get used to a life of celibacy. One afternoon, I was called from the reception desk and told that there was a lady to see me. I couldn't think of anyone apart from U.A that would have come to see me, so I rushed down in my dressing gown, hoping that she had changed her mind.

I was met by an attractive young woman, elegantly dressed and with a big smile on her face. "You don't know who I am do you?" she said as she extended a gloved hand towards me.

No, I didn't know who she was, although something about her face was familiar.

"Sorry, I give up," I said, feeling a little out of place in my dressing gown, talking to this beautiful stranger.

"It's M.I you fool, don't you remember our promises to be friends for ever?"

Yes, I remembered our relationship during our school days when we spent some time together, but unfortunately it never got past holding hands and exchanging timid kisses. We were both too young and inexperienced to progress to anything more serious, kind of an unfinished affair which waited to be completed.

"I am in town for few days, and I am staying at the Atheneum Hotel."

The Atheneum Hotel was one of the most expensive hotels in Bucharest, and very few people could afford to stay there. Besides M.I. was dressed very elegantly and her clothes must have cost a fortune. She asked me if I was doing anything special that night, and if I would have the time to have dinner at the hotel with her.

"No I am free tonight, we finished our fencing training some hours ago. Give me five minutes to change, and I will meet you back here in the foyer."

At the hotel we had a luxurious dinner, being served and looked after by an army of waiters who kept filling my glass with good Romanian red wine. During the meal, she told me that after leaving town she finished her studies and met an older man, a doctor, and they had been married for a couple of years. But she went on to say that the whole affair had been a mistake as her husband was much too old and didn't love her, and that she was very unhappy.

"Why don't you leave him, if you are so unhappy?" I asked.

She looked at me with a sad look and then she told me that the only good thing about their marriage was that she was allowed to do anything she wanted to do, and she could have anything she wanted.

"You see Cornel, as you remember we were pretty poor when I was in Turnu-Magurele. For the first time in my life I can have the best clothes and jewellery.

I realized that she had made her choice, and although she was obviously cheating on her husband, she felt no remorse in doing so. Besides things being as bad as they were, it was pretty unusual to find a rich and understanding husband who didn't mind letting his wife going solo to Bucharest. The hotel room was warm and comfortable. I had drunk a few glasses of wine during dinner and I was feeling relaxed. She stood in front of me and slowly started to take her clothes off.

She had become a woman, a very attractive and desirable woman. I carried her to the big double bed and I made vigorous love to her. She was young and hungry for love. I instinctively sensed that she was starved for love, her husband too old or impotent. I started to feel sorry for her, and I started to stroke her hair gently.

"You know Cornel, " she said, beginning to sob quietly, "I've always loved you, and I hated it when my family had to leave Turnu. I've would have loved to be with you much longer."

"Never mind, we are together and that's all that matters," I said, trying to calm her.

She then offered me some coffee and a small glass of thick yellow fluid.

"Try this home-made liqueur; I made it myself."

I didn't suspect anything and I drank the strong, sweet fluid which tasted very pleasant. I know now that this was no ordinary liqueur and she must have put some gypsy herbs in it, because for the rest of the night I become insatiable for her body, and we had almost continuous sex. The next day I felt like someone had sucked every ounce of energy out of my body and I had to push myself very hard to finish my training sessions. I felt very flat and exhausted. Fortunately for me, she had to leave town and get back to her husband, whose mother apparently had taken ill. It was just as well that she had to go; It would have been impossible for me to keep up with her excessive sexual demands and at the same time to find the energy for my training sessions. However it was an experience one would hardly forget.

MACOLIN, 1955 WORLD CHAMPIONSHIP AND THIN BREAD

We all started to experience the excitement of achieving better results and realized how much we had progressed in the short time from the selection trials late in 1953. It was still hard work, and every session left us most of the time very tired, but we noted with satisfaction how we could do all the work required from us yet at the end of the day, we all could tell how much stronger and fitter we were.

It is hard to explain the transformations your body goes through in the process of training, and how you become a different person not only in the physical sense but particularly how your attitude towards people, and life in general, changes. I started to become more assertive, to challenge more often things I didn't agree with, to stick to my opinions even if this meant another row with Muresanu or the other coaches.

Because we had some 12 members left in the squad, there was a continuous competition between ourselves to prove that we were better than the other members of the squad. Every training session was more like a mini competition, and we all tried to win, to prove to our coaches that we had what it took to make the team. In a way this was probably a smart plan by our coaches, to make us more competitive, but because we all wanted to be the best this wasn't really necessary. Eventually we started to transfer some of the challenges from training sessions to our relationships as friends.

Informing on your friends or even on your own family was one of the most despicable method used by the Communists in Romania, something the Romanian people had never contemplated or tolerated. But this system was widespread throughout the state-controlled institutions and gradually infiltrated all sectors of the community. There was nothing spared or sacred, even little children were asked by their kindergarten teachers to tell "everything" they'd heard being discussed at home. People had to learn to talk in whispers, and to look carefully behind their backs before they dared to say anything.

We were watched constantly by communist secret police, and all our movements were reported to our coaches.

The Romanian Government introduced laws which literally removed any natural rights one would expect in a modern, free society. Until the Russians took over, the Romanian people, although not very rich or influential on the international scene, had a good life, freedom of press and speech, and free elections. We took for granted all these liberties and could not imagine that these rights could be taken away from us.

People could not understand what was happening to them, nobody was able to take a stand or express a view anymore; any comments made in public or even privately against the regime criticizing our "beloved leaders", brought an immediate and harsh penalty. The person responsible would be arrested and dragged away in the dark of night by the secret police. In many cases the whole family would disappear without any trace, never to be heard of again.

In my case, I was an easy target for anyone who wanted to report me to the secret police, simply because my father did not show support for the Communist Party and had a record as a non partisan to the regime. I had to be very careful not to give any reason to be expelled from the Olympic squad by the Central Committee of Sport, and I had to keep a particular watch on what I was saying even when in the company of my close friends.

Once reported to the secret police, guilty or not, one had to have a good explanation not to be expelled from the team.

The race for making the team became more fierce with every day, and the competition between the remaining members was reaching dangerous levels.

Luckily for me, I managed to befriend the youngest member of our team, Wilhelm Roman, who came to Bucharest to study Sport and Recreation at I.C.R and was in my year. He had made the squad through the selection trials and was trying now to make the Modern Pentathlon National Team.

A very shy and modest young man, Willy, as we all called him, had the additional problem of being educated in the northern region of Romania, where there was a large number of ethnic Hungarians, and he had great difficulty learning the Romanian language. I liked Willy for being a very honest and straight person, who in his broken Romanian was able to say what he believed in. I particularly started to get closer to him the day he cornered our "rat", and told him straight to his face that he was no good at anything and that he should try another sport.

But with all my support and encouragement, when the final team to represent Romania in the 1955 World Modern Pentathlon in Switzerland was announced, Willy was left out once again. The team was made up of Victor Teodorescu, Viorel Manciu, myself and Dumitru Tintea as the reserve. Muresanu called me to his hotel room and he told me that he had stuck his neck out for me once again, and despite being a pain in the neck and challenging his leadership, he had told the CCS bosses that I was the one to be nominated team captain. This was a great and unexpected honour, particularly as I was expecting to be told that I had been kicked out of the team because of subordination. He then told me to let Willy know that he had missed out only because his riding test wasn't up to the standard required in international competition.

It's hard to imagine that even after all this time, some 44 years to be exact, certain events and words spoken by my coaches ring clearly in my mind like it only happened yesterday. With fencing becoming my main interest, I tend to remember my fencing lessons more clearly, and the words Mr Galimir would say to me. He was a man who hid under a modest and quiet appearance, a great understanding of life and of people. He was a deep thinker and philosopher, a great teacher with an incredible knowledge of fencing which was his life and passion. Never to be the one to speak evil of others, he would occasionally utter a few words about things he didn't agree with. We had to interpret what he actually wanted to say, almost like solving a puzzle, before we could understand what he actually meant.

Our fencing lessons were held in a large sporting complex, near lake Herastrau, where we had been allotted a large basketball court with ample room to do our fencing lessons and other related activities. Mr Galimir chose the area under the concrete stands where he would give his fencing lessons. Each one of the 12 members in the squad would receive a 10 minute individual epee lesson three times a week. Despite his age, 66, and poor physical condition, Mr Galimir would give lessons to all of us, which took up to two hours. It was hard demanding work which made him sweat profusely, particularly in the summer, when the temperature under the stands became unbearable. But he never complained or took time off and he was always there. He gave everyone the same amount of attention and he encouraged everyone to do their best, even if he didn't like that particular student. He must have noticed my interest in fencing and my eagerness to learn from his lessons everything I could. He started to tell me about the three levels of fencing one can reach in time through assiduous practice: Sport—science—art.

"What we are doing here is just sport, and you don't have much time to even reach the lower level of science, but if you are prepared to spend a minimum of 30-40 minutes a day doing basic exercises, one day, after 3 or

4 years of practice, you may reach the art level." He finished this unusually long dissertation whilst wiping away the perspiration which was running down his cheeks in small rivulets.

According to him, fencing was more than a sport, it was a science with its specific laws, and for a few, this could become in time a form of refined movement and action, which could qualify as art. On that particular summer's day when we had that discussion it had been unusually hot, and during my fencing lesson, because of all the perspiration falling from my face through the wire mask on to the concrete floor, I kept sliding whenever I made a quick lunge. Even so, with all the discomfort and wet floor, this was a rare opportunity for me to have the last lesson of the day. He was able to spend a little time relaxing and talking to me, and I had a chance to ask him things I wanted to understand.

"But how does one know when he has reached the level you are talking about?"

I questioned him whilst still panting from the hard and fast lesson he had just put me through.

"It differs in each individual. Firstly his master will notice the improvement, secondly his opponents won't be able to hit him and finally the fencer himself FEELS that he can do anything he has learned in a lesson, in a bout against his opponent."

"You mean to say Master, that myself and the others are a little scared to try in competition what you have taught us in the lessons, because of the fear of losing?"

He listened to me whilst packing his old rust-stained jacket on top of his epees in an ancient fencing bag;

"Your sport of pentathlon is helping your physical condition, running and swimming will increase your endurance. Fencing on the other hand requires incredible confidence in your ability, courage and quick assessment of the situation; you have to be an opportunist and occasionally you have to gamble and take a chance, but more often you have to suffer the torment of indecision, or the shame of being a coward, of not attacking when you should have taken the opportunity. Yet you must remain calm and totally in control of your emotions, to hate and want to kill your opponent, but not to become the victim of your own anger and blind rage."

He stopped for a minute to collect his thoughts then he continued:

"I am sorry Cornel, I think I am listening to my thoughts instead of trying to answer your questions; What was it that you wanted to know? Ah yes, we were talking about when does one know what stage he or she has reached? That's right isn't it? Well perhaps I will give you a clear aim, something you can try for right now before the World Championships." He took a long look at me then he said

"The day you will take FIVE hits from me without losing any points, you will be ready to beat anybody in the Modern Pentathlon!"

We used to have at the end of our lessons—unless the Master was very tired or rushed for time—a short bout when we were encouraged to try to hit him with any of the movements we had learned or wanted to try on him. It took me a long time before I was able to score points against him as he was very fast and in particular his parry ripostes were deadly. Any uncovered attack or careless preparation of the attack which got us too close to the Master was swiftly punished by a simple direct stop hit to the exposed area. For the time being I could not imagine myself EVER scoring five hits against my Master, and in particular not to be hit by him. He must have read my mind because as we walked back to the changing room he stopped momentarily and added:

"Keep working hard and remember what I told you; It will happen."

He was right as usual and as the time progressed I started to FEEL the movements I was doing as being an integral part of my being.

Before we left for Switzerland, I had my end of the lesson bout with my Master, and we finished 5-2 in his favour. I wasn't ready yet, he told me, more work was needed. I felt I would never know enough to beat him 5-0.

The Championships in Switzerland took place in the beautiful locality of Macolin, high in the mountains, on the grounds of the Swiss Sport Academy.

We had never seen such grounds and facilities. This was a showplace, a Hollywood-like scene, the most expensive Institute of Physical Education and Sport in Europe. I walked through the immaculately kept grounds where one could choose to do any athletic activity. There were numerous running tracks, jumping pits and throwing rings, as well as a shooting range, swimming pool, indoor ball games courts and a bowling alley;

And yet regardless of where you were, you only had to turn round and face the valley and see the most majestic scenery of distant peaks covered with snow. We had never seen anything so beautiful and moving as this place. We had been given excellent accommodation and every little flat faced the magnificent view of the mountains.

I was in seventh heaven as I was able to finally practice my school French and converse with the locals. Most of the Swiss people were tri-lingual and could switch easily between languages. I remember once we had to travel by rail to our riding venue, and in the same compartment there was a young woman and her young boy. As the boy became restless and started to misbehave, the mother spoke to him in Italian but without much success. The boy continued to run and play. Then the mother once again spoke to him but in French this time. This had some effect and he sat down quietly for few minutes, but when he once again tried to get up on the seat, she grabbed him hard by the hand and spoke in German. That seemed to do the trick.

The competition was held under excellent conditions and in particular we were all impressed by the high standard of their horses. They were bigger and stronger than our horses, maybe not as fast as Hungarian horses, but very responsive to the aids.

The riding course was set in a area which had a variety of terrains; flats, hills and forests, and according to the competition rules, the competitor had to cover a total distance of 5,000m and to jump a total of 15 fixed obstacles. Additionally the competitors were not allowed to walk and familiarize themselves with the course, except from a map posted near the scoring board. The map was fairly succinct, and purposely designed not to give too many details.

Most of the 17 teams competing had their riding coaches with them and were able to ask for advice. In our case Colonel Zidaru wasn't allowed to come because of "lack of funding", yet attached to the team were some four secret agents, posing as officials. This was the rule of the day, as some of the top Romanian athletes had started to defect to the free world when they had the opportunity to compete overseas.

I had drawn a beautiful dark horse which reminded me of my poor Satan. In the warm up arena he jumped and did everything I asked of him with great ability. This was a horse I could trust even if I had to ride in totally foreign territory.

The start was placed just outside a thick forest, and for the first few hundred metres I was cantering up the hill, parallel to the forest, keeping an eye out for the small coloured flags which were the only guide on the official track. I had to be careful not to leave the course and incur elimination. Suddenly I had to turn left and enter a small track in the forest; it was just a path, barely wide enough to allow the horse and rider to go through. There were small branches growing across the path, and very little visibility. I was trying to keep the horse on the path and nearly took the wrong turn whilst trying to keep the required speed of 350 m. per minute or a controlled steady canter.

Then without me even realizing it, we took the wrong turn and suddenly I was lost in the dense vegetation and I didn't know where I was going. My horse was stumbling and tripping over dead trees. For a minute I panicked and started to sweat profusely, thinking that if I got lost not only would I be disqualified and score zero points, but I would let my team down.

Fortunately I remembered Colonel Zidaru telling us, in one of the many lectures he gave us on competition, that if we ever got lost and we didn't know how to get back to the correct course, to put our trust in the horse.

"That horse has been over that ground many times and knows better than you where to go. Just hold the reins firmly, place your hands down on his neck and LET HIM FIND HIS WAY."

So I did just that and to my delight my horse immediately settled down, stopped fighting and quickly got back on the course. My coach had taught me well. Thank you coach.

We came out of the thick forest and the horse slowed to a trot down the track and came across a fixed log placed in a difficult position, requiring the horse to jump almost from a complete stop on the opposite bank. I pushed hard with my seat and squeezed with my legs, but there was no reason to doubt my horse. He just collected momentarily and then easily leaped over the heavy bar and started to canter up the small incline and out of the gully.

For the rest of the course, we jumped everything with ease, and I realized how well my horse had been educated and sensitive he was to my smallest command, instantly obeying my directions. By then we had left behind some of the more difficult obstacles like the old loaded cart with a canopy which left little room to jump through; (They even had a few lovely girls dressed in floral national costumes sitting on the front seat of the cart).

By now I knew that I was making very good time so I let the horse travel faster and finish the course in a good time. Just then we had started to approach a triple bench, an obstacle which involves jumping up on three consecutive narrow platforms, each one progressively higher than the previous one. There is enough room on each platform to take one stride and then jump on the next one without stopping.

If the horse travels too slowly or the rider does not maintain "impulsion" by urging the horse to engage his hind legs before the jump, the horse will refuse to jump on the first platform, and then the rider has to attempt the jump again. If he is not successful even after the third attempt, he is allowed to go ahead to the next obstacle. However he will be heavily penalized with points deducted from his final result.

But the worst situation occurs when the horse stops on the second platform because of insufficient impulsion or hesitation on the rider's part. There is no room to gain enough momentum to jump up on the next table and the only alternative for the rider is to take his horse down to the start and do it all over again. This is a very time consuming affair, and many points are lost. So right there in front of me I could see three riders and their horses stuck on the second platform, milling around, cursing, swearing, trying to jump, but all in vain.

I was getting closer with every stride and I could not see how I could squeeze between all those bodies, maintain my speed, and jump on to the next platform; I was getting very annoyed, realizing that I would finish stuck with the other riders.

"Pastele Christosului matii da-te laoparte, misca-te!" I was shouting at the top of my voice in Romanian for the riders to make room, to move to the side. Of course it was all in vain as these competitors didn't understand Romanian, as well as having enough problems with their horses. There was nothing for me to do but to place my horse straight to the middle of the first platform, and urge him with all my might; It worked; We literally landed on top of one of the stationary horses and then pushed our way through and jumped on the next platform, after which we had a free jump on the last platform and out.

For the rest of my ride I could not wipe the big smile off my face, savouring the delight of having such a great horse. It doesn't happen very often in Pentathlon to get a horse you get on with, but when you do you are a winner.

The presentation ceremony was something to remember, our team finishing in second place out of 14 countries. I finished in 7th place, Viorel Manciu finished 4th, narrowly missing the 3rd individual place by some 14 points or 4 seconds and Victor Teodorescu, having a slow ride, finished in 20th place. For the first time our team had won a major placing in an international competition. It had been hard work, with many falls and sore bones, but the moment when the ribbons for second place were draped on our horses, we experienced the greatest sense of achievement, of total fulfillment. As well, we all felt very grateful to our great riding coach, our Colonel, who managed in such a short time to teach us, such complete beginners, to compete in a very difficult event.

The rest of the competition surpassed all our expectations in particular in fencing, where our team scored 22 victories on average, by comparison with the Budapest International where we all scored around 9 victories as an average.

Gabor Benedeck, my prized trophy from the previous competition, must have remembered my desperate attack and took great care not to give me the opportunity to surprise him again, and he beat me after a good technical bout. I was annoyed with myself for losing bouts but I was starting to understand what I was doing and how I was losing; I was able to understand what I was doing wrong, and able to reason what should have been done. I started to accumulate a lot of information and memorize various fencers I was encountering, as to what movement they did, their weak points and good points. For some strange reason I was able to remember accurately what movement I did against one opponent, and how exactly I won or lost that bout. It didn't matter if I didn't meet that fencer for a whole year, When I faced him again, I had complete recall of our previous encounters.

This unexplained ability to have a photographic memory of various actions with the epee was one of the deciding factors in my rapid progress in fencing, as I was able to avoid repeating mistakes or movements which proved to be unsuccessful in previous encounters.

To defeat Gabor Benedek in the future I reasoned, I had to improve even further my knowledge of fencing movements, to the point where I could answer to any of his attacks as well as learning to attack with greater speed and accuracy. Like a game of chess, I had to learn the game well, to be patient and take the opportunity when it presented itself without hesitation; at least I knew that even if he had won this time, technically I had closed the gap and I was "fencing" rather than just "fighting" blindly.

When the competition was over, I had scored 3,800 points, finishing in 13th place with Viorel in 15th place with 3,681 points and Victor Teodorescu in 21st place with 3,457 points. But most encouraging was our team result, 7th overall out of 14 countries with a total of 10,826 points; this meant that we only had to go one place higher in the Olympic Games in 1956, and we would reach our aim of making the 6th place, which meant Diploma of the Games.

Our stay in Macolin accentuated our dislike towards the Communist State of Romania. We were overwhelmed by the freedom and prosperity enjoyed by the ordinary people of this country and the mere thought of returning to the misery of life in Romania made us sick at heart. We all felt sorry to leave but there was nothing we could have done to change the inevitable.

Nevertheless, perhaps for the first time I started to think seriously about defecting, and asking for political asylum.

Although it was never mentioned officially or made public, we knew of some Romanian elite athletes competing overseas in the free world, who had decided to take the big chance and not return with their respective teams back home to Romania. Initially the authorities kept quiet but as the number of defectors increased and started to include not only athletes but also officials and coaches, the government introduced more stringent selection procedures and increased the number of secret police agents who travelled with the official team, posing as competitors or officials, with the express order to supervise and prevent athletes from making contact with local sympathizers.

But more defections occurred to the point where the Central Committee of Sport was forced to change its policy of secrecy and started to make the names of the defectors public. They were portrayed as being the lowest form of traitors, without any dignity or love for their country.

Their names were removed from all the official records, their families were asked to make public apologies and in some cases where the athlete failed to return his equipment or official uniforms used in competition, the family had to pay large amounts of money in compensation.

If by any chance the defector could not survive in the new country and had to return to Romania, he or she would immediately be asked to comment on the experience encountered in the "corrupt capitalist society", to denigrate the social and economic situation found in that country, and declare their undying love and admiration for the "Communist Heaven" he had the opportunity to come back to.

So although I was getting more disgusted and tired with the continuous lies perpetuated by our political system, I was aware that my defection to the free world would be severely punished, and that in particular my family would suffer the brunt of their revenge.

After the Swiss competition ended, we were taken by our hosts and shown some of the beautiful sights of that magnificent country. We were able to buy a few gifts for our families with the money received from our coach Muresanu for our 2nd place in the riding event. On our return home, once again we were met by a large and enthusiastic crowd of supporters who filled the Bucharest Railway Central. My family was delighted with my results and I became the centre of interest, everybody wanting to know how I found life in Switzerland and about their economy and standard of living. We were asked by Muresanu to say very little about our experience in a free country and he warned us that any unguarded statement could mean our expulsion from the National Squad.

My parents wanted to know what I found out whilst overseas and I had to tell them the truth about how miserable our existence was in comparison to their life. I was having a break from training and I was allowed to spend some time with my family in Turnu-Magurele and able to see some of my old friends. It was as always, just a sleepy little town with hardly anything to do, and after one week of rest and good home cooking I decided to go back to Bucharest.

My mother took the opportunity to have a chat with me in private when she asked me a few questions regarding my intentions for the future:

"Tell me son, did you really like what you saw over in Switzerland or were you just trying to impress us; I would really like to know the truth."

She was smiling at me with her loving eyes, so after a short hesitation I decided to tell her the truth, to let her know how much I was tempted to defect and not come back.

To my surprise, instead of accusing me of not caring about what would happen to our family if I decided to defect, she held my hand and spoke with great strength and warmth:

"My dear son, why didn't you stay in Switzerland? Why should you sacrifice your life as well and live forever in this hell? At least you have the opportunity to escape, to start a new life."

She paused for few seconds and then she spoke quietly, thoughtfully:

You should have stayed there, you may not have the same opportunity to leave the country."

I was stunned and bewildered to hear her telling me that I should have defected, that she was not concerned about the repercussions following my defection. She knew what would have happened to our family if I did stay in Switzerland.

"I don't think you understand what these animals would do to you all if I decided not to come back. I thought about it but I just couldn't do it. I love you all too much."

On the way back to Bucharest I could not forget my mother's words, urging me to defect. From that moment on, I knew I would be tormented between the temptation to defect and the pain and the suffering I was going to inflict on my family if I did decide to take that step. For many nights I could not close my eyes and kept going over different alternatives, but the longer I tried to find a solution, to delay the inevitable, the more I realized that life for me had no meaning, that I could not live any longer in this infernal Communist society.

In the final analysis there was only one choice left for me: I had to trade my family for the price of my freedom.

PART FOUR

TOO TIRED TO STUDY

By now we had experienced the hardship of intensive training, the never ending sessions of physical effort to the point where every part of our body refused to take another step, yet we had to push ourselves beyond the wall of pain and finish our given program or there was some form of penalty thought out by our inquisitors.

At no time were I or the other members of the team asked how we felt or offered any form of assistance. Even when we got sick with flu or we strained joints or suffered intense muscle soreness, we were not excused from our sessions; those who got seriously sick and could not cope with the training routine were simply asked to pack their bags and leave the squad.

With every day going by, Muresanu became more intense, more demanding and pushed us harder.

There was less time for anything else apart from training, less time to study, less time to be with our friends or family, and even our free time on the weekends was taken with additional competitions or special training session "to catch up" with our planned progress.

We all became very tense, snapping at one another, using our fencing bouts to release our pent-up anger, but through all this personal torment and silent cry for mercy, we were ignored and left to our own devices to cope with this incredible combination of physical and emotional stress. I think this was the time when I started to hate Muresanu with such intensity that I had to control myself in an effort not to hit him.

A WILD PARTY AND MURESANU'S REVENGE

Alexandru Bruja was one of those people who tend to smile all the time, even if they were not happy; He came into the squad with an athletic background, and had the necessary ability to be one of the top performers but his concentration span was very limited and additionally he did not bother himself with anything slightly complicated. We got on quite well, particularly as he was also enrolled in the ICF, studying to become a future pentathlon coach or fencing master.

One Saturday evening after our meal at the sportsmen's restaurant he caught up with me just as I was going upstairs to my room:

"Cornel, what are you doing this Sunday?"

Muresanu had informed us all that the cross-country run was postponed until the following Sunday so that for the first time in a long time, we could have a free day.

"I don't know Alex, maybe I might go with my brother to see a film or something. I haven't really had the time to do much study and I have to finish a few essays."

"Listen Cornel, enough work and no pleasure. You are going to kill yourself. My two cousins who are studying commerce are giving a party at their flat. There should be plenty of food, grog and gorgeous girls. What do you think?"

It was rather difficult to say no to a little bit of fun, particularly in Bucharest in those days when things were pretty scarce. Besides I felt like a good party to release some of the intense pressure.

"In regula (O.K.) I will come but we must be back before midnight or Muresanu will have a fit. Besides we have to save some energy for the running session."

We met down in the foyer at about 6 p.m. and then we took the tram to a distant quarter of Bucharest, some 20 kilometres from our hotel. The party was already in full swing and there were people everywhere. Alex introduced me to his cousins, two gorgeous brunettes, who in no time managed to make me very comfortable and at ease. As the night progressed everyone was getting more sloshed and I was no exception, especially as I wasn't used to drinking large quantities of red wine and Romanian plum whisky. My physical fitness was vastly superior to that of the average person, but my worst enemy was my insane desire to compete in whatever activity was available. So that if there was a vigorous country style dance, I would be in the middle of it trying my hardest to be the best on the floor, and when someone proposed to see who could drink a full glass of plum whisky without stopping, or taking a breath, I would have to be in it, competing and trying to win even if it was going to kill me. By the end of the night I was totally wrecked and because it was too late to take the tram, there was no other way to get back to my hotel other than walking. So Alex and myself walked the 20 kilometres and we managed to get back to our hotel at about 6.30 am.

I had hardly got into my bed when I heard a knock at the door. It was the usual morning reminder given by Muresanu, who delighted in being the first to get up and make sure that everyone was out of bed and getting ready for the morning's "short" warm-up run, which was more like a decent training session, as we had to keep pace with Muresanu who used to be a reasonable middle distance runner in his youth. I was very tempted to invent some form of illness and not go running, but Willy my room mate, who was up by now and almost ready to go, told me that Muresanu had been looking for me the night before as late as 10 pm., even though Willy had told him some story about me studying with Alex at the university.

"I don't think Muresanu believed one word I told him," Willy said apologetically. "I think you are in real trouble this time."

That was all I needed now, Muresanu trying to revenge his frustration with my interference in his program, which I used to criticize for being old fashioned and not suitable for our sport. So to pretend that I had some mysterious sudden illness was out of question, he would not have believed me, and he would have applied an even harsher penalty and suspended my weekend free time indefinitely. So I had to face the music and go running, pretending that nothing had happened the night before. Muresanu had a very strict code of behaviour for his athletes, and he would penalize any form of excesses such as drinking, smoking and in particular he frowned upon late night escapades with the opposite sex. I had a splitting headache and my mouth was like an ashtray, particularly as I was a very moderate smoker, but on the night I must have smoked at least 20-25 cigarettes. But there was no escape so I did my best to look happy and eager to run, and not let Muresanu get a whiff of my rotten plum-whisky breath.

"I want to talk to you about your late studies at night Cornel," Muresanu said briefly, and I could not detect any threat in his voice. Maybe he did believe Willy and he was just doing his usual check on how I used my time . . . but I was wrong, as I found later that he had been informed by "someone", and he was already planning how to punish me for breaking his laws. At the morning breakfast, after the run, I could hardly eat anything, and the mere sight of the warm steaming food made me very ill. The boys and in particular Victor, who was the oldest member of our team, knew of our escapade, and he made the worst possible effort to hide his delight in seeing our struggle not to puke right there in the middle of the restaurant.

For some strange reason our Communist Sport leaders had been informed that the weather conditions in Australia during the months of November and December, the period when the Olympic Games were to take place, would to be extremely hot, and the athletes had to have some form of training designed to prepare us for the extremes of temperature found in Australia. Additionally our running coaches were trying to copy the methods used by the Hungarian coaches, who had been very successful in international competitions.

They were advocating in those days that an athlete should do his training session as much as possible without any fluid intake, and that the athlete should be encouraged to drink water only at the end of the session.

So there we were, at the running track, in the middle of a Romanian summer's day with the temperature in the high thirties, when Muresanu asked us to prepare ourselves for a slightly different running session for the day.

"I know that some of you are against running at this time of the day, but this is for your own good, you will be much better acclimatized and able to stand up to the harsh Australian conditions."

He stopped for a minute and looked searchingly at our group, then he looked straight at me, grinned, and then he spoke with great enjoyment:

"You are all responsible young athletes who have worked very hard to improve and to lower your times for your running event. Today it is your chance to show me how hard you have worked and in particular I want to test your determination, your refusal to give in."

He stopped for a minute whilst we all listened almost without breathing, and then he dropped the bombshell.

"We are going to do a 3 x 2000m at competition pace, with a three minute recovery between repetitions. However you are asked not to take any fluids until we have finished.

I know it will be hard, but you have done your work and should be ready.

"By the way Cornel, how did your studies go last night? I hope you got plenty of sleep". The bastard knows everything : Alex and I must have been reported to Muresanu by the "rat".

So we were divided in groups of fours according to our ability, and asked to start at one minute intervals so that we were competing against each other as well as trying to catch up with the group in front of us. Because my group had the fastest runners, particularly Victor who was the best in the squad, our group was supposed to set a cracking pace and perhaps set some new personal best results. As the track was exactly 400m, we had to do 5 laps or a total of 2,000 me. before we could slow down and jog slowly for the next minute, then we had to line up at the start once again and start the second 2000 m. This was known as "Interval Training", except that the pace was much higher than the usual training pace. The short rest allowed between the repetition runs were too short to allow recovery, additionally the heat was sucking out our energy.

There was no question that my running had improved markedly since I had joined the pentathlon, and under normal circumstances I would have completed the session tired, but without too much discomfort. But the way I felt that day, I might have just as well done no training at all. My head was throbbing and feeling like lead, my lungs were burning and gasping for air, but the worst was my mouth which was totally parched and dry.

It was a very hot day and by the time we were ready to commence our trials, it was boiling hot, middle of the day, and the sun had settled itself exactly above our heads. This particular stadium was very bare and treeless ; No shade or place to rest from the sun, not that this mattered as we had to stay on the running track. I managed somehow to finish the first 2000 m. and I had to be restrained by Willy from rushing to the drinking fountain to have a long drink. The sun was feeling hotter than before and I was sure that hot irons were impaled into my head.

Muresanu called out something about our pace not being even enough and that we should try to do our 3rd and 4th lap in a faster time. I was by now starting to hallucinate and dream about cool water and a shaded spot when Muresanu called our small group to the start of the second 2,000 m. Victor and Willy were striding happily at the front in a blistering pace, whilst myself and Dumitru Tintea who hated running, were dragging our feet and trying not to lose contact. It's hard to explain to someone else what happens when your body reaches its physical limit, when you feel that every step you are taking burns deeper in the flesh. You become aware that there is nothing left in reserve, and there is an imminent threat of actually dying. This is when one has to face one's fears and there is no room for pretence, when there is nothing to reach to, when there is no help from anywhere. It is a fight for your very existence, which you have to look straight in the face. Your body is imploring you to slow down, to stop, yet the other part of you, your brain, the one which holds all your dreams and expectations, the one that has been planning and hoping that one day you will be the best in the world, or that one day you will be free and leave the Communist hell, tells you that you CANNOT STOP, that you have to finish no matter what.

I swallowed hard and kept running, but just before the last lap my stomach refused to listen to my orders and it let loose; I was sick as a dog on the side of the track and brought up this horrible mixture of food and plum whisky from the night before. When I finished, I looked up and saw my group approaching the finishing line; Muresanu didn't say anything, he was just looking at his stop watch. I started running once again and stumbled across the finishing line. Muresanu looked like nothing had happened and simply told me to hurry up and get ready for the last 2,000m run. This was a well planned revenge by my coach. He was finally able to see me on my knees and the only thing that I had to do was to beg for mercy.

"Come on Cornel, you are supposed to have the best endurance in the squad," Muresanu said with a thin cruel twist of his mouth. "I hope this is not too much for you"

He was obviously enjoying his revenge, proving and reaffirming to the rest of the squad he was the undisputed master. Suddenly I relaxed and a strange feeling invaded my body. The pain started to dissipate and I started to feel better, to feel my energy coming back.

It was a great feeling, and I was able to complete my last sprint in a good time and keep up with Victor. Despite the pain and discomfort I learned a lot on that day about effort. I also realized that there was something much more powerful than just the body, that the mind is capable of things we never dreamed possible, things which at time appear to be just our imagination. I know now that there is but a thin line separating the average performer from the champion, but in order to cross that line, one has to have the courage and the determination to hang on just a little longer, and to accept the pain. My body had responded magnificently all considered, and I promised myself that I would not abuse my body in the future and definitely not party before a competition.

YOU ARE READY TO WIN

Our fencing coach Aristide Galimir, was a man of great experience and he would, during the lesson, talk about things totally unrelated to the fencing lesson, or at least that was how it appeared. He was a deep thinker and a good judge of human character and behaviour, able to treat everyone with courtesy and admirable patience. He was, I realize now, a true example of a noble mind in an old and unfit body, proving his superiority and endurance against all obstacles. For a man of his age he was quite remarkable, and only many years later I started to realize how difficult it must have been for him to give some 12 individual lessons of 15 minutes duration in a hot airless room, having to wear a heavy teaching plastron, and never stopping for more than few minutes when he had a quiet sit down and a smoke. We were all extremely fit and capable of intense effort, so that as the time went by and we became better fencers, the lessons became faster and more demanding.

It was customary for Master Galimir to finish a fencing lesson with a short contest when we were asked to try some of the new movements learned, and score if possible a hit against him. It was exciting to actually fence against such an experienced fencer. He had a magnificent light hand, and although his legs didn't carry him too well, the swordhand was lightening fast, and it was almost impossible to hit him with a simple direct attack; he would parry and riposte with such speed and elegance that he would hit you before the front leg would land in a lunge position. But we got better and started to refine our movements and having the advantage of fitness and youth, we started to score an occasional hit (touch) on our master. He would gracefully accept the hit, like a true competitor, and praise our efforts.

One day after I'd had a particularly good lesson, when my Master did not have to tell me what to do, when to attack or how to respond to any of his preparation attacks or stop hits, a lesson called "a la muette, (a quiet lesson without words,) he rested briefly whilst drying the perspiration dripping from his face, he looked at me and asked me if I remembered what he had told me some time ago about being ready for the big time:

"Remember what I said to you about being ready some time ago, when you would know you are ready to beat the best in the world?" How could I have forgotten what was almost burned with an hot iron in my mind?

"You told me that the day I could take 5 hits from you in a bout without losing one hit, then I would be ready . . .

He looked very pleased and happy, obviously impressed with my recollection of something he had said a couple of years ago.

"Yes that's right, and today you are going to find out how you have progressed and if you are ready for the Olympic Games. Would you like to have that bout now or next lesson?"

I had been waiting for a long time for this moment. I had worked longer and harder than any other member of the squad. This was the time to find out if everything I had learned and thought about was of any value. The bout that followed was intense, skillful, and fought with great emotion. For the first exchanges I was reticent to hit my dear old Master. How could you hit someone you love and respect, someone who taught you everything?

At that point he stopped and talked to me, but obviously for the benefit of the whole squad which had stopped training and was watching us:

"You see Cornel and the rest of you, one cannot be a winner unless you are prepared to hit your opponent. Fencing is actual duelling and even if we cannot physically kill one another, that point of your epee is just as damaging when it hits the target and the electrical box indicates a hit. You have no choice: You either kill your opponent or he kills you. All your ability amounts to zero unless you have the desire to hit your opponent."

He stopped for a second and flexed his old blade against the ground and then he looked up and said to me in a gentle but steel like voice:

"As much as I like you and the others, I am not going to give the bout to you: YOU HAVE TO WIN IT BY HITTING ME!

I put my mask on, feeling relieved, and then I fenced my Master the way he had taught me, moving continuously, feinting, taking the blade, lunging and the occasional fleche.

In the end I won the bout 5-0 and the Master came forwards, took his mask off and shook my hand with great emotion. He was totally exhausted and on the verge of collapse, but he happily uttered:

"Yes by God, I think you are ready now, and nobody will stop you."

Not long after that bout his predictions started to prove true, and I hardly lost another bout in practice or competition.

FIRST ROMANIAN MODERN PENTATHLON CHAMPION

The place selected for the running of the first Modern Pentathlon Romanian Championship was Sibiu, the beautiful and prosperous town where I was born. Our squad used this town right from the beginning for its excellent facilities necessary for our training and in particular for the use of the horses belonging to one of the last Romanian cavalry regiments. The preparations for this event started earlier so that everything was ready and in place for our first national event, when our new sport had to show the country that it was indeed ready to take its place between the competing nations of the world.

Being a new sport we didn't have a great number of spectators but it didn't deter the competitors from contesting with great zeal all the events. I was ready for the event, and the only problem I had to deal with as usual, was the shooting event. Almost every other member of the squad had problems with their shooting technique, which wasn't working well, particularly under competition conditions. This was the direct result of being taught to shoot for results before our shooting technique was properly learned and under pressure we were unable to control our nerves. In shooting the beginner has to learn to perform each component part of the total shooting action before he starts to worry about scoring. We didn't have the time to do that and in fairness to our young shooting coach, despite the big rush to get us ready and not having the time to gradually get used to the competition pressure, we managed reasonably good scores.

In pentathlon the competitor has to shoot at a moving target which faces the shooter for a duration of three seconds then abruptly turns away for the next seven seconds. The shooter lowers the pistol or' revolver to 45 degrees and waits until the target turns and faces the shooter once again for another three seconds. The pistol is lifted, the aim is taken, the trigger is released smoothly and without jerking . . . well at least this is the correct way, but in practice there is very little time to perform the whole movement. In the back of your mind you worry about how much time is left to pull the trigger, then you pull the trigger or at least that's what you think you are doing, but somehow the connection between your brain and the trigger finger is interrupted, and the more you try to release the trigger the more the gun starts to shake. You feel the perspiration starting to run down your face, and you have a nightmare starting to calculate how much faster you will have to run or swim to compensate for the loss of 200 points! Finally the bullet leaves the barrel of your pistol but by then the target has already turned away or your hand has moved so violently that instinctively you know that you shot has missed the target completely. A feeling of despair overcomes the shooter, and he knows that his final score in shooting will jeopardize his overall total.

We all suffered from competition nerves in some way and failed to shoot as well as expected. Some of us adopted a philosophical approach and tried not to let this event become too overpowering. Others, like Victor, designed their own system. It wouldn't have been so funny and perhaps we should have tried to help Victor, but as he always had a smart comment to make and he was supposed to be experienced in all areas, we did enjoy his shooting predicament. Victor was a magnificent cross-country runner, but he could hardly swim so that it was essential for him to do the other events very well. He could not afford to lose points in shooting and the pressure was greater on him because he scored low in swimming.

His fear of scoring low in shooting started to become obvious and we all made jokes about what he would do next, what new theory he had evolved to deal with his nerves.

I think it was just before one of the competitions in Macolin, we were all were looking for Victor who had been called to his shooting bay, but nobody could find him. Eventually we located him in the locker room, sitting in front of a towel stretched out on the floor, on which he had carefully placed all the bits and pieces that make up a pistol.

"Victor, do you realize you have five minutes to get ready to shoot? What are you doing.?" He looked at us like we were all stupid and didn't understand what he was doing taking his gun apart, and said:

"You know my pistol has been playing up. How can I shoot well with a faulty weapon?" By now we all were totally mesmerized and could not believe what we were seeing: The man had flipped, how could he take his gun apart only minutes before he was due to shoot? But the funniest thing was that he felt totally vindicated and could not see how illogical his actions had become. We helped him to put his gun together, and of course he shot badly but he had a very good excuse.

"How could I shoot well, having all that worry about a faulty pistol that I could not trust and had to be put together seconds before I had to shoot?"

Victor was much happier after the incident, and he continued to be late for his shooting and able to reason his inability to shoot until the day when we decided to hide his pistol and prevent him from doing the dismantling trick.

When Victor realized that his pistol was missing, he started to rush around asking everybody if they had seen his weapon. We tried to stay serious and suggested things like: Maybe you left it back at the hotel or perhaps it dropped out of your bag in the bus?

Victor was almost beside himself when he heard the last call from the range official to take his position or be eliminated. Only then Alex came forward holding Victor's gun:

"Here you are Victor, gee you're lucky—I found it in the changing rooms under the seat. Somebody could have taken it away. Here, go and do your shooting."

Victor mumbled something about the pistol not being properly set for the competition, but there was no time to do the usual trick and take the pistol apart. He had to shoot straight away or he would have missed the event.

Well, as you probably guessed, he shot miserably as usual but when the shooting was over and we asked him what his reason was this time not to shoot well he replied,

"What do you expect me to do: my pistol was missing, I was rushed to do my shooting, how do you expect anyone to do his best?"

After that incident we dropped the issue and let Victor do his thing without trying to make him see his strange conduct. But Victor wasn't the only one to behave strangely when it came to shooting. In my case I was praying a lot.

"Please dear Lord, just this time, let the bullet be on the target, even if it is only a five, but let it be on the target."

In reality we all wanted to do well, to shoot high scores, but shooting is a very unforgiving sport which does not allow for nerves or emotions. You have to have a perfect technique, complete confidence in yourself, and not to fear the outcome.

How could we have been confident or not fear losing a target when our very existence depended on getting good results? How could one relax and enjoy the competition fully knowing that if we didn't perform we would have been kicked unceremoniously out of the squad and back to the ordinary miserable life available to the average Romanian citizen?

I was particularly determined to stay at the top, to be in the national squad and to score the highest possible result. It was the challenge of my life, to be the first Romanian Modern Pentathlon Champion. The competition was fierce, particularly in the fencing and we all fought like gladiators in the arena under the critical eye of our selectors, not giving any quarter to our training partners; everybody was fighting for their very survival and showed no mercy. It hurt me in particular to hit Willy who was one of the kindest people I'd ever known. But it had to be done . . .

It is a long time ago and I have forgotten the details of the various events and results obtained in this National Championship with exception of the shooting event where I remember shooting well up to the third round but in the last round of five shots I waited too long to get the perfect sight alignment and jerked the trigger. The barrel of the pistol moved crazily and I was sure I'd lost that target; I started to silently ask for help and not to have a complete miss. The recorder called the shots on the target and to my surprise all five shots were there. What a relief.

When the competition was over I was the first Romanian Champion and although the points difference was just minimal, once again my score in fencing put me ahead of Tintea and Teodorescu.

IS MY SHOULDER BROKEN?

In 1956, the Olympic year, we were working even harder to get ready for the Melbourne Olympic Games. Our training sessions were more demanding, but we all felt we were getting stronger and more skillful. I was finding less time for my last year of studies at I.C.R and my marks in various subjects were just above the average, enough to pass the tests and retain my bursary. Sandu my brother was doing reasonably well with his journalism studies and had started to get more assignments from sport journals, particularly as he was getting some excellent action sport photos. My private life had suffered to the point that I had very little time to see or talk to anybody, and every minute was dedicated to some form of training or competition. My body was leaner and stronger than ever before and in particular my running improved to the point where in the annual university cross-country run I won easily against all the top runners in the University. This gave me tremendous satisfaction, remembering how at the start of the course in 1952 I had finished somewhere in the middle group, minutes behind the winner. This time I was confident and able to control my pace at the start, then gradually moving faster forward and passing the slower runners. Towards the end, where there was a steady long hill, I increased my pace further and easily passed the remaining runners; I could see in their eyes how surprised they were when suddenly I appeared on their shoulder and then moved ahead. Obviously they had not seen me competing in university running events, and they didn't think that we in the Modern Pentathlon had time to concentrate on one particular event. Nevertheless this was the first time I realized how well we had been trained by Muresanu, and how much I had improved.

The situation in Romania was gradually worsening with more people out of work, less food and in particular increased lack of freedom. There was only one political Party and the elections were a total farce, people having the "freedom" to vote for the candidate. The problem was that there was only one candidate: the Communist candidate who was nominated by the Communist Party. Probably the hardest thing we had to learn in the new regime was that your life meant nothing and nobody was safe.

The Communists controlled the press and allowed only items of information which praised the Communist countries or denigrated the "Capitalist" countries. They continued to stir up a lot of hate and resentment against the US and England, accusing these countries of being responsible for all the problems of the Communist regime. Although Romanian people were usually kind and hospitable, they never accepted foreign rulers, and were fiercely proud of being a free nation.

It became obvious as the time went by that the Communists, at the urging of their masters in the Kremlin, would gradually try to transform Romania into another Russian Republic, and destroy our very national origin. So is it any wonder that the Romanian nation hated with passion anything which was supported by the Communist regime, that they wanted to destroy the new regime and return to our previous system of democracy and freedom.

We know now that it took some 40 years before the Communist regime and its miserable puppets were overturned by a popular uprising in 1990, with the loss of some 70,000 Romanian freedom fighters. Although I resented intensely the regime and I spoke on various occasions against the dictatorial regime, I finally had to admit that sooner or later I would finish in prison and the only way out was to do well in pentathlon and one day defect to freedom when competing oversees. As time went by I had to face the problem and I became more stressed as I could not reconcile defecting with having to leave my family. However hardly a day would go by without something foul being done by the Communists—yet another restriction or freedom taken—so that I knew that there was only one way out, that unless I left the country I was likely to do something stupid.

This continuous silent challenge between my love for my family and the desire to flee to the free world started to take its toll, and I started to have blinding headaches which would last for days. To add to my distress I decided not to talk to anybody about my plans, not even to my family. I knew what had happened to other athletes who spoke to their parents or close friends. After they defected, the secret police would interrogate the family left behind and if they found out that the family had known but did not report the impending defection to the security forces, the family would be put in prison. As I could not tell anybody, I continued to train and study whilst my mind become aflame with contradictory thoughts. I don't know how I didn't go crazy or kill myself, but somehow I managed to continue the daily routine.

The Romanian Olympic Committee directed various Federations to conduct their selection trials and nominate those athletes who would represent Romania in the Games. Our Modern Pentathlon team selection was held in Bucharest in the month of September and was conducted under the international rules and conditions expected to be encountered in Melbourne. Muresanu and the other coaches selected the most difficult conditions, particularly in the running and the riding event. In fencing our Federation invited top Romanian epee fencers to compete against us although their score did not count in the final classification. As usual the first event was the steeple chase event over a distance of 5,000m and 15 fixed obstacles placed around and inside an old quarry, requiring firm control of the horse and plenty of determination to tackle some of the bigger obstacles. Colonel Zidaru was openly not happy to put us over an obstacle course which required a lot of riding experience as well as better horses which we didn't have. We didn't realize at first why Muresanu directed Zidaru to set this almost impossible course, probably harder than anything we had jumped overseas where they had much better horses than ours.

Over the years since 1956 many of the rules and the very format of the Modern Pentathlon competition have been changed so as to remain in the Modern Olympic program and acquire more "spectator appeal". These days all of the five events are run in one day, the time for fencing bouts has been reduced to 3 minutes per bout, the shooting is done with air pistols at 10 m. but the biggest change has been in the riding event which is now run in an enclosed arena with an ordinary jumping course, where the obstacles are not fixed and can be knocked over. The ground is smooth and covered with soft grass, and there are no trees or old brick walls to be jumped. The horse and the rider are quite safe and the majority of the competitors will finish the event without any serious injury.

The riding event was well attended by spectators, Romanian people being very fond of any sport, not unlike the Australians. Beside there was the added excitement of seeing the future Olympic Team in action. After the initial official opening, the draw for the horses took place, and every competitor took their number out of the hat. The numbers were called out and the horses were brought in the main arena by their handlers. It was always very exciting to see the horses paraded in the main arena as they looked well groomed with shining coats and flowing manes, walking or trotting smartly, pictures of strength and suppleness.

We were divided in two groups of about 15 competitors, group "A" to ride in the morning and group "B" in the afternoon. I finished in group A, and my horse was an old gelding, very tall and rather stiff in the joints. This was one of the horses used by our squad in regular training, so that I knew from the start what he was like over the obstacles. Snagov was an honest horse but being over 17 hands tall, he was rather awkward, hard to turn, and did not bother to lift his legs properly, occasionally tripping over the smaller obstacles. I had to make sure that this horse was well warmed-up, and "awake". Colonel Zidaru was watching me in the warm-up arena smoking his usual cigarette stuck in a long holder, which made look like a Hollywood director on the set. He never shouted at us or tried to cover the distance by raising his voice, he would call you right next to him and tell you what he wanted done:

"You have an honest horse but not quite fast enough to win, Agree?" He continued before I had a chance to agree with him. "If you become to demanding and try to do a better time than Tintea or Manciu, you're going to have a problem. Don't do it. Be satisfied with a clean run with no mistakes, no refusals. You may not win the ride but you are here for the five events. Agreed?"

As the Colonel was talking to me, my horse started to nibble his hand; At times I felt badly about pushing these old horses over difficult courses, when they should have been retired a long time ago to a nice grassy paddock. But this was not the time to feel emotional and be too soft; I would be careful and make sure that the horse was not hurt, but the two of us would finish this course, no matter what. My ride was good enough to score me over 1000 points with the exception of a big incline covered with loose earth and rocks where Snagow spent a few seconds looking at the drop and refusing to go down. I had to give him a mighty hit with the crop which made him jump forward and then literally slide all the way to the bottom of the quarry on his tail. Well at least we both arrived safely at the bottom and completed the rest of the course without any other problem. I was unsaddling the horse when Colonel Zidaru come over and told me that he was pleased with my ride.

"This is what I have been trying to teach you all—understand the horse and then use the right approach to suit the horse. Well done, perhaps you can be around this afternoon and help Willy who has your horse for his ride."

I was very relieved to have finished the riding event without injury or loss of points. This ride would have placed me in a good position for the second day of the competition, the fencing event. Willy was getting ready for his ride and I was telling him couple of things I had to do during my ride:

"Look Willy, you know the old fellow, just don't be too kind to him or he will stop on you; Take particular care at the big slide, don't let him slow down too much."

Out of all squad members Willy was the hardest worker, always trying his heart out, always trying to improve himself; He never complained about anybody, just plodded along happy to be a member of the National Squad. He had improved greatly, particularly in the last few months, and he became a definite contender for the Olympic Squad.

But his riding was his weak point, and he lacked the natural aggressiveness required particularly when having to push a 600kg animal over an obstacle. He was very worried and just before he was told by the official that he could start his warm up and mount, he looked at me and said that this time he was ready and he would do his best run.

Willy had finished the usual sequence of walking and trotting around the yard and some figure of eights when he suddenly guided the horse towards one of the warm-up fences. It was only a low straight bar about two feet off the ground which any horse would have flown over, but Snagov, being a lazy horse, did not lift his front legs properly, stumbled over the jump and landed on his knees. Willy must have been relaxed and not holding the horse properly with his legs because he slid forward over the horses neck and landed with a thud on the heavy wooden bar. The horse righted himself and started to munch on some grass growing near the obstacle. We were watching Willy who was still lying on the ground, making no sound. We all started laughing and calling out to him to get up:

"Come on Willy get up, didn't you sleep last night?"

But Willy didn't move or say anything until the official walked over to him. The official then turned around and called out to those of us outside the rails:

"I think he wants to talk to Cornel, he wants him to have a look at his shoulder."

I leaped over the rail and ran over to Willy. He was obviously in pain and his right shoulder was covered with dust.

"Cornel I don't know what I've done but I can't move my right hand."

He looked at me with the eyes full of fear. "Please have a look and tell me what is wrong with me, I want to know the truth."

It wasn't hard to diagnose his injury. He had landed very heavily on the wooden bar and broken his right collarbone. It was the worst possible accident as it was impossible for him to lift his arm, to shoot or to swim. He could have had his shoulder strapped and do his ride, but he wasn't capable of competing in the remaining four events. I didn't know what to say except that I couldn't tell him what I thought, I couldn't shatter all his dreams, I had to think of something else.

"Willy it looks bad but you will have to wait for the results of the X-ray. It may not be that bad . . ."

Tears started to slide quietly out of his eyes; I could not hold mine much longer when the team doctor finally arrived and took over.

Willy had a very bad fracture of the collarbone and missed out the selection. He never had the chance to compete in the Olympic Games, and although he continued to compete for the next few years, I don't think he ever got over the accident. He got married and become a physical education teacher in his native town, but one day when he was returning from work on his motorbike, he hit some loose gravel and hurtled into a tree. He was killed instantly.

My dear Willy, I will always miss you. God rest you in peace.

THE TEAM IS ANNOUNCED

The selection trials were over and according to our coaches and the reports in the press, for the first time since 1912 Romania would have a representative in the Modern Pentathlon in the 1956 Olympic Games. Muresanu had proved his point and despite criticism from other Federations, in the end he had justified his confidence in the future of this new sport and predicted that our team was capable of doing well and occupying the 6th place in the team event and a possible placing in the first 15 individual positions. I won the selection trial and Dumitru Tintea and Victor Teodorescu filled the 2nd and 3rd place. Viorel Manciu, who was a team member in the 1955 World Championship, managed to secure 4th place and was nominated as the reserve.

Muresanu called us together before our fencing session on the following Monday after the competition, and congratulated us for our continuing success:

"This was an excellent show and has given Modern Pentathlon a much higher profile with the Central Sport Committee. However there is still room for every member of the team to make further progress, to concentrate and try to improve their weak points." He took a long look at us and then he continued in a slightly softer voice:

"You may be in the team but don't forget that nobody is irreplaceable and I will not hesitate to replace anyone of you with a better performer."

So he hadn't changed his harsh attitude. Just one small mistake, one weak moment and you were out with no second chance. It was win at any cost. Those who were weak or ill had to make room for the strong, it was a fierce struggle for survival.

After the meeting Muresanu called me and gave me a short lecture about how lucky I was not to have been kicked out of the team, but he felt that I could do better particularly if I stopped asking too many questions and trying to undermine his authority; Then he stopped for few seconds and looked at me with a searching look:

"I don't know if I did the right thing but I recommended you to be nominated the captain of the Pentathlon Team? What do you think?"

I couldn't believe what I was hearing. After all the criticism he had always thrown at me, he was actually admitting that I was the best in the squad; That must have taken some hard thinking, or perhaps he had no choice. Actually I found out later on that he had to justify the inclusion of everyone in his team, for their success as competitors but he also had to vouch for their clean political pasts and that they would were not potential defectors. When he was told about my father's anti-Communist stand, Muresanu apparently had told the Selection Committee that unless I was allowed to go, there was no point sending a Pentathlon team to Melbourne. He had to personally guarantee me.

DREAMS AND OUT OF BODY EXPERIENCES

It was after the selection trials that I started to have a recurring dream. It was always the same. I was looking at the immense body of a passenger ship anchored to a pier, with hundreds of people already up on various decks, waving to the crowd below on the wharf.

I had never been on a boat until the dream, yet the details were very clear and vivid; I could not tell what my role was in this picture but a silent thought was telling me that I was to go on this boat soon, and travel across the seas to some exciting and distant places.

This was something I had not experienced before and I could not explain why it was happening to me and in particular I did not understand its significance. Back in those days there was very little interest in supernatural or magic, particularly as the Communist regime was strongly against anything suggesting the existence of a supreme being or things which could happen without a scientific and well-documented explanation. In fact the Communists closed most churches, persecuted local priests and prohibited religious activities. Additionally they removed the main celebrations such as Christmas and Easter and replaced them with dates which celebrated the Russian revolution, day of the International Proletariat and of course Lenin and Stalin's birthdays.

But the people kept celebrating the religious dates even if it wasn't made public, and continued to attend religious services. Romanians are very traditional people who stubbornly stick to their long established traditions. They resent changes and oppose anything different or foreign to their customs. Although the Communist Party tried every possible method to take the church out of people's lives, even after 40 years of indoctrination and persecution, the Romanian people have continued to follow the old traditions and remain faithful to their church and religion.

In my youth I had very little respect for people who believed in predicting the future or those who believed in the existence of the spirits. Like most of us, the youngsters, we had witnessed on numerous occasions our mother or aunts, who after drinking little cups of hot sweet coffee ("cafeluta turceasca), would proceed to read the future in the dregs left at the bottom of the cup. But the most respected fortune tellers were the wondering gypsies who travel through the country, stopping here and there, and making a living from fixing old pots or selling old herbal remedies. Many years ago I remember seeing an old man with a venerable look and a long white beard, who stopped by our home in Abrud and sat on a wooden bench in the yard. My mother fed him and when the old man had finished, he started to tell my mother about the future. Between the things he told my mother I clearly remember what he told her about my future. I was to be, according to this old man, a great warrior and that I would leave the country and travel far away to a distant land, and I would never come back. My mother became very upset and told him to go, but somehow we both kept the memory of this incident and never forgot old man's predictions.

There was very little reading material on the subject of the metaphysical, and of course no television to fill our minds with all the ideas which seems to dominate the majority of program these days. So I don't know how to explain a most bizarre experience one summer back in 1948, when I spent few weeks with my father in a mountainous region of Romania called Viseul de Sus, where my father found work as a construction engineer and was responsible for laying out a new railway line through what had been an inaccessible part of that region. I was to do my work experience, which was a requirement for all secondary students in Romania, and learn at first hand about the organization and financial running of a government-funded program.

This was a great experience, mixing with the local people, finding out about their simple unadulterated lives, their centuries old customs and culture, and joining the local youngsters in various sporting contests. Many times in the evening after work, I would cross the brook running behind the little timber house with the thatched roof where we were staying and start climbing up the nearby hill from which I could look across the valley. This was a fairly steep hill to climb and it took me some time before I started to feel that I was getting stronger and could run part of the way.

One such evening, as usual I went for my climb feeling quite good and after walking for part of the way, I started to run. Suddenly, without any warning I felt myself left behind, struggling to keep up with the person in front of me who was moving faster up ahead in front of me. But that was not possible. There was nobody else climbing with me. The hill was deserted. Then it hit me with an incredible force that left me shivering: It was my body running in front of me and I was left behind, still running but falling further back.

I started to call out "Wait for me, wait for me!", when after few more seconds I knew that I was once again inside my body. By then I was almost at the top. I stopped and sat down to rest with my heart beating hard. I could not understand what happened to me, how it was possible to see the back of my body, when I wasn't dreaming or drunk. Even to this day I fail to see the significance of that event except that since that day I became less critical of people talking about strange experiences and as I grew older, I found more evidence of things or actions which cannot be explained.

HUNGARIAN STUDENTS ARE RIOTING

My studies were completed and I had passed all the exams required to obtain my Diploma of Sport Medicine, which entitled me to either go into tertiary education and become a lecturer, or take a position with one of the large sporting organizations such as the army or financial institutions. Or I could do another year of studies and become a physiotherapist. There was also another option which attracted me, and that was to do a further three years of study at the School of Medicine, and become a specialist in sport medicine. I had an interview with the Dean of the medicine faculty, and he received me very warmly, being very interested in my interest in a multi-sport discipline, which was little studied or documented in those days.

"Well Mr. Vena we will be glad to have you here, as we need people who have first-hand experience at these new sports. How about we wait until you come back from the Olympic Games, and then come and see me again. I am sure that there is room for people like you in our course."

Things were starting to fall into place. I had a promising future, my pentathlon performance was going well and additionally my family was doing much better. The I.C.F. administration made a list of all the students selected in the Olympic Team and told us that they will make a special dispensation for all of us; we had to sit for a final exam called the State Examination, which was something introduced by the Communist Party, an exam which tested the allegiance of the candidate to the ideals and aims of the Communist Party. It did not examine the knowledge accumulated by the student, it was interested only in finding how committed the candidate was to being a faithful enforcer of communist principles, in short it was a political test of suitability for high-placed jobs. It was also the last chance at the disposal of the political leaders to eliminate or prevent anyone who did not fit the requirements of the Communist Party. Even the slightest suggestion of capitalist leanings—if your family had anything to do with having any profit making business, even if it was generations ago, you were regarded as being a potential capitalist, an exploiter of the working class. Many of the students in my course were anti-Communists but feared to be too open about their hatred of the regime because they would have been immediately removed from the university and in some cases put in prison. Occasionally we heard about other University centres such as Cluj, an old University in Romania, where apparently there had been some open unrest between the students, who started to demand some human rights, and criticize the government for their inflexibility. Because there was no free press, and any news about any form of disagreement between the students and the government was suppressed, we only had some sketchy reports about student unrest in Cluj. Not long before our scheduled departure to Melbourne in October, we heard that the students at the Budapest University in Hungary had rioted and barricaded themselves inside the university building. It was only a rumour, and although we were deliriously happy about this first real sign of revolt against the Russian yoke, we didn't have any real proof, as all the papers continued to publish the ever boring litany about the achievements of the top workers, the Soviet advance in technology and the "hell" of the corrupt and decadent capitalist system.

TIME TO SAY GOODBYE

Our team continued their preparation for competition and at the same time we were all fitted for the official uniforms for the opening and closing ceremonies. This was the first time most of us had the luxury of having a proper tailored and fitted suit. We started to experience the pleasure of being comfortable and well looked after. Muresanu was becoming friendlier and allowed us more free time. But he never dropped the iron curtain which he had set in place right from the beginning. There was no communication between him and the team members, all his concern was to keep us in top condition and make sure that we did our best.

I was more than ever before torn between what to do, particularly as I knew that what was happening in Hungary—our next door neighbour—would change the attitude of our Communists, and they would increase the dictatorship and limit even further people's rights and freedoms. How much longer I could take this suffocating lack of freedom, this shameless pretence of "everything for the working man", when all the signs pointed to the rapid elevation of Communist Party members, their domination and rapacious accumulation of anything of value under the pretext of taking it from the old exploiting society and giving it to the working class. They had the audacity to claim freedom of the workers, yet they prohibited any form of unionism, right to call for a meeting and have more than two people together at any time, public marches or demonstrations, and in particular they came down severely on anyone striking for better conditions. Long prison terms were the rule of the day, and the judicial system was a mockery of justice, in most cases giving long sentences for any politically motivated action.

The day finally came when we had to leave Bucharest by a domestic plane which was to take us somewhere else to a bigger airport where we would board the Air India airliner, which would then take us to Melbourne via Switzerland. Bucharest's airport was a small building full of team members, their relatives and a large number of well wishers. We were all asked to wear our new ceremony uniforms, and were allowed to spend a little time with our families before boarding the plane. My father could not leave his job so he sent his best wishes through my brother Sandu and his wife, Florica, whilst my mother Zina was crying softly and holding my hand tightly.

"You see my boy, how accurate that old gypsy was and now you are going away."

Inside I was crying. I knew somehow that this was the last time I would see all of them, that I would not come back to Romania after the games. I would compete and do my duty to my team and my country, I would do my best, but after that I would have to decide where to go . . . perhaps to the United States or maybe Canada. I didn't know much about Australia as the only books allowed to be kept in the library were "Power without glory" and "Botany Bay" which I found very interesting.

Finally we were called to board the plane, and I had a final embrace with my family. My mother squeezed my hand and said once more:

"God be with you Cornet, don't forget us . . ."

My eyes have filled with tears of sadness as I write these lines; I feel those moments with the same intensity, the suffering of seeing my mother and sister-in-law crying, but most of all how small and defenseless my mother looked. I had to part with everything I loved and grew up with, to leave my family and my country of birth, to start a new life in a totally strange and foreign country. I started then to realize the enormity of my decision and fear the consequences.

HOW IS YOUR BROTHER IN SYDNEY?

We were in the air for a short time, and from my flying days I could tell that we were heading in a north-west direction somewhere towards Resita, an busy industrial town, usually covered by thick clouds of smoke and soot belching from the city's many furnaces.

I don't know why we flew to this place except that everything done in those days had to be done in great secret, so that nobody knew what was happening. When we disembarked from the smaller plane, we noticed a huge plane parked away from the main hangar. It was a beautiful Super Constellation—a plane of the type used by the Americans in the war to bombard the Germans. Despite its enormous size, and its six engines it looked sleek and very aerodynamic. The whole group of competitors, officials and secret police were asked to line up with their hand baggage along the long fuselage and have the official Olympic Passport which we had all been issued ready. We were the only ones to have such a privilege as travelling overseas was prohibited in Romania, and no passport could be issued to any ordinary citizen. The only people allowed to leave the country were Communist leaders attending conferences or highly qualified professional and lately leading sports people who were competing in overseas competitions. We were very privileged and we could not believe that we actually had an official document to prove that we were representing Romania in the Games. The line of people started to move forward slowly to the steps leading up to the huge plane where a security officer dressed in his best ceremony uniform politely asked each person to present his or hers passport. But we were a little uneasy at the sight of two ordinary soldiers standing on each side of the gangway, holding on to the strap of combat rifles with affixed bayonets. They looked very business-like and did not smile;

One by one, competitors from different sports were allowed to enter the plane. The officer was very friendly and we could hear him, after checking the credentials, congratulating the competitor and wishing them success in the Games. I was getting closer to the officer when he started shouting at one of the competitors whom I didn't know:

"You think you can fool us and get away, you traitor. Step aside and wait over there"

The girl started to cry and called out to the officer who by now had turned his back to her and was inspecting another passport:

"What have I done wrong? Why you won't let me go? I've done nothing wrong."

The officer stopped briefly and nodded to one of the guards who immediately grabbed the girl by her arm and took her to the main building. The officer then continued to smile and greet the next competitor, like nothing at all had happened. So that's what happening, I thought. They lead us to believe that we are going but they will stop some of us just before we board the plane. Why would anybody put another human beings through such emotional distress? Why didn't they tell people earlier that they could not go for whatever reason. I wondered if they had found out about my father's opposition to the Communist Party and they were going to stop me and send me back in disgrace. By now I only had couple of people in front of me. One of them was asked to show his documents. I knew him only from pictures. He was our greatest high jump champion, Ion Soeter, who was possibly the best jumper in Europe at that stage, and it was expected that he would bring back home the first Romanian Gold Medal in athletics. The officer obviously knew him because he addressed him like a respected friend.

"Comrade Soeter! What a pleasure to finally meet our greatest champion, I am really honoured . . . You must be so happy to go to Australia at last."

Up to that moment, we the people behind this admired athlete could only share his pride at being greeted so well by this officer, who obviously respected this remarkable athlete. Ion Soeter came from the German part of Romania, and he looked the typical German, having blond hair, blue eyes and white skin. But he was much loved for his humble attitude while being a great competitor and I had never heard anyone talking against him. He was a decent citizen and an excellent athlete, what else was needed to allow him to compete in the games?

Then the officer stopped smiling and started to talk to Ion like he was almost spitting at him:

"So my shifty friend, you are all set to go to Australia or perhaps to Sydney and meet your dear brother, and then who knows you may even decide to join him and stay in Australia? Wouldn't that be nice?"

By now we all froze, not being able to comprehend what was going on. We didn't know about his family in Australia, but the secret police must have searched everybody's records and found every possible detail. I hadn't seen many grown people cry until then, but Ion become suddenly an image of despair and deep emotional hurt.

"You think you are a great champion and you're going to cheat us all, but you are nothing but a common traitor, and you will never have the honour to represent your country. Get out of my sight! Move!"

Tears of despairs and humiliation were running down his cheeks. He moved slowly to the side and did not say another word. So this was the way they were going to punish us. It wasn't enough to kick us out of the team, they wanted to continue the suffering and destroy whatever pride in ourselves we had left.

I am not going to let them get away with it, I said to myself. If this pompous prick of an officer tells me to get off, I am going to punch him up right there and then, I will shut his filthy mouth. It was my turn to present the passport to the officer who once again was smiling and trying to be terribly friendly. He looked at the passport then smiled and looked up at me:

"Ah, this is the new sport we are trying for the first time. I hear that it is based on a military experience?"

I couldn't say anything, I was totally surprised not to be told to step to the side.

I mumbled something in the affirmative, when the officer handed my passport back and asked the next person to step forward. Shortly I was glad to see that our whole team was on plane. We were on our way. At last I knew that nobody would stop me now, I also realized that this was my last chance to leave the Communist hell.

FIRST TASTE OF FREEDOM

Perhaps it is almost impossible for someone who was born in a free, prosperous country like Australia to really appreciate what it means to feel free and safe, without the continuous threat of being punished for the slightest sign of individual expression, or the smallest attempt to do things which are not listed methodically in a severe code of action. Not even the most skilful film directors can capture the full gamut of the frustration, fear, despair and uncertainty which becomes part of everyday life, inescapable and unavoidable, the continuous feeling of being watched and spied on, subjected to humiliating experiences, asked to act against every decent moral standpoint, reduced to a miserable skeleton of a human being reduced to begging for mercy and a little food. How can I describe how I felt inside this magnificent flighing giant, which had every possible comfort starting with the luxurious interior and finishing with the beautiful Indian flight attendants, dressed in colourful national saris, greeting us all like important dignitaries. Within minutes our young team made itself comfortable and changed from official uniforms into our new competition tracksuits and started to circulate in the plane, talking to other teams, laughing, congratulating and playfully having little wrestling matches. It was something so spontaneous and happy, that made us all feel like little children back in the school yard playing, enjoying a beautiful morning without any fears or responsibilities.

The Head of Delegation and Minister of Sport, Comrade D.S. was the brother of the Chief of Staff of the Romanian Army and was assisted by some 10 high officials from the Department of Sport. It was almost weird to see this elite gathering, people who in Romania could decide with a stroke of pen the future of anyone in that plane, people who normally you may see or meet once in your life time, people you only heard about, people who controlled your life and death. But proximity tends to dissolve barriers, and now with the added freedom and the knowledge that we could not be sent back to Romania, we were all sitting in the same plane, even if the leaders were occupying the back seat of the plane, presumably to be able to see us at all times.

We started to act more naturally and became noisier and more boisterous to the point where Muresanu and other team managers were immediately called to the back of the plane, where they had a short conference with the high officials. Muresanu came back, his face red and his normally long and nose looking even longer.

"You are all warned to settle down; your carrying on is embarrassing the Minister; he wants you all to keep quiet and not to leave your seats without my permission."

For once his message did not get the desired result and to his surprise none of us stopped smiling. He and all of us could feel the change in the air, the slight rebellion, the defiance which for a long time had been subdued. Things were going to be different now that the regime of terror and fear could not be enforced by our inquisitors. We were free to speak and act without any apprehension. The plane was moving swiftly by now, leaving behind the beloved land of our country whilst we were starting to settle down and enjoy the rich scenery below us. We were at last on our way to freedom and nothing could stop us.

PART FIVE

FLYING OVER A FREE COUNTRY

Our flight was heading west and the light became dimmer as the evening approached. The most favoured topic of discussion in the plane was about our next stop, and what was happening in Hungary;

Nobody could give a correct answer to any of these questions so we were speculating and trying to guess between ourselves what would be the outcome. The Romanian language is of a Latin origin, having its roots in the language spoken by the Roman legions which under the command of Emperor Trajan, defeated the territories north of the Danube, the Geto-Dacian ancient land, following the war which ended in the summer of 106.

It is a language closely related to French and Spanish but more so to the Italian, and consequently Romanians can learn without any difficulty these related language, but they have some difficulty with languages of Anglo-Saxon origin, such as English and German. The Communist regime in Romania had introduced compulsory learning of Russian in all schools and even in the university, and curtailed the learning of customary languages taught until their arrival such as French, German and Latin.

English was spoken by few in Romania simply because there were few teachers who could teach this language, but it was immensely popular, and many of us would have welcomed the chance to learn it. Even trying to find self-taught books was out of the questions as the Communists had purged all the libraries and book shops of any classic or ordinary book dealing with English or American history or culture. Already we had started to realize how difficult it was to converse with the flight attendants who could speak only English and very little French. I realized then that this would become a very important issue, and that I would have to learn to speak English as soon as I got to Melbourne.

The pilot said something on the intercom in English, which was translated by our official translator:

"He is saying that we are going to land soon in Bern, Switzerland, where we are going to refuel and that we are going to be in the airport for about one hour."

Muresanu didn't want to leave the plane, and I was the only one from our team asking permission to go and have a look around the place.

"Just be careful and don't take too long", said Muresanu, "We don't want to leave without you".

What a great sensation to be on my own in the free world without somebody watching me; I had experienced only briefly a similar experience in Macolin the year before when we had a free shopping day, when we were allowed to spend a little time in town. The airport was a beautiful sight to see; people of all races and colours moving around, talking in different languages, brightly lit shops and windows loaded with expensive goods. If this was the "Imperialist hell" then it looked much better than our "Communist Paradise". But I had to find a newsagent, to see if I could discover what was happening in Budapest. I finally managed to find a news agency which had a display of a variety of magazine and newspapers in French, German, Italian and Swiss. The paper I picked was in French and had splashed across its top page Russian tanks are encircling Budapest. A thousand students are dead!"

So it was true. The Hungarians had finally had enough of the Russian yoke and they were rioting. This was such incredible news I had to let the others know what was going on, but I didn't have any foreign currency to buy the paper. The girl behind the counter must have seen me looking because she came over smiling and asked me if I needed any help. I told her that I was a Romanian athlete on my way to the Olympics and that I would like to buy the paper but I only had Romanian currency. She got very excited when she heard we were going to compete in the Olympics and wanted to know what sport I was in and what my chances were.

We chatted for a while then I told her that I have to go or the plane would leave without me. She wished me good luck and asked me to take the paper:

"I like to wish you and your team good luck. "Bonne chance"

I thanked her and hurried back in the plane and told our team what was happening.

BOMBAY AT NIGHT

Our plane was flying smoothly and most of our competitors had settled down and were enjoying the pleasure and comforts only dreamed of and never before experienced. By now most of our competitors had found out about the riot in Budapest, and we were all appalled by the ruthless action taken by the Russian army. The question on everybody's lips was if the Hungarian team would be allowed to compete in Melbourne. As we found later, they were given permission only because their Sports Minister was a great lover of sport and was confident that his team would perform well. A man of courage and integrity, something our Romanian leaders could have learned and put in practice.

After dinner, the noise in the plane subsided, and when the lights were dimmed, most of the young competitors were asleep. We had all been subjected to an unforgettable experience which would remain with us for the rest of our lives. I could not take my mind of the degrading and inhumane treatment given to those poor competitors who were kicked out just at the last moment. What kind of people were these Communists? I thought I knew the Romanian people well, I was one of them, yet to see how cruel they had become, lacking the most common decency, to treat their own compatriots like dirt, it was hard to comprehend.

That power corrupts become more evident, people who you never imagined to be anything but kind and friendly changed almost under our very eyes, a real Jekyll and Hyde transformation. I could not sleep, my mind was full of anger and despair, because it had become more obvious that I would never be able to accept the restrictions and the injustices enforced by the Communists, and yet I could still not decide to leave my family behind. Early in the morning I went to sleep only to be woken when the pilot announced that we were going to land in Bombay.

Talking about a change of scenery, one minute in a moderately civilized country and only few hours later in a totally different environment. Unfortunately our stay in Bombay was very short, but we spent the whole day walking and visiting as many places as was possible, enjoying immensely this great cauldron of human existence, observing the great variety of people. Despite looking poor and undernourished, there was hardly one face which did not smile back at us. These people obviously had a hard life, a continuous battle for their daily needs, but they seemed still able to go on and accept what fate had given them without complaining. In particular I was moved by the large number of very young children who were doing heavy physical work. They had little time to enjoy their young life, they were already treated like adults.

The day went very quickly and we had to return to the hotel for our evening meal.

In Romania none of us had ever experienced tropical fruit with the exception of oranges which used to be imported before the war from southern Italy. We were served a great variety of Indian curries. For desert we asked to select our choice of fruit from a big long table. We didn't recognize most of the beautifully presented tropical fruit with the exception of the oranges and some apples. Our hosts encouraged us to try something new, such as bananas. I ate one, so as not to be impolite to our hosts, only to find minutes later that my stomach did not enjoy at all the mixing of the curries and fruit. So for the rest of the evening I kept trotting to the toilet, feeling very nauseated. Later during the evening as the heat was too oppressive for us to go to sleep, we decided to go for a walk along the strand which started just outside our hotel. We could hardly see where we were going as it was a moonless night and for some reason all the street lights were turned off. We stumbled in the night along the building's wall when sudden cries of anger and pain started to come from under our feet. We realized that we were walking over people lying directly on the ground, spending the hot night near the cool breeze of the ocean. We abandoned the idea of our short evening walk and returned to the hotel.

In the morning we avoided anything which resembled fruit or curry, and asked for some boiled eggs and toast. Once again we boarded our huge and beautiful Air India plane and shortly after that we were on our way to our final destination, Melbourne, Australia.

1956 MELBOURNE—OLYMPIC CITY

Before arriving in Australia, most of us had only a very sketchy idea of this country apart from a few geography lessons when Australia was mentioned as being a very distant land where there were few people living in a enormous expense of country. We had heard about a great variety of strange animals, birds and sea life (by our European standards) but probably the most intriguing information was the existence of an animal called the kangaroo which apparently was so plentiful that we could expect to find some right in the middle of Melbourne, mingling with the people.

My scanty knowledge of Australia was accentuated by the lack of books or works dealing with the past or more importantly, with modern Australia. As I mentioned earlier I had the pleasure to read two books about Australia, one called "Botany Bay" which was a record of the experiences of the first group of convicts and soldiers who were sent out from the British prisons and the incredible hardships they had to go through in establishing the city of Sydney.

It read more like a great adventure and I was looking forward to visiting a place with such an incredible past. The other book was Frank Hardy's "Power without Glory", which was published in Romania because Hardy was considered to have some sympathy for the proletariat regime. Perhaps Hardy was at that time regarded by the Romanian Communist Party as a Communist, however it was a book which showed a little more of Australian society, but still too far back to give a true indication of this new country.

We were all filled with great curiosity and perhaps a little apprehension at the thought of coming face to face with a place which we didn't know much about, but it sounded very original.

My intention of defecting from the team was becoming stronger with every day, and I had decided that I would compete for my country, I would lead my team by example, and when I crossed the finish line in the cross-country run, only then would I make my move and leave the team. Because I knew so little at that time about Australia, I was very much in favour of going to America or to Canada after the Games. But the future was to be totally different to what I had begun to plan.

When finally our plane started circling and getting ready to land in Melbourne, we could hardly control our emotions; we couldn't believe that we had finally arrived in this distant place. Through the night we kept flying a steady pace and after hours of inactivity, we were all getting restless, and wondering how much longer it would take to get there. Finally the plane made a smooth landing and minutes later we were thanking and saying good by to the lovely crew and the pilots, who stood proudly at the bottom of the gangway and wished us good luck and success in competition.

Essendon Airport in those days was the main airport in Melbourne. It looked big to us although this was just a huge metal hangar with rows of tables where smiling officials greeted us and asked for our passports. The whole process went quite quickly and before long we were all processed and issued with our official passes. It was so friendly, more like a party or celebration, where hundreds of people move about, eager to meet the new arrivals and to make friends. The Australians were well prepared for the arrival of competing teams and although we couldn't talk to them in English, they had Romanian interpreters who helped and explained what was required. Before long we were out of the huge Nissan hangar, and we boarded the bus to take us to the Olympic Village in Heidelberg.

What impressed us almost immediately were the well built houses, the neat, colourful gardens in front of most houses—in general a very modern town.

What was all the rubbish we heard about a semi-civilized country with wild animals running through the streets? This was much better than what we expected and more developed than our own country. By the time we arrived at the village we were all impressed by this clean and well kept city. The entrance to the village was flanked by the flags of the competing nations, all bright and new and fluttering in the slight breeze. The place looked fresh and exciting with many new houses which were going to accommodate the competitors and the officials.

Our team consisted of some 51 men and 15 women who were to stay in the village between October 29 and November 31, 1956. The Heidelberg Olympic Village was designed to accommodate some 6,500 people who were to live and train there for the duration of the Games. Our team was given an area which was near the main hall, at the end of a court. We had the Austrian and the German team at one end and the Hungarian team at the back. I shared my room with Victor and a member of the canoeing team, Leon Rottman. As soon as we were settled in our rooms we were asked to assemble outside our headquarters, the slightly larger building where our officials set up their reception and conference rooms. We lined up outside this building, looking our best in the new team uniforms and waited for the Romanian flag to be raised by a small guard of four Australian soldiers. This was one of the most moving events in my life; It would be difficult to explain how it felt as this was an unique combination of deep emotions, pride and realization of the great responsibility placed upon us to represent our country with dignity and best results. The sight of our national flag slowly being raised to the top of the metal pole brought tears to many of us, perhaps some of us realizing how much we loved our mother country and how much we suffered to see our Romanian nation being oppressed and persecuted. To me it was also a kind of premonition of the things to come, having to leave my country and my family, never to return to the place of my birth, to the place where I grew and where I belonged. I felt like a person condemned to execution, aware of the finality of the irrevocable course to be taken, and yet determined not to show pain or fear, to go with my head held high. This was the moment I had trained and suffered for, the moment of achieving my greatest dream, to be selected to represent my beloved country, Romania, in the Olympic Games.

Perhaps in another time I would have been ready to enter the gladiators ring and fight for the glory of Caesar, or to lower the visor of my helmet and prepare to charge the infidels with my double-handed sword, once again having to find the deepest resource of my energy and skill, and prove in open battle my convictions and my worth.

We returned to our rooms deeply moved and even more determined to do our very best for the glory of our country.

I THINK I WILL TAKE THE ROMANIAN TEAM

Having arrived in Australia late in October, we had almost one month to acclimatize and train and get used to the Australian conditions before our competition started on the 23rd of November. Modern Pentathlon requires a lot a travel between different venues and it was essential that we had a good means of transport to take us every day to the respective venues—from swimming at the Richmond Pool to riding at Oaklands Hunt Club and finishing back at the indoor hall in Richmond for our fencing lessons. From what we heard later on, the Australian organizers had to ask local people to assist with transport for athletes and officials. As expected the Melbournians responded enthusiastically and offered their help by providing private cars for transporting competitors to their training venues.

The Modern Pentathlon teams were allocated their transport and at the time of our arrival apparently there were two teams left to be taken, the Russians and the Romanians. Mr Norman King, a respected and successful businessman and avid sports lover, was the only person available on that day, and he was asked by the transport manager which team he would be responsible for transporting. Apparently he thought for few seconds and then he selected our team for reasons we could never make him divulge. Perhaps he wasn't so comfortable about what was happening at that time in Budapest, perhaps it was something else, however it must have been our luckiest day, as he became our best friend and adviser.

We met Norman the next day, when we were told by Muresanu that our official driver had arrived and was ready to take us to our scheduled training venues. Naturally we had imagined a car or a minibus type transport to be made available for us. So we all gasped in admiration when we saw his elegant, brand new Jaguar sedan. We hadn't seen cars like that before in the streets of Bucharest and realized that this was unusually beautiful and expensive car. A middle-aged man stepped forward with a friendly smile on his face and introduced himself, speaking in a gentle and quiet voice:

"My name is Norman King and I will be your driver for the day."

We must have all looked puzzled and confused because he spoke again:

"Does any one of you speak English"?

A short embarrassing silence followed and then I managed to say that I could speak French or German or perhaps Russian. Mr King made a gesture of despair and then laughed heartily, announcing that the only foreign language he remembered was a little school French, but it wasn't much use. He started to use his hands to demonstrate how little he knew:

"Un little peu, moidmoiselle, merci, beaucoupe, au revoir . . . ?

For a moment we didn't know what to say then it suddenly hit us all how ridiculous the whole situation was, this nice Australian didn't have a clue what he was saying but he obviously had a great sense of humour. Within seconds whatever language barriers may have existed, were broken by a uncontrolled and healthy laughter. From that day on, "Uncle Norman" as we affectionately called him, became our punctual driver, English language teacher, tour guide financial adviser and driving instructor. He became very interested in our team and this new sport he had never heard of before and apart from taking us all over Melbourne he became involved in the training routine we followed.

A real friend and supporter of our team, he became our dearest friend in this new environment, helping us to adjust to the customs and the type of life which was so different to anything else we knew back home.

Norman was a man who inspired respect although he never demanded it. He was calm, patient and sensitive to all our painful attempts to speak the new language, and in particular quick to fathom the differences between us and our Communist leaders. However he was too smart to show our leaders his real feelings about their attitude to the competitors. He continued to gain the respect and friendship of everybody so much that even years later he would receive cards for Christmas or New Year from Muresanu, and the assurance that he would always be a welcomed friend and visitor to Romania.

Our training routine continued unaffected for almost a month. It was almost impossible to realize how exciting life was in the Olympic Village, and it is hard to comprehend now in retrospect where we found the necessary energy required for our long training sessions, yet in the evening we all managed to drag ourselves to visit the Main Hall of the village where one could meet people from every country in the world. Perhaps we all realized how precious this period of time in our lives was, how we had to make the best of every minute, fully knowing that this may be the last time we have such an opportunity. Perhaps it was even more exciting for us, young people coming from behind the Iron Curtain, not only being able to see and do things which we could have never done before in Romania, but being free, being able to enjoy the sheer pleasure of not being terrorized or punished, to be able to sleep at night without waking up covered in perspiration, expecting to be arrested and thrown into prison over some trivial matter.

MY ARM IS MY SWORD

We were concerned about not having our regular coaches in the most technical events of the Modern Pentathlon, fencing and riding. Colonel Zidaru and Mr Galimir had been left behind in favour of two extra secret agents brought to Melbourne for the express purpose of keeping a close eye on the competitors. Fortunately for us, the National Fencing Coach who was in Melbourne to train and look after the Romanian fencing team, was available for lessons and assistance to us during the official competition. I had never met Mr Csipler until then, but we hade heard about this remarkable coach who had already trained many National and European Champions.

He coached for many years before the arrival of the Communists, but his efforts had never been rewarded more handsomely than now, when sport in Romania started to progress rapidly due to the large amount of funds injected into sport, and the opportunity given to our athletes to compete and gain experience through participating for the first time in big international events.

Master Csipler or "Csipler Baci" as we called him, was a medium sized man, with wide shoulders and penetrating vulture like eyes, a short black moustache and dark hair brushed back. We met him at the Richmond Pool in a hall next to the indoor swimming pool, after our daily swimming session. He had already finished giving lessons to the Romanian National Fencing squad, and was wiping the sweat off his face with an old towel when he called us to him:

"My name is Csipler and you have probably heard about me. I am glad I have the opportunity to work with the pentathlon team, however I deeply regret your coach, Master Galimir not being here. He is the best epee coach in Romania or perhaps in Europe."

He stopped for a minute, looking at us with a piercing look then he stopped and spoke again, accentuating each word:

"I don't intend to teach you any new movements or change the style taught by your Master, you will have to tell me what movement you need to practice, and I will give you exercises designed to improve the speed of execution, to become so fast that not even you will know when the attack you intend to do on your opponent has started.

The looks on our faces must have made him doubt if we understood what he was trying to convey to us so he shrugged his shoulders, smiled and then told us not to worry.

"You will get used to my Hungarian style of fencing even if I have to pretend that I can teach the French method."

I was asked to have the first lesson with Csipler Baci, who before starting the standard lesson, spent few minutes asking which were my favourite attacking movements if I had any, and he encouraged me to tell him without any hesitation if any of the things he was going to teach me were different in any form to those taught by Master Galimir. He must have realized my feelings towards him, that I doubted his ability to match that of the older Master. "Look Conrade . . . Cornel (he corrected himself instantly), I would like you to show me what you would do if I make a certain movement, a certain attack or preparation of the attack.

I want you to react as if you were in a competition, responding to the Hungarian or French competitor; Imagine you are in a real competition and you are only interested in scoring."

"This man is good, very good," I thought to myself as I tried very hard to hit him with some of my more successful attacks, but he managed to parry most of them. The bout-like lesson must have tired him because he stopped me just as I getting closer to the target.

"That's enough, I can see you have a good technique, but there is room for improving your reaction speed. We are going to work on a lesser number of movements, but we are going to repeat them until you can do everything without any hesitation, without having to think. I want you to improve your basic movements to the subconscious level, and allow your conscious reasoning mind to be able to concentrate on the TACTICAL aspect of any given bout."

I didn't understand the real meaning of what Master Csipler was telling me but as the time went by, and more lessons were taken, I started to feel not only technically correct but my reflexes become razor sharp as well being able to respond to any movement he gave me, quickly, accurately and above all INSTINCTIVELY. With every training session I could feel my body becoming more responsive, more alert, moving almost instantly when the need arose, effortlessly changing between attacking and counter-attacking movements, only to execute a quick and a counter-riposte.

Our lessons become more demanding but true to his promise the Master kept everything simple and direct and only when I asked him for a particular movement I wanted to improve, he would do so.

My approach to fencing has always been one of wanting to know more, to repeat a movement until I felt that I had been able to dissect its very nature, and understand the smallest detail. What was more amazing was that I never knew I had any talent in this sport nor had any previous experience prior to joining the Modern Pentathlon squad.

I've asked myself many times since then where I got that inner knowledge of this unusual sport? How was it possible for me to learn in such a short time a sport which requires years of preparation, considering that I am a slow learner and it takes me a long time to perfect any skill?

But the most amazing experience was still to come. One day during my usual lesson with Csipler Baci, as he tried to push me back with a "froissement"(a sharpening like movement) preparation on my blade. *I had the weird feeling of actually touching his arm with a quick disengage-stop hit, not with the point of my epee,* **but with my index finger**. It *was as if* **my arm had become one with the steel blade**, *except that the hard steel was now part of my arm.* I didn't say anything, thinking that maybe I was getting dizzy with too much work, except that the Master stopped, took one of his long piercing looks at me and said:

"What was that Cornel? How did you manage to hit me when I wasn't even near you" Instinctively a good Master senses when his student enters a new level of performance, it is something which comes with many years of teaching, sweating and experiencing the full gamut of human emotions caused by failure or success. There was nothing I could tell him simply because it was something I had never experienced or heard of before.

It was almost scary not to know what your body is doing, a little like that time many years ago when I saw my body running up the hill in front of me. But I had a great warm feeling in my chest, I instinctively knew that I was on to something wonderfully exciting, something none of my teammates had experienced before or heard about. I kept this sensation to myself, I could not tell anybody. It was something which I knew didn't come to everybody, it was a unique and moving experience.

In the days that followed, I discovered a new set of reactions. I was doing things I had previously only dreamed about. I felt absolutely in control, performing even the most intricate and complex sequence of movements without any apparent effort. Until that time I used to sweat profusely during bouts and lessons, which is quite normal considering the extreme level of concentration required by high competition fencing. I was sweating less and instead of being tired or sore after practice, I felt strong and relaxed, as if by some strange miracle there was no effort and everything was done with a minimum of effort yet the results were deadly.

A combination which reminded me of putting together the efforts of a sprinter taking off from his starting blocks with the suppleness of a ballet dancer, the leap of a triple jumper, the precision of a surgeon cutting near a small artery, and the mind control of a chess player. Yet, to the untrained eye, fencing is only visible when the so called duellists attack one another with large obvious movements, which can be seen by the spectators.

In a top fencing competition bout, the movements are extremely small for the obvious reason that anything big is easily seen by the defender, and consequently can be parried with ease. Additionally if the attacker uses large movements, automatically he has less accuracy with his point or he is easily parried and hit by an immediate lightning like parry-riposte. So it is rather sad to realize that most people will never be able to understand how a good fencing movement is performed as it is very hard to see.

In the old days when there was no electrical equipment to decide who scored the first hit, it was always very difficult to find competent judges who could see the initiator of the first movement, and to award the hit to the right person. Modern fencing, particularly epee, is much easier to judge these days when they use an electrical box connected to the fencers' weapons which clearly indicates when there has been an actual hit. Even so there is the occasional "Double Hit", when the two fencers lunge simultaneously or extend the arm at the same time, and the electrical circuitry which is designed not to separate on hits delivered within 1/20 of a second, indicates that each fencer has scored.

In ordinary fencing, where they have the luxury to fence for 5-15 hits in a bout, in the case of a double hit, a point is allotted to each fencer. In pentathlon as there is only one hit it becomes very important not to let your opponent score or to allow a double hit which wilt score zero points for that bout. This is why pentathlon epee is probably one of the hardest events in fencing. There is no second chance. Once you are touched by your opponent you wilt not have the chance to redeem yourself until the next competition.

Csipter Baci kept his promise and did not try to change my fencing style as most fencing masters would have been tempted to do. Instead he made me do the same movement over and over again until I was reacting with a speed I'd never experienced before. He must have been pleased with what he saw because one day he approached Muresanu and told him that as the Romanian team did not have a representative in the individual event of epee, I should be allowed to compete in the fencing competition as well as pentathlon. But Muresanu did not think that I had time for anything else except pentathlon and refused.

LIFE IN THE OLYMPIC VILLAGE

As much as Muresanu tried to control all our actions, he wasn't able to deter our boys from being very interested in the social life which was blossoming in the village. The men and women's quarters were separated by a high wire fence, and we were told from the start not to enter the women's quarters at the risk of being expelled from the village. But as usual the passion and the fire of the young heart is always very hard to control. As soon as we arrived in the village, hardly taking the time to unpack our equipment, we were already attracted and fascinated by the incredible excitement, the sheer electricity running through our young bodies, fuelled even further by an enormous level of personal energy induced by rigorous training and total abstinence from alcohol and sex. Despite restrictions imposed by various team managers, almost overnight new friendships started to blossom, bringing together young and old people. Words cannot describe our exhilaration and the state of mind we were in. It was as if by magic we had entered a magic land of wonder where everything was bigger and larger than reality. We were experiencing the intense joy of celebrating our success, our superior achievements to the point where we were acting in an trancelike fashion, an exaggerated state of euphoria, where anything was possible. In those days we did not know about drugs, yet in retrospect we all were acting a little like we were drunk . . . drunk on life.

One of the most desired things in Romania in the 50s apart from having an automobile, was American jazz music and dancing in their style. Even with all the restrictions and heavy penalties imposed by the Communists against playing or listening to "decadent Imperialist music", most of us managed to listen to the BBC or other European stations and dream and imagine what it would be like to dance to the tune of Benny Goodman's Band or Satchmo's trumpet. We were so hungry for listening to the English language that quite often when we walked through the main streets in Bucharest near the big international hotels, we would risk being arrested by stopping near groups of tourists and absorbing with all our pores what appeared to be the tones of English language. Some of us, including myself, were mimicking what we thought sounded like English speech or songs; I was quite popular at parties when I was asked to "talk like an Yank", which I gladly obliged, even if nobody knew what I was talking about, but it sounded good. At parties we also tried desperately to dance "American" style, and we created our own strange routines of dance steps which quite often ended in terrible bruising for our poor dancing partners, taken totally by surprise by our unpredictable steps. So now we didn't have to close all the doors in the house or to pull the blanket over our heads and listen to the small crystal set, barely audible due to the distance and the local stations distorting the foreign signals. I in particular sat quite often in the main hall of the village, listening to the smooth sound of the visiting bands, feeling wonderfully relaxed and pleased and wondering how I had managed to live until then without such incredible live music. I don't think people living in the free world will ever understand that they had the greatest admirers and potential friends in the millions of people caught behind the Communist Iron Curtain. As history was going to prove some 40 years after, not even the harshest jail sentences and intense torture succeeded in curbing people's thirst for a free life, for being able to choose what they wanted most and resist to death against the Communist orders.

NORMAN AND ENGLISH LESSONS

As he had done for the last few days since our arrival, Norman had parked his gleaming new Jaguar in front of our quarters, and was waiting patiently for us to go to the morning training session. Mursanu as usual was urging us to hurry up and get in the car, and after much shoving and pushing, we were finally seated in the car ready to go to the new shooting range at Williamston. Through all this hubbub "Uncle Norman" was waiting patiently, puffing unperturbedly on his short pipe which was never out of the corner of his mouth.

Norman was a man of average height, solidly built, of fair complexion and blue eyes, in his early fifties. I say probably because he was a very reserved person when it came to talking about himself; He lived with his sister and brother-in-law and their daughter, and it appeared he did not have a family of his own.

Travelling in this luxurious and comfortable car was something we all looked forward to, the soft red leather upholstery, the quiet music wafting from the elegant timber console, the adjustable seats with the head rests, the smooth running engine, the precise automatic transmission, this was a car fit for a king. Now and then we would look at one another silently as if asking if this was not the ultimate in comfort and opulence? It was almost like a dream to be surrounded by such wealth and comfort, when only a few days ago we would consider that riding on a bicycle was better than the public transport. We would have loved to show just for few seconds to our family and friends at home, how life was treating us now.

During our trips with Norman we usually talked between ourselves whilst Norman drove and listened. I was sitting in the front seat next to Norman, trying to establish some communication. I tried to explain to Norman what we were doing, how we were going in English. I had purchased a small Romanian-English dictionary, which I studied furiously. But it was very difficult to exchange even the simplest form of information, stopping to look for the required word, then trying to decipher the meaning of the next word. Norman was a marvellous teacher, having a particular ability to remain calm and attentive to our babble. His intelligent blue eyes would watch intently and in an inexplicable way he perceived what we were trying to explain to him, even if the language we used was an incredible mixture of some Romanian, some French or German and some distorted English.

He instinctively would work out what we wanted and then suddenly he would say one of two words which summarized our frenetic attempts. Gradually we were able to communicate a little better and make our wishes more clear to Norman. But words were not necessary for any one of us to understand the soul of this noble man who was generous to a fault, good humoured, brimming with friendliness and tolerance of our shortcomings. He became very dear to all of us, more like a relative, a member of our family.

After I finished my shooting practice at Williamston Olympic Range, I spent a little time with Norman out in the car park whilst waiting for the rest of the team to finish. My English was getting better with every day as I studied furiously my little dictionary; I was starting to put some sentences together and pass the point of "How are you today? Good thank you." That particular day I was trying to explain to Norman the meaning of the word "Fluent" and "effortless" in relation to the shooting action we had to perform. It was an impossible exercise trying to explain a QUALITY rather than an tangible object. So for the next 10 minutes I tried every possible avenue to convey to Norman the meaning of the word flow, but in sheer frustration I had to eventually give up.

I have never felt so frustrated and annoyed with myself to have to face the impenetrable barrier of silence. Finally Norman gently put his hand on my shoulder and said something which I did not understand, but it was the warmth of his gesture, the feeling of compassion that I felt he had for me at that moment . . . It was as if my own father was trying to tell me how much he understood my plight.

We sat in the car silently for a while, listening to the shots fired on the range, when Norman looked at me and simply said:

"You happy? Muresanu not good friend?"

How did he sense what was going on in my mind, the torment of deciding what to do, the suffering which went on day and night because I was torn between the desire to escape from the Communists yet I felt responsible for the future of my family?

"Not happy Norman," I said, trying not to show how miserable I felt. "Not good". He took a puff of his pipe then blew it out slowly and nodded his head in agreement:

"That is not good. You must tell what's wrong. O.K.?"

Muresanu and the rest of the team returned to the car and were still talking about the finer points of how to shoot in competition without losing your nerve. Muresanu must have sensed that something else had been happening, because he looked at me and asked what was going on.

"Oh nothing special coach, just trying to explain to Norman the word "flow" and we spent the last 20 minutes getting nowhere. This has to be the hardest language in the world to learn." The boys started to laugh and did their best to explain to Norman what it meant. As in the previous cases, I noted with amusement how people believe that if they speak their own language a little louder, with more firmness and a little use of hand gesticulation, the other party should be able to comprehend a totally foreign language.

"Unchiule Norman asta inseamna ca merge usor, fara greutate, intelegi Domnule?" Norman was trying not to look confused and nodded his head in agreement.

"You see Cornel", Victor exclaimed with delight, "Uncle King understand everything I tell him, I have better control of the English language than anyone of you"

We all started to laugh and settled down for the trip home. I felt a little better, perhaps I could confide in Norman, but I had to learn more English and quickly. There was little time left before the competition started and it may be too late if I left these matters unresolved much longer. We were back in the city driving along the Alexandra Avenue, a beautiful street lined by majestic old trees, parallel with the Yarra River which flows through the heart of Melbourne. Suddenly I turned to Norman, I pointed to the water running smoothly, and I moved my hand in a wave like action:

"Water flow, water flows?"

Norman's face lit up and then he repeated with a voice full of emotion "Water flows, I understand Cornel, I understand you very well".

It was as if by magic all the barriers between us had been removed. I felt that I had a friend for life, someone who I could trust implicitly.

ARE YOU OK?

We had been in the Village for almost two weeks and we were getting used to our exciting new life. Muresanu after the initial fear that he was losing his "total" control over us, as he was used to back at home, was actually starting to relax and even managed to smile occasionally. But he did not reduce the intensity of the daily routine and we were driven with the same ferocity, which we were by now used to. I was training and feeling well; Physically I was probably the fittest I would ever be, but the continuous worries caused by my secret plans to defect from the team after the Games and to seek political asylum were starting to take their toll. I could not sleep properly at night, tossing and turning in bed all the time searching for a solution, a way to avoid hurting my family. But needless to say all my endless searching did not succeed in finding any solution. As the time got closer to the start of the Games, I was getting more concerned about my future, and what I was going to do. It was becoming so unbearable that for the first time in my life I started to have continuous headaches ;I did not like taking aspirins or sleeping tablets, so I did my best to cope with the sleepless nights followed by energy sapping sessions of training;.

The hardest thing of all was not to be able to talk to anybody in our team about my intentions for the fear of causing a lot of troubles for that person, who would be penalized severely by the Communist leaders once it was found out that my intentions were known but the person responsible refused to report what he found out to Muresanu. It would have been a lot easier if I had managed to make my decision and then just stick to the plan, however I was my worst enemy by not being able to cut my connections with Romania, with my family.

Another thing which was hard for me to understand was Muresanu's inability to sense that I was acting differently, that I wasn't the same person. He ought to have known better after nearly three years of training us, being with us almost everyday;. I can only conclude now that he had very little knowledge and understanding of human nature, or perhaps he was scared he would be regarded as being too soft in his relationship with his athletes and lose his position of power. It was much easier, as is almost always the case, to pretend total ignorance, to avoid any close contact with us, to hide his own feelings behind a wall of apparent disinterest. Whatever the reasons, at that time I could not trust him, I could not talk to him as I had realized long ago his inability to show any warmth or friendliness to us and I doubted he would have the slightest intention of helping me with his advice, considering he would have an even harder task to explain to the leaders the reason for my defection. So I continued to suffer the torture of indecision in silence, concentrating on my training sessions during the day, and going through the sleepless nights, until I felt that I was getting on the verge of going out of my mind. At this point I was starting to get very depressed and began to realize that I could not go back to Romania and continue the rest of my life under the odious regime of terror and slavery; For the first time in my life it became obvious that life without freedom was not worth living and I would much rather be dead than continue to survive under those conditions. That kind of thinking worried me very much. I was startled by the intensity of my own feelings, the desperation of my thoughts, the negative and self-destructive solution to my problems. It was time to make the big decision even if it meant that I had to leave my family behind in the hands of the Communists. I had to take this big step which would alter the fate of my family and myself with the destructive force of a hurricane, and prepare for a long and painful period of regrets. There was no choice, I had to decide or die.

That particular evening I decided to go to the Recreation Hall, and spend some time listening to the live bands which provided great relaxation and enjoyment for the hundreds of competitors who would train hard during the day and look forward to an evening of friendly encounters, new faces, different languages and cultures and perhaps meeting that special person. By the time I got to the hall the music had already started and the floor was milling with hundred of pairs dancing to the tune of a very lively melody. The village was full of many lovely young women, who were looking for a little fun and perhaps hoping to find someone different, someone special. We all felt also the urgency of the moment, we were going through probably the most exciting time of our lives and we felt that this opportunity may not present itself again. Many friendships were formed only to be broken the following night, a kind of a long continuous party where everybody was having an incredibly good time.

I had already made good friends with Lois, an Australian discus thrower, but I couldn't see her in the hall. Not far from where I was standing there was a group of very noisy girls who seemed to be having a great time. I couldn't hear what language they were speaking so I walked a little closer to them and realized that they were Americans. They were all pretty but one in particular attracted my attention. She was a tall brunette, slim and elegant with her hair tied back, standing almost defiantly, a little of that look typical of a matador ready for the encounter. It was an image of feminine grace and the harmony of a Greek classic sculpture. She was emanating an exciting air of warmth and physical attractiveness. I had to meet her even if I would make a fool of myself. So I started to walk towards their group when our eyes made contact.

"You Americans girls?" I muttered, going a little red when they all stopped talking for a second and looked at me with big friendly smiles.

"Yeh, yeh, we are from United States," and they all burst into uncontrollable laughter. I was getting very nervous and ready to walk away, when this tall brunette suddenly stopped laughing and asked me where I was from and language I spoke.

"Romania, speak little English (showing with my fingers how little), French, some German, little Russian and very good Romanian.

There was more laughter and various attempts by all the girls in the group to say some old forgotten school French or German words:

"Parle vous Francais? Merci beaucoup? Sur le pont D'Avignon. Sprehen sie Deutch?" Everybody was talking and laughing and almost instantly we were like old friends who haven't seen one another for a long time. The only one not talking was this tall brunette and myself. I could not take my eyes off her and she just looked back at me with these great shiny brown eyes. The band had started to play again, a quieter melody which I knew I could manage without stepping on my partner's feet.

"Dance?" I asked her rather hesitantly and took her hand.

"Yes, dance" she said, and we both stepped onto the crowded dance floor where almost immediately we were pushed and shoved by countless couples. We started to dance and my partner asked me something which I could not understand, then she pointed her finger to herself and said "L.A", and then touched my chest and asked simply "You?"

"Ah yes, I Vena Cornel."

She obviously had incredible patience because it took her most of the dance to explain to me that here in the English speaking countries one has to say his Christian name first followed by the surname.

You say Cornel Vena not Vena Cornel, understand?"

"Yes," I said, but I still could not understand why people here consider their Christian name more important than the surname. I pointed to her and asked what her name was. "L.A.".

From then on we just danced for the rest of the evening, enjoying each other's company, laughing and spending a lot of time trying to explain even the simplest thing. It should have been very frustrating but strangely enough we both must have sensed that this was no ordinary meeting and we persevered with our attempts to understand what the other was saying.

The night went very quickly and I walked her back home to the women's quarters. For the first time in a long time I felt that I was not lonely anymore, that I could talk to someone and express my deeper emotions. We both hesitated to part at the high security gate, when she said something about having a good time:

"You O.K., you good man, " She smiled as she said that.

I didn't quite know what O.K. stood for so we had to spend a few more minutes before I knew what it meant. That was good, I said to myself, because I thought she was saying "In Regula" which is the approximate equivalent of O.K in Romanian language.

. I told her that I would like to see her again at the hall and then she had to go because the guard at the gate called out to her, urging her to get in before the gate was closed for the night.

L.A, started to walk to the gate when I called out to her:

"You O.K., like you."

She turned and looked back smiling then she waved goodbye and entered the yard. I went to our apartment where everybody was in bed and asleep. That night for the first time since I left Romania, I slept soundly.

TRAINING "AGAINST" VLADIMIR KOUTS

After meeting the American girl, I started to get my interest back in doing my daily training routine and generally regained my desire to compete and to improve my performance to the highest possible level.

All of us in the team had made excellent progress in all five disciplines of the Modern Pentathlon although proportionally we had spent more time on improving our running times than any other discipline, which in the long run proved rather costly. The Olympic Village at the time of the Games had an excellent running track situated near a little creek running at the back of the village. Muresanu, who was always in search of the best possible training grounds, had secured permission for us to conduct our track speed sessions and timed trials at the brand spanking new red cinder track which was only minutes from our quarters. Although due to a total lack of overseas news about any item of interest including sport, we didn't know much about the performances of other athletes particularly if they were from the U.S.A. or England. Basically I knew almost by heart all the results obtained by top athletes from the Iron Curtain countries, people like Rozsavolgyi Tabori and Kovacs from Hungaria, or Pipine Soukhanov, Bolotnikov and Tcherniavskii from the USSR. As for top performers from Europe we had heard some reports about Jazy and Mimoun from France, but apart from that we had no idea about all the great runners who were getting ready for the biggest event of their lives.

Occasionally, when we moaned about the intensity of our running program, Muresanu would mention the enormous amount of work done by the top runners in the world, the new and more demanding systems of training, such as the interval training favoured by the Russians and the Fartlek system devised by the Nordic competitors; And if that wasn't enough to motivate us, he would throw in some facts and figures but it was difficult to believe that any human being could go through such exhausting routines and still be alive at the end.

One of the latest system of training used by the Russians was the Interval + Speed Variation program, a " secret weapon" which the Russian coaches hoped to use with great success against the rest of the world, in the 5,000 and 10,000m.

It was based on the principle of running at the front of the pack, dictating the pace of the race in such a way that every two or three laps the front runner would increase the pace, already at a breakneck speed, and literally sprint a 400m lap and then revert back to the basic speed;

Apart from the element of surprise, changing pace in long distance running was frowned upon by the true greats particularly as demonstrated by the great Finish runner Paavo Nurmi, who won most of his remarkable races in the 1920 and 1928 Olympic Games by disciplining himself to keep to an even pace throughout the competition. He even had a stop watch in his hand, and refused to look around to see where his opponents were, he knew that by keeping his pace he would kill any resistance.

We had heard some stories about a new Russian athlete, a sailor in the USSR Navy, discovered during one of the usual annual cross-country Navy events, which used to be compulsory for all personnel. Vladimir

Kouts apparently did not have any training as a runner, he was rather stocky and short, yet he managed to win the race ahead all the top runners, some being regular members of the National Russian Athletic Team. This particular afternoon I was having a special running session with Muresanu at the village track, whilst the others had gone to a swimming session. For some reason Muresanu felt that I wasn't trying hard enough when training with the rest of the team, so he decided to give me a taste of a one-on-one session, to keep an eye on every move I made and to push me harder if F showed any sign of slowing down. After I finished my warm-up I was told by Muresanu that I had to do 12 times 400 m sprints with a 400 m recovery lap in between each sprint. Every fast lap had to be done at almost my maximum speed, somewhere between 61 and 62 sec. per lap. The recovery lap had to be done jogging and no walking at any time was allowed.

It did not start to hurt or be too difficult to keep the required pace until the 5th or the 6th repetition when your body starts to run short of oxygen and every step you take starts to demand extra energy and determination to keep the pace set at the start. I was feeling strong and my endurance had improved greatly over the last few months so I was striding with long powerful steps and covering each lap with ease; Muresanu must have been pleased with my effort because after every sprint he would call out the time and make an encouraging comment:

"Good, 60.7 sec., keep your head still and move arms a little higher."

These were the usual technical points which he liked to mention to his runners, however he would have changed his attitude and tone, if I couldn't have kept the required pace.

His voice would have changed almost instantly to a short icy snarl which would grow in intensity and become an ugly howl if we didn't pick up the pace and return better times. He was almost like a conductor in charge of his musicians, quick to sense any deviation from the required script, demanding absolute perfection and not hesitating to admonish his charges. But today he was in a good mood because he even said few nice words, which normally did not enter in his repertoire.

"That's good, keep up that pace."

I was on my 7th., repetition and was just taking the corner when suddenly a shortish runner appeared from nowhere on my right shoulder and started to move slightly ahead of me. He was a short athlete who had good shoulders. His hair was rather long and of a reddish colour. He was running smoothly and without any apparent effort. But what impressed me was his enormous stride, which would have been expected from a much taller runner. I tried to keep up with him but he gradually moved in front of me and disappeared around the next corner. By then I was crossing the usual starting line of my sprints so I slowed down to a jog. Muresanu called out to me in a surprised but rather pleased voice to "SLOW DOWN"

That was something I've never heard him saying until then, to anyone of us:

"Slow down, you still have another 4 laps to go. You won't be able to keep the same pace." I knew he was right but by now we had learned to be very competitive to the point of total exhaustion if challenged; So the next lap once again I was caught by the same runner, and despite my frenetic efforts to stay with him. He left me behind. It was infuriating and I felt humiliated to be passed with such consummate ease by this running machine. But to make things worse I noticed that whilst I was doing my recovery lap and getting my breath back, he kept running round the track at the same pace' I didn't know who he was so I thought that maybe I had slowed down too much so I asked Muresanu the time of my last lap:

"You're are still too fast, you did the last one 58 seconds!"

I couldn't believe my ears, this was about the fastest repetitions I had ever managed. The only other time I did a better time for a 400m sprint was in the company of Victor Todorescu, the best runner in our group, when I did the distance in 56 seconds, but then we were tested specifically over this distance and we didn't have to do any repeats.

Who was this man and how could he keep this infernal pace without any variation? But I kept jogging and at the end of the rest lap I had to do my next and last repetition "If he catches up with me this time I won't let him pass me even if I drop dead. He is not going to beat me again no matter what," I said to myself.

Once again he caught up with me just before the 200 corner, when I increased my pace and managed to keep level with him for some 50 metres. We were running shoulder to shoulder when he turned his head towards me and smiled. It was almost as if he was trying to ease my anger with this simple smile, then suddenly he took off and by the time he crossed the finishing line he would have gained more than 30 metres on me.

When I finished and crossed the line I was almost breathless and every cell in my body was asking for mercy. Muresanu come over with a funny look on his face and told me that I had run my best ever 400metres.

"This is very good Cornel, maybe you should take up middle distance running," he said with a grin. "You covered your last 400m in 54 sec!"

I was too tired to be pleased with this unusually good time for me, besides I was curious to know who was this "dwarf" with the legs of a giraffe who could run like that.?

"Do you know who that fellow was?" I asked Muresanu.

He looked at me and asked who I was talking about. I was sweating profusely and felt very tired so I moved my arm towards the runner who was going unperturbed around the track.

"Him, that bloody "ogar" (greyhound)" I said, pointing weakly to the nimble figure with even longer strides and flowing hair. Muresanu took a look in the direction I was pointing and then he burst into laughter. "You don't mean Kouts?" he said, unable to stop his laughter.

"What's so funny?" I said, not seeing anything amusing in my question.

Muresanu finally stopped his cackling and started to talk to me in an amused tone.

"Now I know why you did such good times today. You were trying to keep up with him, and that should show you that you are capable of much better times, as I have been telling you for a long time." He stopped for a second and then said in a almost respectful voice

"That was the greatest Russian runner, Vladimir Kouts. He is going to rewrite all the World and Olympic records over the 5000 and 10,000metres."

He stopped again, looking at the lithe figure moving smoothly over the red cinder and then he said to me:

"Remember what it is like to run against the best in the world."

Vladimir Kouts went on to be one of the world's greatest long distance runners and won both the 5,000m and the 10,000 metre races. His best race which will be remembered for a long time was his run against people of the calibre of Jozsef Kovacs of Hungary, Allan Lawrence of Australia and Gordon Pine of England. His remarkable performance in the 10,000m race in Melbourne will be remembered for Kouts' sheer destruction of his opponents due to his ability not only to keep a constant fast pace but to be able to sprint almost at will whenever his opponents managed to get near him. Unfortunately I wasn't in the Main Olympic Stadium to witness this memorable race but fortunately for all sports lovers, David Wallechinsky, the author of "Complete Book of the Olympics", had described very well how the race took place:

"Kuts took off like a flash and completed the first of 25 laps in only 61.2 seconds. Slowing down only slightly, he had outdistanced everyone but Pine by the seventh lap. Kouts ran the first of the race so quickly that he passed the 5,000 metre mark at 14.07.0 which almost equaled Emil Zatopek's Olympic record for that distance. And he still had another 5,000 m. to run. Between laps 8 and 20, Kouts tried a variety of tactics to rid himself of stubborn Pine. Several times he sprinted out at a seemingly insane pace, only to have Pine catch up each time. Alternatively, Kouts would slow down, move to the outside, and wave Pine past him. But Pine refused to bite, preferring to remain at Kout's shoulder.

Suddenly at the end of the 20th lap, Kouts stopped so abruptly that Pine was forced to take the lead. Relieved of the pressure of having Pine on his heels, Kouts rested for half a lap while he studied his adversary in front of him. Then, just as suddenly as he had slowed, Kouts burst past Pine to take the lead for good. Pine struggled to keep pace, but with four laps to go, he gave up, eventually dropping back to the eighth place. Kovacs and Lawrence finished strongly, but Kouts was never in doubt."

Kouts went on to win the 5,000 metres as well, when he took the lead from the start and finished some 70 metres ahead of Pine. His incredible stamina gave him the edge over the other competitors, but unfortunately the excessively hard method of training which was required of him by his Russian coaches took its toll. He had his first heart attack in 1960 and by 1975 at the age of 48 he had his fourth and final heart attack, which killed him.

I've asked myself many times in the years that followed, what is the ultimate limit of human endurance? How much can the human body take? Before doing competitive rowing and Modern Pentathlon I thought that some of the running events I had taken part in demanded the absolute effort and that I could not ask for more energy at the risk of dropping dead.

But I was wrong. I found out that I could do a lot more than what I thought humanly possible. I found out that under certain circumstances, when there's no way out and when a good coach knows how to extract from you the last ounce of energy, one can go well beyond the self-imposed limits of what you can achieve.

Suddenly you enter a different state of reality, a little like an out-of-body experience; you past the point of intense pain imagining that the next step you take you will die, but, to your great amazement, at that moment of intense pain and fear of the unknown, suddenly you are liberated and able to go on feeling refreshed and ready to go forward once again. But there are times when you can hurt yourself, particularly if you receive the wrong advice from those who are supposed to know what they are doing.

CORRUPT LEADERS AND ROMANIAN PLUM WHISKY

There is no doubt in my mind now that Muresanu was experimenting with us, without fully knowing what the ultimate result would be of the high intensity program we had to follow. Those of us who had some previous experience with efforts of high intensity managed to scramble through the whole period of training without doing too much damage to ourselves, however a small number from the initial intake became ill and had to stop training with the squad. Ultimately this type of training was designed to achieve results at any cost, the health of the athlete not being considered as part of the equation. You survived and performed, or you were not good enough to be in the national team. This was the reason why the Communist countries of that era suddenly made a great leap forward and started to defeat other countries with a long tradition in specialty sports. They perpetuated the biggest lie—amateurism—athletes training with no gains or benefits to themselves, when in reality if you were in a National or Olympic Squad you received assistance varying from free meals, free equipment and unlimited access to your respective venue of training. Additionally you would be sponsored and helped to travel overseas for international competitions. So all the time when they complained bitterly about "professionalism" and accused other countries of being corrupt, they were relying entirely on rewarding their athletes and perpetuating the methods of full professional sport.

Most of our sport "leaders", the high priests of Romanian sport, had little or no experience in sport organization. They were nominated to the top administrative and financial positions simply because they were members of the Communist Party and they were related to some high placed official in the Romanian Government.

Until our arrival in Melbourne, we had never had the opportunity to meet our Minister of Sport or any of the high officials in charge of the Modern Pentathlon We did know however that the Minister for Sport, who happened to be the brother of the Minister for Army, and that he did not have much experience with sport. So for the first time since we had been associated with the Olympic Squad we had the opportunity to see these "invisible faces", the people in charge of our life and destiny, with the power to destroy any one of us with the smallest amount of energy. It was almost disappointing when we actually came face to face with tovarasul D.S, who was a short, fat little man, with a big head, a pathetic individual who spoke to us as though he was still back in Romania, expecting to see all of us falling on our faces and kissing his feet.

He was accompanied by another big name in sport, the head of the Romanian Rowing Federation, Tovarasul B.Y. There were a few others in this group of "leaders" but I will leave them out as they don't deserve a mention. They were there only to follow meekly the orders of D.S.

After the initial flag-raising ceremony we did not see our leaders again as they seemed to always be in a meeting or elsewhere. Muresanu was the only one who was allowed to go and see them. So the day we were getting ready for our riding practice at the Victorian Police Farm at Oakland in Broadmeadows, he told us that our riding gear and in particular our saddles had not arrived.

"What do you mean they haven't arrived?" Victor asked, annoyed with not having his favourite saddle.

"They were packed in those big wooden crates in Bucharest and put in the plane. They should have arrived here in the village a few days ago."

Muresanu was obviously unable to cover up the mismanagement of the whole affair so he had to give us (not his normal method of dealing with us) a plausible explanation:

"I don't want you to go around telling others, but they filled up the crates with gifts and casks of "Tuica" (Romanian plum whisky); we don't have any riding gear but I have already arranged with Sergeant Lloyd from the Police Academy to lend us some gear."

I must admit that even Muresanu for once had dropped the pretence and did not try to cover up for our leaders.

"You mean to say that they left our gear home and brought all this liqueur and gifts, when they knew that we couldn't compete without proper equipment," I said to Muresanu, trying very hard to hide my sizzling fury.

"These people are totally incompetent and they should not be here."

Muresanu suddenly moved to the door of our flat, opened the door carefully and looked to see if anyone was listening at the door. Then he came back into the room clearly upset and he spoke to us in a way he had never done before:

"You may say or do things which we all know are not going to help any one of us in the long run; We are here because they let us, because I went on my knees begging to be given a chance. So don't ruin what we have achieved, don't throw away your hard work and say something we all going to suffer from. Do your training and compete well, that's your job. As for the rest, leave it to me. He stopped for few seconds then he spoke again:

"You must know by now that each one of you have a "supervisor" and anything you do or say they will report. Be careful with what you say and who is listening to you, or you are going to regret it when you return home."

It was a surprise to hear Muresanu warning us as I never thought he had any interest in us apart from our sporting performance. I wondered why he had talked to us in those terms, then it occurred to me that regardless of his personal motives, he was right. If anyone of us challenged our leaders too much, they could easily send us home on the first flight.

So I decided to close my mouth from then on and wait until I had finished my event, represented Romania to the best of my ability, and only then do what I planned to do. From now on I was going to pretend, to lie, and to convince our Communist leaders that I had the best intentions at heart.

A few days after that particular discussion with Muresanu, I was called to see the Minister and some of the other leaders. They were sitting at a long table with the minister at the far end. Muresanu was also in the room, sitting a few seats away from me.

The Minister, met me with a big smile. He told me how impressed he was with my results in Modern Pentathlon and then he regurgitated the usual garbage about the Communist Party, the best regime in the world, the corrupt capitalism system and how it was our duty to show this decadent society how superior the Communist regime was. Finally he came to the point:

"We had some reports about some of our competitors who appear to be fascinated by what they've seen here, and believe they may try to stay here. Can you believe that?

After all the Party has done for them, all the advantages, the coaching, the travelling?"

He was, like most of the Romanian Communist leaders, a true performer, performing for those present in the room, pretending to be deeply affected by these ungrateful people, hurt by their ingratitude. Once again he launched himself in a long song of praise to the Communist Party and finished looking very emotional.

"So what you are going to do Cornel? Are you going to compete for your beloved country and lead your team with skill and courage?

YOU ARE WITH US OR AGAINST US ?"

There was a silence in the room and for one moment every fibre in my being asked to tell the truth, to tell how much I hated everything he stood for, but something stopped me, the image of our team being sent home in disgrace, all that effort for no avail.

No, I would tell him nothing of my true self, I would give him what he deserved, a big lie."

I will compete first for my country, and for all the hard work I put in, then and only then, when I finished the competition, I would tell them what I think of their regime.

I spoke then in the typical jargon taught to all of us irrespective of age, a litany to the glory of the Romanian Communist regime. By the time I finished the long empty address, I could see the faces of our leaders smiling encouragingly, almost on the verge of applauding. Later back in our rooms, Muresanu told me how pleased the leaders were, and they fully endorsed my nomination as the Captain of the Romanian Pentathlon team.

At that moment I had made up my mind and decided that I would never go back to the misery and the wretchedness of Communism. I would rather die than go back. That was final. Suddenly I felt free and the pain and mental torture of the last few years started to dissipate.

It was going to be hard to forgive myself for the damage I would cause to my family, but I had no option, I had to decide or go mad.

Eventually we found out the whisky and gifts packed into the crates were ironically used to welcome ex-Romanian visitors to the Olympic village in an effort to impress and show these refugees from the Communist regime how wonderful and prosperous it had become. But according to what we heard from many Romanians residing in Australia and eager to hear the latest news from back home, they were just as suspicious and critical of our leaders. We were asked to take money or gifts to their families back home. I avoided offering my services but the other members of our team, in particular our reserve Viorel, having more time to spare, met many Romanians and I believe he made many friends during his stay in Melbourne.

THE FLYING PRIEST

The pace of our daily activities in the village was getting progressively faster and more tense with the approach of the start of the Games. Our training was progressing well and Muresanu started to allow us a little more freedom and occasionally he would go by himself into town and we would do our running training by ourselves. The small stadium in the village was frequented by many athletes, many of them trying to put the final touches to their preparation. When I had finished my running session I would watch and try to learn as much as I could from other athletes, many of them being national champions or the best in the world.

One of the most spectacular sessions to watch were those performed by an American athlete who would spend endless hours training for the pole vault event. A man of middle stature who seemed to have the agility of a monkey and the strength of a weight-lifter, he spent hours perfecting his approach and the take off. Now and then he would raise the bar to what appeared to be an impossible height, only to clear it with consummate ease.

As part of my physical education studies back home, we had to be conversant with all athletic events and we had been showed the correct pole vault technique.

It is a very difficult event which demands great speed for the approach and incredible strength to be able to push off the pole at the highest point of the elevation to clear the bar. I think the most we could do at the university in Bucharest, including our teacher, was around 3 m. By comparison, this athlete was doing his warm up at heights which could have been a Romanian National record every time he went over.

I wanted to meet this great athlete so I went over to the jumping pit and spoke to him in my broken English:

"You good. How jump so high?"

He had a very friendly face and almost immediately I felt at ease with him.

"I am American and my name is Richards, Bob Richards. What's your name?"

He told me about being a pole vaulter and a decathlete, and in private life he was a minister of religion. There was something calm and confident about this man, and I could feel his strength and control. We got to know one another quite well, although due to my language difficulties I could not talk about more interesting things but I was very interested to hear from him about life in the USA and if it was difficult to get there.

Only years later when I was able to read through the results of ex-Olympic champions, I found out more about this remarkable athlete, the "Flying Vicar", who had already won the 1952 Olympic Games pole vault event in Helsinki, with a Games record of 4.55 metres.

The only other vaulter who was considered to be well ahead of his time and to have done better than Bob, was another American, C. Warmerdam, who in 1942 set the world record at 4.77 metres, a record which wasn't broken until 1957.

The importance of meeting people like Bob was the opportunity I had to establish contacts with the outside world, to practice my English and to gradually formulate a plan of action so that when the time came, after the Games, I would act decisively and according to a plan.

TOMORROW'S THE OPENING DAY

The Opening Ceremony took place on Thursday, November 22, 1956, in the Olympic Stadium in Melbourne. Preceding this grand event, the torch relay carrying the sacred light from Olympia in Greece, became an emotional and moving act which involved thousand of ordinary Australians. It commenced with Qantas Airlines who gave safe passage to the flame to Darwin, which was then carried by the Royal Australian Air Force plane to Cairns on the north-east coast, the starting point for a relay of some 2,830 runners who would carry it day and night to arrive at the Main Stadium in Melbourne at exactly 4.32 on the afternoon of 22nd of November.

The route of the relay was planned to pass through Brisbane, Sydney and Canberra.

It took month of careful planning to organize the details of the journey of the flame.

The flame was carried day and night for several weeks along the Eastern coast of the Australian continent, being greeted everywhere by hundreds of people lining the highway, waving flags and cheering on the runners. In many towns everything stopped, and people packed the streets to see and welcome the torch. Brisbane was the first of the big cities to receive the torch and according to reports "people were swarming over every possible vantage point" On the way out of Brisbane the traffic started to intensify and by the time the convoy reached NSW, the road was blocked by cars and the police had to step in and force the traffic to the roadside to allow the Olympic Torch convoy go through.

Sydney was even more difficult to negotiate, roads being blocked for up to 25 km. North of the city. As a result the official reception had to be kept short in front of the Town Hall. By November 19th the torch had reached Canberra where an impressive reception was organized, with all the flags of the competing countries unfurled and the Torch taking centre stage.

By November 2 1st, the torch had reached the Victorian border where it was received with great enthusiasm. By the time the Olympic Torch passed through the Victorian towns of Wangaratta, Benalla and Shepparton, people were literally infected with "Olympic fever".

PART SIX

The Opening Ceremony

Thursday 22nd November 1956.

For the opening Ceremony, we had to be ready to board the buses by 1 p.m. and leave the Olympic Village at Heidelberg. We were taken to the assembly area which was the Richmond Cricket Ground, situated only a short distance from the main stadium, where the various Nationals Teams waited for the procession to start. There were so many happy faces, so many national costumes and uniforms, so many champions and renowned sportsmen and sportswomen. One competitor stood out in particular, the US heavy weight lifter, Paul Anderson. He had such big arms and legs that his uniform looked ready to burst, but the funniest thing was his beret which looked minute in comparison to his strong head and neck. There was my gymnast friend, looking very elegant and slim in her tight fitting blue skirt, but we pretended not to see one another and attract more criticism from our commissars.

When the march commenced the teams had to enter the main stadium, turn to the right and then follow the red cinder track, passing in front of the packed stands. The Royal Australian Navy and the Australian Army Bands combined to provide continuous march music whilst the teams marched. The Romanian Team assembled, the honour of carrying the National flag being given to Ion Sarbu, our small bore rifle champion, followed by the three top Romanian officials, then the girls, members of the highly successful gymnastic team, two fencers and the high jump champion, Iolanda Balas. In total our team consisted of 33 men, 11 women and 11 officials. The men were arranged in three lines with the water-polo players at the front, followed by our pentathlon representative; I was placed fifth from the front in the inside line, Tintea was last in the same file, Manciu and Muresanu were in the middle file, whilst Teodorescu was in the middle of the outside file. We hadn't had any practice in marching together as a whole team, but we immediately fell in rhythm with the tempo given by the bands, and marched very well.

We were following Puerto Rico into the stadium and whilst we were approaching the entrance we could already hear the powerful distant roar of the crowd and the beat of the fanfares; it sounded like a thunderous sea building in big swells and then suddenly crashing with a deafening, deep echo which made the whole surroundings shudder.

I stepped inside the arena, to be greeted by the greatest spectacle I had ever seen in my life. As if by special command, the sun had come out, bathing the whole spectacle in a bright glorious light which enhanced even more the huge stadium with its immeasurable sea of smiling animated faces, the scintillating spectrum of flags, and the brilliant colours of uniforms. It was all so overpowering that for a few seconds after stepping on to the fresh new red cinder track, I felt slightly dizzy, trying to adjust my senses to a feast of colour, sound and sensations which embraced my whole being with an incredible, lively force.

The whole place was full of animated exhilaration, an inspiring and deeply moving experience. We were so proud, so aware of this special moment of great physical and emotional elevation, that we marched like we had never done before, like one single body which moved proudly and effortlessly, rejoicing in the exultation which had engulfed competitors and spectators alike.

Team after team entered the arena and marched along the track in front of the official box, giving the salute to the Duke of Edinburgh, marching to the lively music, waving to the excited crowd, and finally assembling in the allocated area in the middle of the field, facing the main stand. The excitement grew with every team arriving in the arena to the point when every person anticipated the arrival of the Olympic torch with an ascending roar of applause, laughter and jubilation. The Duke of Edinburgh was then asked to officially open the Games. He simply made the pronouncement:

"I declare open the Olympic games of Melbourne, celebrating the XVI Olympiad of the modern era."

When all the teams had finished marching and lined up in the middle of the field, a fanfare of trumpets was sounded and the Olympic flag was raised. At the same time thousands of pigeons were released and filled the stadium with more colour and movement. A salute of 21 guns followed. Then as if responding to a secret signal all movement and noise stopped and an expectant silence fell upon the whole arena.

The young athlete Ron Clarke, the Australian junior mile record holder, took over the sacred flame at the entrance to the stadium where it had been brought by the long relay of enthusiastic and dedicated runners. Carrying the torch high, he circled the track and climbed the steps to the top, where he lit the cauldron.

I will always remember how moved I was watching this young man, running with elastic long strides, holding the torch high with sparks of fire falling on his bare arm, urged on by the delirious crowd and competitors. He was obviously in pain, the flame was burning his arm, but in an almost pagan form of sacrifice he kept running, climbing the steps, and finally leaning forward in to the huge cauldron and lighting the Olympic Flame.

The jubilation and exaltation had reached its peak, and by now everyone in the stadium felt complete, we all knew that in many different ways, each one of those present to this unforgettable, magnificent display of human emotion and ideals, would never be the same again.

An assembled choir made up of some 2,400 singers, all dressed in beautiful white robes sang with great feeling the Hallelujah Chorus and the flag bearers moved forward and formed a semicircle around the main rostrum where the Olympic oath was taken in the name of all the competitors by the captain of the Australian Athletic Team, John Landy. The National Anthem was played by the Royal Australian Air Force band and sung by the choir. The most moving ceremony I have ever experienced came to an end almost abruptly, and we all felt like we had been awoken from a dream, brought back to reality by our officials asking us to march out of the stadium. We boarded our buses and returned to the Olympic village, tired and emotionally drained, but savouring the unforgettable pageantry.

RIDING ON A GREEN HORSE

<u>Friday, November 23rd.</u>

The euphoria of the Opening Ceremony had left us slightly dazed and perhaps a little numb, a fact which Muresanu must have recognized which made him order us to start moving, to get all our gear ready for the first event of the Modern Pentathlon competition, the riding event. As already decided, our team would consist of Victor Teodorescu, Dumitru Tintea and me, with Viorel Manciu as our reserve.

The riding event was to be held on the grounds of the Oaklands Hunt Club situated some 25 km. outside Melbourne. The course to be covered by all the competitors was 5,000 metres, over a rough country terrain, through a dry creek, up a small hill and through a small wooded area, finally having to ride through a large dam just before the finishing line. On the course there were some 15 fixed obstacles, many awkwardly placed. Overall the course was not as difficult as the one we had to do in Macolin in 1955;

It was very open and there was little chance for any of the riders to take the wrong turn. What we had found out during the weeks preceding the competition was the total difference between the Australian and European horses. Basically the European horses tend to be easier to control, they respond more accurately to the correct impulse and the to the rider's aids. The Australian horses were much stronger than the European breeds, and tended to be less responsive and obedient to the rider's directions. The Australian organizers had some 84 thoroughbreds in training and after careful selection they selected forty-five for the actual competition.

Many years later I was told by the people in charge of the riding event that out of those 45 horses, five were added to the final list at the last minute, and they were not of the required standard. So this was the moment we had been waiting for, the moment of truth when we had to show what we have been doing for the last three years. We had to do well in the riding event, as we didn't have the same ability for the physical events such as the swimming, and we needed the points from the riding to lift our total score.

The competitors lined up ready to draw the name of their horse from a hat;

Once the piece of paper was handed to the riding official, he would call out the name of the horse. When the drawing ceremony was finished we were allowed to go and have a look at our charges. My horse didn't look too bad, and through my little English I tried to find out from his handler, the horse's good and bad points. Unfortunately I couldn't understand much of what he was trying to explain to me except that this was a good young horse which "could jump."

After saddling the horse I was allowed to enter the warm-up arena, where each competitor was given 20 minutes to ride and get used to the horse. We were also allowed to jump a couple of little obstacles placed in the arena.

Almost from the start I knew that I was going to have a royal battle with this powerful brown thoroughbred. He wasn't a "nasty" horse, trying to get rid of me, he just had too much energy and he wanted to go at great speed. He was a hunter, used to being asked to gallop at great speed and take the fixed obstacles in his way without any hesitation. Our system of riding in pentathlon demands that the rider "finishes" the course without damaging the horse or himself; Additionally the pentathlete cannot afford to suffer injuries which can eliminate him from the event or make him unable to continue the next event. It was difficult to me to know what to do as my horse became harder to control, and I would have dearly loved to have our regular coach, Zidaru to give me his experienced advice.

Muresanu, who could not ride, was unable to give me any help so that I had to decide what was the best line of approach; In fact the only thing I could do was to keep the reins short and try to hold him back.

I started with a sudden jolt as my horse literally jumped over the starting line and immediately put his head down and charged the first obstacle. By the time I managed to shorten the reins and try to lift his head up this pulsating dynamo had already barged through the wooden bars of the obstacle and reduced them to splinters.

From then on he literally pulverized any obstacle we were supposed to jump, fighting with me to get his head and go even faster. Gradually my arms started to go numb with effort, and I was unable to stop this mad horse from going faster.

We had already walked the course before the actual ride, so that I had a fair idea where I was going to come to strife, where my horse wouldn't be able to go through the obstacle. This particular obstacle was made out of a pile of heavy railway sleepers positioned just on the lip of a dry creek bed, when the horse didn't have much momentum left and had to collect momentarily before engaging the hind legs and jumping over the obstacle.

As I imagined, he rushed into the dry creek, and on the way up he caught sight of the huge obstacle looming above our heads. I tried to push him to the take off position whilst my horse was nervously trying to avoid facing the obstacle.

But in pentathlon we are taught to avoid refusals at all costs which means loss of time and additional penalty points, although after three trials we are permitted to go on to the next jump. But I didn't want to lose more points by letting this wild animal stop, beside it was very awkward to go back in the creek and then try to jump; I had to get him going whether he wanted or not, I had to impose my will on his and not let him refuse.

Besides, by now I really hated this animal, his total refusal to listen to my commands, his sheer brute strength which made it impossible to ride him correctly, so I said to myself "Go on go and break your stupid neck, see if I care".

Eventually he realized that I wouldn't let him stop so he lifted almost from a standing start and tried to clear the obstacle. Normally horses extend their legs forward over the obstacle when they jump, this horse did something I have never seen before:

He tucked his legs under his body, and just managed to go over the top of the obstacle and then slid over the obstacle and landed on his head.

I was holding on the rains as taught, and did not let go of the reins in case the horse got up and ran away, which would mean a lot of time lost before I could remount.

For a few seconds we were both lying on the ground, me still in the saddle with my right leg trapped under his body, and the horse on his right side. At first I thought he had broken his neck as the head was literally caught in a sickening position under his body, and it was making these sad little noises trying to get his breath.

Not far from the obstacle there was an official watching our plight helplessly. He wasn't allowed to render any assistance as that would have meant immediate elimination. Somehow I felt like the time had stopped, that this was the end of my competition, that the horse had broken his neck and we couldn't continue. Besides the amount of time lost in the fall was almost beyond repair.

I started to feel sorry for this poor animal and gently tried to pull his head from under his body. Almost immediately he started to move and kick with his hind legs, then weakly he got up and gave himself a good shake. It was hard to believe that this horse was still alive, and getting better by the second. I stroked his neck and cleaned some of the dust from his face, then I spoke gently to him and placed the reins over his neck and slowly mounted him. He was much easier to mount, and willingly started to walk forward when I asked him to do so. Immediately after the creek the ground started to elevate to a small hill; My horse broke quite unexpectedly into a small trot and then amazingly into a controlled canter. I couldn't believe that this was the same horse that a few minutes ago was more like a sumo wrestler fighting and refusing to do anything I asked him to do.

At the top of the hill we jumped smoothly on to a wide wooden table, made a perfectly controlled landing and then we went down the hill in a comfortable school canter.

I started to enjoy myself, even if I knew that whatever thoughts I had before the start of the competition of scoring well in this event were hopeless, and that I should just be grateful that at least I didn't injure the horse and that apart from a sore hip, I was unhurt and able to continue the next day with the fencing event.

When we finally arrived back at the flat area where hundreds of spectators were gathered around the most interesting obstacle, the water jump, I was almost on the point of letting go of the reins, my hands being totally cramped and without any power.

The water jump was to be entered from the side of the dam by jumping straight in the murky brown water over a low bar. Most competitors got into trouble at this final obstacle due to the physical fatigue, and anticipating the finishing line awaiting just metres away from the dam. My horse by now was responding admirably to my aids, and he took off exactly from where I had reasoned the water would be most shallow. Even so I didn't realize how muddy the dam was and the horse slid in deep, barely keeping his head above the water. Momentarily I lost the grip on the reins, and I could feel that we were in a spot of trouble. But once again I was pleased to feel my horse half swimming half running through the water, and heading towards the exit point. Seconds later we crossed the line dripping with water and perspiration. I was so happy to have finished that I hardly noticed the smiling faces of my team and Muresanu's attempts to shake my hand.

As soon as the ring official allowed me to dismount and have the saddle checked for the correct weight, I went to thank the handler for the use of the horse, which is customary in pentathlon. To my surprise he looked very annoyed and started to speak to me in a harsh tone and kept pointing to the horses legs; Suddenly I understood what he was on about. He felt I had been pushing the young horse too hard, and as a result the poor animal had scraped the skin of his lower legs to a bloody pulp. There was nothing to explain to him and for once I hated my inability to speak English, so I said the only word I could think of: "Sorry".

I was glad the ordeal was over, not realizing at that moment how difficult this event had been and that many other competitors not only could not finish, but that some of them had been badly hurt. Bjorn Thofelt who was the World Junior Pentathlon Champion, fell after his saddle strap became loose, then remounted only to come down again as a result of the loose strap. He was dragged by his horse for some distance and suffered a nasty head concussion which necessitated hospitalization. Carmona (Chile), du Plessis (South Africa), and Ferreira de Silva (Brasil) were injured during the riding and took no further part in the competition which meant elimination of their teams. Our team finished 6th out of the 12 teams, with a total score of 1,160 points, well below our 1,954 points in the World Championship in Macolin. Tintea had the best ride and scored 777 points having taken 11.29 minutes to finish and losing another 60 points for a refusal; I managed to score 442 points due to losing 80 points for the fall and 557.5 for taking 13.10 mm. to finish, whilst Victor who took 18.10 mm. to finish, scored zero points. It wasn't a good start for our team and we all knew that we would have to try very hard the next day in the fencing event and get some extra points.

A RECORD IS SET

<u>Saturday, November 24.</u>

After the ride we all felt a little deflated, disappointed not to have scored better, particularly as we had such an encouraging result in Macolin. Of course it was pointless feeling dejected and upset for something which was not in our control. Although many of us worked hard to improve our riding skills, we all knew that in the draw one can pick a real donkey and score badly or conversely, be get lucky and pick the best horse in the draw.

So we did our figures and realized that the bad ride placed us at disadvantage in the Individual classification, and it probably had already ruined our chance of finishing in the first 10 places. But that's pentathlon. The only event which could now change our position was the most technical event, the fencing. To make things even more difficult, we were very disappointed not to have Master Galimir with us, left behind in Romania to make room for another political spy.

The morning of the fencing event we did as usual a warm up run very early in the morning in the village, trying to get rid of some of the sore spots. My right hip was slightly stiff but by the time we finished our run it was feeling hundred percent. The fencing event was to take place in an old building in Melbourne, the Exhibition Building, which had ample room for the organizers to set some 8 fencing strips in three separate halls plus the warm-up area. A field of 36 competitors were to contest the event. Under the Pentathlon scoring system, every competitor has to fence all the other competitors for one hit only. For each victory gained, the fencer receives an equivalent number of points which is determined by the total number of competitors, so that the equivalent of 75% of victories or 26 victories, would represent 1,000 competition points. For every bout above or below the standard number of 26 victories, a total of 37 points would be added or deducted from the 1,000 points.

Up to that moment the highest number of points accumulated in the fencing event since 1912 when Modern Pentathlon had been introduced to the Olympic Games, was 1,068 points(actually the ratio), a score obtained by Grohagen of Sweden in the 1912 Olympics in Stockholm. He had scored on that occasion 24 victories or 77.42%. But I don't think that one of us was even remotely thinking that this record could be broken, and we would have been quite happy if we scored around the 800 points mark or 20 victories.

In the team event, due to the elimination of competitors in the riding event the previous day, there were eight teams left: USA, Finland, Hungary, Mexico, USSR, Great Britain, Ireland and Romania. Sweden, Chile, Brazil and South Africa fenced only for the individual event, not having the regulation three competitors to represent their country. We were all very concerned about the state of health of the young Swedish champion who was still unconscious in the hospital. He in fact never recovered completely from the fall and stopped competing altogether which was a real loss to Swedish Modern Pentathlon.

Our new Master, Csipler Baci, was there to give us all a good warm-up and final preparation before the event started. This shortish, tough man had a confident manner about him, something of a "Don't argue with me, I am right" attitude which removed any doubts. He was confident that we were going to do well despite our lack of international experience. Perhaps he was more aware of our potential than we were, as he had coached many national and international fencing champions. He had the experience and the knowledge. Muresanu was very excited and as usual was busy checking to see if all the technical details were looked after, finding out who was in charge of the Jury of the Appeal in case of any disputes, where the canteen was, which team we had to fence first, and all other small details which can be so important and determine the final result.

I had changed my attitude and preparation for this event. After many hours of inner mental search and examination of the results obtained until then in competition, I realized that I had to adopt an approach which had to be fault proof. I had to use a method which gave my opponents very little chance to catch me unprepared. By then I had formulated my plan of action which I did not mention to anyone. It was my own design and was based on a few simple principles:

1. CONCENTRATE: meaning that from the moment I stood on the metal strip ready to start the bout, and for the whole duration of the bout (some 5 minutes), I would concentrate intensely,

imagining that my opponent was actually starting an attack NOW, THIS INSTANT. This meant that instead of expecting to sustain an attack from my opponent some time in the future, 30 seconds or perhaps one minute after the president had called us to start, I was maintaining a continuous state of alertness, not the usual mental conditioning of a fencer which normally calls for extra alertness once the attack starts.

I would defend myself when my opponent made his movement or even while he was starting to put his plan into execution. This would give me a time advantage which will be sufficient to stop his attack and possibly score with a stop-hit or a parry-riposte action. A successful attack in fencing depends on a number of factors such as distance, correct choice of movement, and understanding your opponent's faults and good points. But by far the most important factor in overcoming a good defense, is "TEMPO". It encompasses the total combination of all the factors being executed at the right time. It means that unless the attacking fencer FEELS the right time, selects the very split second when his opponent is most unguarded and not fully balanced, he could miss the moment and not have another chance for some time. It is easy to see how important it is in fencing and particularly in Pentathlon fencing, to FEEL the right moment for an attack, or to catch your opponent in the middle of his attack and stop him.

2. RETREAT AND DEFEND: As long as my opponent attacks or moves forwards with preparations of the attack I shall move back cautiously, defending by covering correctly my fencing lines, and performing parry-ripostes or other defensive movements like time-hit or stop hits, awaiting for the opportunity when the opponent loses his calm and becomes reckless and uncovers his own lines.

3. ATTACK WHEN THE OPPONENT STOPS: I decided to attack only when the opponent stops moving forward or he tries to get a little rest. That was to be the moment when I would start pushing him back, carefully, methodically, until I could see an open line or make my opponent make the wrong movement.

4. BE PATIENT AND WAIT FOR THE RIGHT MOMENT: Rather than try to finish my bouts in the first few minutes, I would make every bout go the whole distance, in order to get my opponent tired and careless.

5.   STICK TO MY PLAN REGARDLESS OF THE OUTCOME.
In the past I had been fencing well at the start or towards the finish,
but I didn't manage to keep the same standard of concentration
and correct execution of movement right to the end. This time
I wanted to keep the same style and performance right from the
start, and not worry about how many bouts I won or lost. I would
do the counting at the end.

I told Viorel Manciu not to tell me under any circumstance my
position (bouts won/ bouts lost), during the competition. I didn't want
to lose my concentration, to become too confident or lose my positive
mental attitude.

So everything was ready for the fencing competition, which was to
last between 8.00 a.m and 5.00 p.m. involving a total of some 600 bouts.
Our first bouts had to be between the members of the same team, to avoid
competitors favouring their team members in the Individual Classification.
My first bout was against my good friend Victor Teodorescu. We saluted
one another with the traditional fencing salute, we both smiled but as
soon as the masks were lowered over our faces, I had only one thought in
my mind: I WILL BEAT YOU NO MATTER WHAT!

It was probably the hardest I had to fight in the whole of the fencing
competition to beat Victor, who was particularly fit and a good fencing.
Like a good chess player he would make a plan of attack and gradually
he would push his opponent into making one mistake which he would
immediately exploit then score. But this time my concentration and
patience eventually wore him out, and he faulted by launching a direct
attack to my flank which I parried and then I riposted swiftly to his
unguarded shoulder. We were both covered in perspiration and very tired
when we finally stopped and shook our ungloved hands as is customary
in fencing.
    "What are trying to do to me" I said laughingly to Victor. "This is
only the first bout for today".
    "Yeah, but you didn't want me to beat you" he said with his usual
wicked smile." You could have let me win this one at least as a good
friend".
    I stopped smiling and I looked at him with a determined face:

"Not today Victor, today nobody is going to win a cheap point from me."

The bout against my other team mate, Dumitru, followed a similar pattern. It was a hard bout but I found it very easy to defend his attacks and towards the end, when he tried to rush me with a balestra, (a jump and lunge movement performed in quick succession), I could see him coming well before the final movement and scored easily.

From then on I started to fence with such ease and lack of tension that I stopped perspiring altogether; Normally I would sweat profusely and have to change my T-shirt at least two or three times during the competition. I would have expected to lose a lot of fluids on the day because of the heavy fencing jacket we had to wear for our protection as well as the double thickness plastron, which is compulsory in fencing, and protects the upper body. The mask also prevents the fencer from breathing sufficient air, and before long the fencer becomes bathed in his own sweat in the sauna-like uniform.

Our first match was against the Russian team which had the reputable Igor Novikov, one of the best fencers in international pentathlon fencing. In fact the whole Russian team had been meticulously belting us over the last three years, and they were expecting to give us Romanians a good hiding. Fortunately for us I had to fence first against Novikov. He was a tall and powerful man, with an enormously long arm which seemed to be so well covered that there was no room to hit anything. As planned I waited for his movements, parrying his preparations, moving away just a split second before he could start his attacks, and generally not giving him a chance to use his mercurial lunge. He was very technical, and did not make any mistakes, but I had to make him commit a mistake and place my epee point exactly under his guard (coquille), to reduce his arm length advantage. I finally caught him with a beat feint on the blade, which momentarily opened his defense and allowed me to hit the exact spot on the glove behind the metal guard.

Igor stopped when he heard the electrical buzzer signaling a hit, and he realized it was his light which was on, meaning that he had been hit. He took his mask off and looked at the glove with an incredulous stare, refusing to admit that he was hit on that spot, when he knew that he was perfectly covered. I was enjoying this moment of success, remembering the many painful defeats suffered at the hands of the Russians. It was even more pleasing because I hit him exactly as I had planned. Muresanu and the rest of the team were delirious to have won against Igor. That gave them all more confidence in their ability and for the first time our team became a real threat to the Russian team.

My next bout against the second Russian, was almost too easy, as the Russian panicked a little and tried to force the pace. His technique was not as smooth as Igor's and I found his uncovered arm during one of his out of distance attacks, and stop hit him. By now our team was leading and Csipler Baci, our coach who was of Hungarian origin, could not hide his delight. There was the last bout for me against the last Russian, Alexandre Tarassov, who I had never fenced before. He was one of the new champions who came through the Russian nursery of world champions and started pentathlon from an early age. He was a good fencer but like the rest of the Russian fencers, did not have a style of their own. They had tried to copy the French, the Italians and the Hungarians, and produced a style of fencing foreign to their own national temperament. As a result they were fencing like well programmed robots, but were unable to reproduce the brilliance of the other fencing schools which they copied.

Tarassov was the typical white Russian, with blue eyes and long blond hair. He didn't seem to have a care in the world and kept a permanent smile on his face. Perhaps I was getting a little confident, but I did everything as planned and when the moment arrived I took his blade and lunged, directing my epee to his forearm.

I engaged his blade and performed a scrupulous attack with opposition on his blade, and my point like the head of a cobra was ready to apply the bite on his exposed arm. At that instant his point landed on my guard, stopped for a split second and then as I continued my lunge, flicked from the coquille unto my glove. It happened very quickly and there was nothing I could do to prevent it. I should have started my lunge closer to the Russian to avoid his point altogether, but for once a little luck was necessary. The Russian jumped with joy realizing his luck and come forward apologizing and thanking me for the bout. Well I was annoyed but I reminded myself to stick to the plan and added another rule to my battle plan: DO NOT ATTACK UNLESS YOU HAVE TO.

However we were all flabbergasted with such a good start, this was the best we had ever started, particularly against the Russians, who were second only to the Hungarians, the 1952 Helsinki Olympics champions, and considered then the best pentathlon fencers in the world. Muresanu had a broad smile on his face although he was careful not be seen by the Russians enjoying himself too much, as this in the long run would have been regarded as an affront to the "Russian sport supremacy".

Strangely enough I was for once unaffected by the whole spectacle, I could only think of my fencing, of my plan of execution and nothing else could penetrate my armour. Even when Viorel Manciu, our reserve, came over and asked me if I needed anything, I had to pretend that I needed something to drink so as not to make him feel useless.

"Would you like me to get some oranges for you?" Viorel asked.

"Yes that would be great" I said and looked forward to the fresh juicy taste of the oranges.

"If you like I could get you some black coffee" Viorel said, being glad to be of any assistance. At that stage I wasn't aware of the terrible danger of mixing fresh oranges with coffee, and being a typical Romanian who likes his coffee, I greedily accepted his offer. Manciu disappeared to the canteen to get what we wanted whilst we moved to the next match against the US team.

The bouts against the Americans presented less difficulty and we found that we could hit them without much trouble. As I fenced them I started to get that incredible feel of one oneness between my fencing arm and epee. It felt quite natural and I had no difficulty *actually touching my opponents with the steel point of my epee. It was as if I could reach out with my arm and place the tip of my index finger on that fencer, I could hit that person any time I wanted to . . . I could not believe it, but it was happening.*

The gruelling riding event had been won the previous day by the American George Lambert who was very tall, even taller than Novikov, with long thin arms and rocket like attacks. This time I didn't have to fence first, in fact I had the advantage of seeing Victor fence this American first and observe his style.

So that by the time I had to fence him myself, I had already made a plan of attack, and I knew what he was going to do and how to provoke him into doing that movement, which then I would use to my advantage.

It worked almost exactly as I wanted to; I took my time, doing very little attacking, letting him take the initiative, retreating, pretending to be intimidated by his reach. Gradually he became more aggressive and careless, taking less care with the distance and covering his own arm and body. I had already decided not to attack unless my opponent had stopped moving forward altogether, so I waited patiently for his attacks and the moment when he would uncover himself and offer the best opportunity for me to hit him without taking any unnecessary risks.

That opportunity came sooner than expected when Lambert decided to put all his cards on one attack, and surprise me with an attack called a fleche.

Fleche comes from French and means arrow. It is a running attack which supposed to catch the opponent by surprise, so that there is no time to retreat or to parry. Performed correctly and from the right distance, it is almost impossible to avoid being hit. I used a lot of these attacks in the beginning until I realized how potentially suicidal they could be when one fences just for one hit. Quite often during the rush and a flurry of blade movements, both fencers get hit, and they are both credited with one hit. In the early stages of sword fighting these attacks were called by the fencing masters of the day, "Coup de Deux Veuves," or the widows' hit. Indeed there is no winner, both fencers losing a hit and apart from having the satisfaction of "killing the other fencer" score zero points.

So it was better to play safely I reasoned, not to take any chance unless it was absolutely necessary. I realized then how far I had moved from my early desperate attacks, when I used to throw caution to the wind and blindly launched myself in a nervous attack. It is a great feeling to be in control of your opponent in fencing, to examine calmly his moves, fully knowing that no matter what he does he is going to be hit.

Finally when Lambert could wait no longer he commenced his fleche and I could easily see his blade travelling closer to my chest; I delayed my parry to the very last moment, so that when I did take his blade and parry counter-six again, he had already passed my chest with his blade. All this time we were running—he was going forwards and I was running back. In the next few tenths of a second, we could see one another's eyes—his unmistakable fear of being hit, of not being able to disentangle his blade from the outside of my epee. That only lasted for a split second, then suddenly, still holding his point outside my body, I pointed my epee to his chest and extended my arm, hitting him in the chest. Just then I felt I had done this movement some time ago, a deja-vue sensation. I was slightly sorry to have to hit this nice American once again, but it had to be done.

By now we were going so well that there was little doubt about scoring our best fencing result. Although I wasn't keeping a close check on the number of victories obtained, by the time we had fenced six other teams I had lost only two bouts out of 18 encounters. Viorel Manciu was beaming with pride for his team, running around all of us trying to fulfill any need we may had had. I felt very strong and alert, I didn't need anything, I just wanted to fence. Finally Manciu come back from one of his trips to the well stocked canteen, carrying a bag of oranges.

"This is for you champion, have some, get your strength back," said Viorel with an inviting smile. "Come on, I know you love oranges, have one."

I finally succumbed to the temptation and ate two oranges. I ate quickly as I had to fence again against the only French competitor, Jean Claude Hamel, who had a lovely classic style. By the time I returned to our area and sat down, Viorel had already brought me a strong cup of black coffee. I was getting a little thirsty and having few minutes rest before fencing against the Finnish team, I drank the delicious brew quickly and started to make some adjustments to my equipment.

Normally during a long competition, more often than not the electrical equipment breaks down and the fencer has to have at least two other weapons (epees) ready to replace the faulty ones. Back home we had a qualified electrician who looked after our equipment, but he also could not be included in the team, and we had to look after our own gear. Up to that stage everyone else had changed their weapons at least once except for me. This was an incredibly strong weapon which seemed to have nine lives; it worked perfectly and passed all the weight and pressure tests which the President (person controlling the correct and safe run of the fencing bout) had to do before the start of a new bout.

Suddenly I felt very sick. My stomach felt like it was about to explode. I dropped everything and I started to run; I just managed to get to the toilet where I had a violent attack of diarrhea. From then on, for the next half an hour, I kept running between the toilet and the hall, trying to get back in time for my next fencing bout. Obviously it was difficult to maintain the same concentration as before, when I could hardly control my bowels and I was in great discomfort.

So for the next 5 or 6 bouts, I fenced with great difficulty and could hardly wait to finish the bout and run to the toilet once again. Fortunately for me I finally started to feel better and got back to my normal state. By then I had lost some four bouts out of eight bouts! My early advantage had been reduced and I had to get back to my plan immediately.

We continued to fence well and Manciu had to tell us that our team was running second, equal with the Russian team, and that the Hungarians were the only team ahead of us. He tried to tell me my score when I chased him out of the arena, threatening to kill him if he ever came near me again with coffee and oranges.

It had been a long day of competing, and everybody was getting tired and the fencing was getting slower. I felt just as fresh as if I hadn't fenced at all, getting more accurate and performing smaller and more precise attacking and defending movements. It was almost 5 p.m. when we started to get ready for our last match for the day against the Hungarian team. By then most of the competitors had finished their scheduled bouts and gathered round the strip where the match was going to take place. This was to be the real test. If we had any claim to be the better fencers, if we truly wanted to beat the Russians and the Hungarians, this was the moment when all our training and preparation for the last few years had to demonstrate if it all was of any value or just an unfounded dream.

In past fencing competitions I would get very nervous and doubted myself particularly when I had the right opportunity, yet hesitated to attack, only to realize that I had missed my opportunity and allowed my adversary to survive a little longer and eventually score against me. But today everything was different and we had changed roles. We fenced with no fear and superior technique and speed. With every bout won against the other teams we became more confident, more aggressive and believed even more in our ability.

We were looking forward to finally meeting the Hungarians, the 1952 Olympic champions, the most feared fencers who made the other competitors look like dilettantes.

Romanians and Hungarians are very competitive, particularly when they compete against each another. There is a certain amount of old defiance and desire to prove who is the more competitive, the better opponent; besides for our young and inexperienced Romanian team to beat the Hungarians in the fencing event of the Modern Pentathlon was unimaginable, something we could only dream of. The two teams had finished all their scheduled bouts, and this was the last match of the day.

Despite my strict instructions not to tell me how we were going, Manciu could not control his emotions any longer and came over to tell us what was happening:

"Listen you lot, do you realize that you are equal second with the Russians and if you win 6 more bouts against the Hungarians, you could come first in the team event."

Victor laughed sarcastically and said something about pigs flying and we all laughed.

"No, really you're killing everybody, and you Cornel, you are well ahead of Gabor Benedeck." Manciu looked very serious and we finally believed he wasn't making it up.

I knew instinctively that I had fenced well, but I thought those four bouts lost during my stomach attack would prevent me from gaining a place. This time I didn't chase him out of the halt, and we all became very quiet. It was what we had been training for and dreaming about, yet it was happening to us now, the dream had become a reality . . .

Muresanu made sure that we all had everything we needed, and then in an unexpected show of pride and team spirit he told us that he was very proud of us, even if we couldn't destroy the Hungarian team.

"Cornel you have the first bout, and you know what to do. But remember that the way you fight this bout is more important than any other bout you have fenced today. It will set the example for the whole team and it will make the Hungarians lose their confidence. Do it for your team!"

Where have you been until now, why didn't you talk like this before? You respect me now and you ask for my utmost but it would have been different if you could have shown me that you cared, that you have emotions like us all. Yes I will win, but this time it is because nobody can take away what I have worked for, nobody can snatch from me what has been achieved through a lot of blood and sweat. My first bout was against Janos Body. It was a good fight but lacked the usual fire and aggression for which the Hungarian pentathletes were known. I felt his caution verging on fear. He had a few opportunities to launch a damaging attack but he hesitated. It reminded me of my great annoyance with myself for not attacking, and I felt slightly sorry for him. He must have been advised by his coach not to force the pace and to wait for my attacks. So I deliberately put on a big display of extreme caution, avoiding his movements and continuously retreating; As expected he was confused and unable to work out for himself what to do next. The bout was coming to an end and unless one of us could score, it would count as double defeat. It would have advantaged the Hungarians as they were slightly ahead of us. My little acting had the desired effect and soon after the President stopped us and informed that we had one minute to go. When we recommenced fencing, I suddenly moved forward, enveloped his blade with a double counter in 6th, and lunged deep with opposition to his torso. It was over in a split second, and my light on the electric box indicated a hit in my favour.

"Fantastic Cornel," said Master Csipler with his usual energy, "Where did you learn that movement; I cannot remember teaching you envelopments in the lesson." He was obviously pleased to see my result.

"No you're right. This was one of Master Galimir's special movements. He wanted us to use them only against fencers who keep their arm straight and rigid."

I looked around our team and I could feel how much we all owed our dear Master, left behind, simply because he spoke his mind, was a Jew and had relatives in Israel. The reality of the unfair situation back home hit me once again, and reminded me that the clock was ticking away, and that soon I would have to decide which way I will go. But as soon as the bout was over, Viorel come over to me and told me that even if I lost the next two bouts, I would win the Individual fencing competition!

I pretended to be annoyed with him and said in a stern voice:

"I told you not to come and tell me how I am going. I don't want to worry about scoring; I just want to do my fencing. Do you understand that?"

Viorel smiled and then told me that he had kept his promise up to now, but the way I had been fencing had placed me at the top:

"Cornel, you are the champion, nobody can beat you today. You must forgive me, but I cannot keep this from you; I wanted to be the first to let you know."

He looked so happy and pleased that I just smiled and then I told him not to worry because I knew I could beat Benedeck and the whole Hungarian team today.

The excitement was growing with every bout our team fought. The Hungarians, true to their reputation, were giving everything to prevent us from winning more bouts. Viorel and Dumitru tried very hard but could only score another one victory between the two of them. My second was against the younger member of the Hungarian team, Antal Moldrich whom I didn't know that well. I decided to use a different approach and surprise him with a balestra attack, immediately after the command normally given by the President to start fencing.

In international fencing events including the Olympics, they use French and many of the Presidents were of French origin. I spoke good French, and I had no problem understanding our French President, but this was not the case with the other competitors who spoke very little French. From the previous bouts I noticed that this young Hungarian didn't seem to understand French and relied on their team translator to ask questions. I also noticed that he took a little longer than the others to respond to the President when asked if he was ready. So this was my plan: As soon as we were asked to take on guard and the President asked in French if we were ready—Vous etes pret Monsieurs ?, I would immediately answer first and wait for my opponent to give his answer; I was hoping that for a second or two he would try to say the words (Oui Monsieur) as well as he could, and perhaps he would be more concerned about the correct pronunciation than my next movement.

Then as the President would impatiently tell us to start—Allez—I would do an enormous balestra, (step lunge) and cover the distance between us. Normally most fencers take a couple of steps and then lunge at the start, the distance between fencers being set at four metres for the very purpose of preventing fencers from lunging simultaneously and causing a serious accident. But even with a balestra I could not reach his body except if I hit him under his coquille, exactly where the glove is exposed. The main difficulty laid in covering the unusually large space separating the fencers at the start, as well as the placement of the point exactly on an area no larger than a five cent coin. It had to be successful or the Hungarian would have me completely at his mercy at the end of my attack, unable to counter his immediate parry and riposte from such close quarters.

It was a risky movement which normally I wouldn't have tried, but I felt so strong and confident, I knew I could not miss.

"Take on-guard Gentlemen" the President said, indicating with his hands our starting positions behind the On-Guard lines. After we settled and took our on-guard positions he asked in a clear voice if we were ready:
"Are you ready?"
I immediately said in French: READY!
He then looked at my opponent and asked once again:
"Are you ready"?
Yes, he was ready but he had quite a job to say so in broken French:
"Yes, ready."
The President then quickly added the usual : "ALLEZ", (Go !)
At that exact moment I commenced my balestra and before anyone even realized what was happening, I flew over the distance separating us, and placed the point under his coquille. I knew I had hit my target and confidently stood up from the deep lunge and took off my mask, smiling, and extended my ungloved hand for the customary shake. For few seconds everybody stopped moving and the whole arena was frozen, then different people started to check their positions and try to assess what had happened. Moldrich was looking at his glove where I had hit, not believing that I had touched him and was shaking his head with great anger. My team was jumping with joy, Muresanu was shouting something, and Master Csipler stood up applauding. The President asked us to stop (we had actually stopped a long time ago), and stepped forward to the recorders and time-keeper's table and tried to find out if there was had been a hit. An Australian girl was in charge of the electrical box which registers and indicates a hit by mean of a coloured light. Mine was the green light which I had seen with the corner of my left eye just as I hit. But

the suddenness of my attack must have surprised the girl and she pressed the button to cancel the light almost as soon as it came on. The President then proceeded to establish if there was a light and in particular which light had come on.

At first, the girl who was obviously inexperienced and rather overawed by the occasion, said that she had pressed the cancel button because she thought that she had forgotten to cancel the light from the previous bout. The one thing she was sure was that the light was green.

In the meantime Muresanu had jumped forward and begun to argue with the President to try and convince him that the hit was given and that I should be awarded the bout. But the President wasn't going to be rushed and asked for an interpreter. At that moment I was getting a little tired of waiting and wanted to get on with it, so I told the President that it didn't matter and I would fence him again if he wanted. Muresanu got very annoyed and was moving from the fencing strip to the official table, shouting half in Romanian, half in broken French:

"Non, c'est ne pas possible. Domnule ce magarie, je n'avait jamais vue un choice comme cet. Spunele Cornele ca sau gresit."

(This is not possible, I have never seen anything like this. Tell them Cornel that they are wrong.)

Finally the President managed to sort out what had happened and explained in broken English to the teams and the spectators:

"No light on box before. Green light only. Hit to Roumanie. Next please."

I was awarded the hit and didn't have to fence the Hungarian again.

The President had fortunately remembered that in the previous bout the Hungarian fencer scored against Tintea and the red light was on. So he knew that the hit recorded on the box could have been only a new hit as it was the green light.

My final bout was to be against Gabor Benedeck the Hungarian National Pentathlon, also one of the top three fencers in Hungary. He could have fenced as a member of the Olympic Hungarian Epee team, but he elected to represent his country in the Modern Pentathlon, event he and his team won in the Helsinky Olympic Games in 1952.

By now all the bout have been completed and this was to be the final bout of the day. The spectators and team competitors were gathered around the metal strip where the bout was going to take place.

I had many times in the past thought about this encounter, about having to face this skilled and experienced fencer; I had won once and lost once against him, but I knew that today it had to be a complete show; Lack or chance would play a very little part in the outcome, it had to be a controlled bout, one where there will be no room for silly mistakes, or sudden desperation attacks;

It had to be perfect and without leaving anything to chance; It had to be final and not relying on another chance; This was real, do or die duel, hit or be hit, win without allowing your opponent to get near you.

The President did the usual weapon check to see if everything was working properly and without favouring the other fencer. My beautiful trusty weapon, once again passed easily all required tests, and I was ready to start.

We saluted one another with the graceful old classic salute, then we took on-guard. He had a good position, with the legs well bent, straight and slightly effaced body, presenting minimum target, right arm gracefully curved above his head and the shining epee blade pointing directly at my arm. I started to move softly towards him, gently engaging his blade, and maintaining a good safe distance; We changed roles swiftly and took turns at attacking and defending, trying different preparations of the attack, short lunges and the occasional half speed Fleche which did not finish. To every movement there was a counter movement followed by an immediate continuation of the attack, all done without stopping, without hesitation. If it wouldn't have been so deadly one could have admired the beauty of it all, but we both knew that this was for real, that the smallest mistake would have brought a swift and deadly finish to the match.

I was enjoying immensely this bout, and I appreciated my opponent's skill, his perfect sense of distance and his impeccable style. He was showing me that the Hungarian style of fencing did not lack the finesse of the French school, and he had a great repertoire of movements. The bout was drawing a great variety of sounds from the crowd, which was totally captivated by the display. We fenced for the full five minutes without slowing down or giving ourselves any rest. I didn't feel at all tired, and it felt as if I had just started.I had watched Bendeck fencing before against Victor and Dumitru who he beat with ease, and I had realized that I could hit him if I got him tired and particularly if I attacked him with a simple indirect attack at the right time; Timing was going to be the thing that would beat him.

"Arettez-vous s'il vous plait Monsieurs" The president asked us to stop and told us that there was one minute to go. We both took our places once again behind the white on-guard lines, saluted, and took on guard for the last time. The game was over and I was ready to for the final hit.

"Vous-etes pret Monsieurs? . . . Allez"

As soon as we commenced moving I started to force Benedeck back, pushing him with a flurry of preparations which did not allow him to settle in his position. Once again I was using his inability to react correctly against repeated beats and engagements on the blade.

Suddenly I stopped, giving him the impression that I had exhausted all my movements and perhaps had temporarily given up. He responded by relaxing just for a second, taking a little rest, getting his breath back, perhaps relieved that I hadn't scored: This was the moment I had been waiting and preparing for; that instant he was vulnerable and at my mercy. I made a simple direct feint to his chest which he tried to parry with the usual counter-riposte, but it never found my blade which by now was doing a circular disengagement and had already arrived on his chest, exactly on his heart.

If that would have been a duel fought with sharpened blades he would have died almost on the spot, but although there was no blood, he was mortally wounded, he was hit. He slowly took his mask off and placing it under his left arm he came forward to meet me in the middle of the strip. He smiled with a tired smile and shook my hand:

"Vous-etes le meilleurs".

We shook hands and the spectators clapped warmly for what had been an unforgettable bout. I thanked him and told him how much I had enjoyed it. All our team were delirious with joy, not quite accepting what had just happened. I was the Individual winner of the fencing event with a score of 29 victories and 6 defeats, giving me a total of 1,111 points, and placing our team in second position, equal with the Russians and behind the Hungarians won the first place in the team event.

It was late in the evening and a small group of Romanian competitors and officials walked outside the old building in the garden, and took a picture in front of a water fountain. I had just experienced the greatest victory of my life and I was on top of the world.

How can words explain or depict the great feeling of achieving the impossible dream? How can one express his deep sense of gratitude to those responsible for his success? I will never be able to show my gratitude to the man who made me a world champion, the man who humbly persisted in convincing me that I was something special. Thank you Master Aristide Galimir, may God rest you in peace wherever you are, and perhaps if there is some truth about reincarnation, I hope to meet you again, but this time to have you by my side when I win.

I SHOT MY BEST TOO EARLY

There is nothing like success, everybody loves you and all the old differences and disagreements are conveniently put on hold. I was suddenly a national hero and my name was mentioned with pride in many articles written in the Romanian newspapers.

Our Sport Minister, was gloating with self-congratulatory praise, because he was the one with the vision and courage to "risk" my inclusion in the team and nomination as the team captain. Norman was enjoying our success and laughed often, mentioning about making the right choice in selecting our team ahead of the Russian's. He had been a true supporter and unconditional friend, always ready to assist with whatever was needed. By now Norman was totally accepted as one of us and even Muresanu, who was normally a cold and unapproachable person, warmed to him and trusted his actions.

By now Norman understood my intentions and was quietly working in the background to prepare for the time when I was ready to leave the village. I had made it clear to him that I would not do anything until I had finished competing, only then I would make the final decision. In the meantime our friendship became stronger and as I could speak more English he was able to get a better picture of the situation which I had left back home. I could sense his compassion and understanding; he was like a father to me, and I felt that I had a real friend to rely on in times of need.

Before the Games started our team made numerous visits to the pistol shooting range at Williamstown, which was one of the new facilities specially built for the Games. Norman and I spent time walking the short distance to the shores of Port Phillip Bay which bordered the range. There was also a large car park where there was enough room for those of us who wanted to learn to drive the automatic Jaguar made available by Norman.

*   *   *

One week before the actual competition started, all the Pentathlon Teams in the Village were invited to a pre-competition challenge on the new range, to test the new installations under real competition conditions.

The shooting event in Pentathlon consists of shooting twenty shots on a silhouette resembling the upper torso of a person, marked with concentric circles from a high ten to the low five. The shots are fired at a moving target placed 25 m. from the shooting line;

After a sighting series of five shots allowing the competitor to make any necessary adjustments, the actual contest starts. Shooters are asked to load five shots only. At this stage the targets are facing fully, and each shooter can rise the arm and take aim, settling in the usual position. Care must be taken not to fire whilst lifting and lowering the gun, as this will be penalized heavily.

When the whole group of shooters seems to be ready, the range officer asks : "Are you ready" ?, and if no one is asking for extra time to get settled, he then calls "Targets away"!

As the targets turn away facing only with the edge, the shooters must hold their extended arm at a 45 degrees angle, and wait for seven seconds before the targets turn facing the shooters; Only then are the shooters allowed to lift their arms, aim and fire at the target before the targets turn away again; So the shooter has only THREE SECONDS to do all that, or he will miss the target altogether for as great loss of points, each target shot lost representing two hundred points . . .

Quite often I was questioned by people who only compete in shooting events, and don't understand the mental pressure placed on us the Pentathletes during the shooting events;

The series consist of five shots, after which the targets are checked and the scoring is recorded. A total of four series are completed with short rest in between to allow for target checks and marking. The maximum possible score is 200 point of 200 possible or 20 bull eyes, a score only achieved once in the history of the Modern Pentathlon Olympic Competition.

A lot of people who do not do the pentathlon but they shoot, cannot understand why is it so difficult to score well in the Pentathlon event; That is because unless you compete in all the five events, where every point counts, you cannot understand the incredible emotional strain placed on the Pentathlete to score well and get the maximum amount of points; But the greatest fear we all have is not to pull the trigger too hard and "jerk" the shot, or release the trigger too slowly and miss the turning target . . . It is a very precise technique which can be learned in practice but during the competition the emotions and fear of losing can completely change the shooter's technique.

All our team suffered from "nerves" and in particular Victor who would do anything to avoid the actual shooting phase and pretend that his gun wasn't functioning normally. But he wasn't the only one to fall victim to this event; I found out years latter that even George S.Patton, a 26-year old lieutenant, who became very famous as a general in the U.S. Army during the World War II, ironically, when he competed in the 1912 Stockholm Olympic Games, and finished 5th overall, in the shooting event he only managed a mediocre 21st position out of 32 competitors.

He did complain and argue that one of the bullets in the series, went through the same hole made by a previous bullet, and not missed the target completely as decided by the officials. Would have his claim be accepted and proved correct, he would have won the gold medal . . .

This first invitation event for the Modern Pentathlon competitors, was eagerly attended with most teams itching to find out how they have been training. As expected, all the scores on the day were well above the normal average, and our team performed well above all expectations.

I was shooting very calmly for once and did not allow my mind to wander off and do all sorts of quick calculations; I tried not to think of anything except my technique. Wait . . . breath easily . . . start to lift . . . aim and commenced the pressure . . . release the shot just as the sights settled in the centre of the ten . . . follow through . . . lower to 45 degrees . . .start counting the three deep breaths . . . hold and wait . . . start to lift . . .release the air gently . . .go through the trigger release and follow through . . . do the whole routine five times, then stop and get ready for the next round . . .

In principle it was very easy and on that day I managed to maintain concentration right to the last shot, not allowing any foreign thought to enter my mind, except my set technique . . . It worked because on that day, I won the shooting event with 198 points out of 200 possible, shooting only two 9 s . . .

*   *   *

Unfortunately during the actual shooting event in the Games, I had a continuous mental barrage of thoughts, fully knowing that if I shot above 195 points, even with my bad score in riding event, I could have finished in the top 10 places. I could not empty my mind, concentrate on my technique and forget about scoring. I started well but after the second series my arm started to shake and I could not control it. I don't how, but I managed not to lose any shots and finished with a score of 182, not a disaster but well below my expectations. Victor scored 177 points and Dumitru 184, which placed us in 6th place on the teams aggregate. The winner was Almada Felix of Mexico who scored 193 points, whilst Gabor Benedeck came second with a score of 191.

MY WORST EVENT

Norman was keen to show us as much as possible of Australia and managed to take us around Melbourne and its surrounds. But his desire to look after us went much further as he made great efforts to introduce us to his own family and treat us as his own. Perhaps because he wasn't married and had no children he saw us as a ready-made family, but most certainly as far as he was concerned, we were his best friends. Romanians are very hospitable people and were renowned in the past for their warmth and friendliness to strangers, but Norman was indeed something special because he continued to look after us better than anybody else. We were invited to his home for a traditional Australian barbecue where we had a great time as well as being able to meet his own family, his sister Hilda and brother-in-law Ted, who proved to be just as friendly and helpful. That was the time I started to change my ideas about where to go if I decided to defect; America was a distant inviting land, but I had found so many good, decent people here in Australia that it was getting harder to decide to leave.

During one of these parties, Norman told me that he was going to invite his brother Jack, a doctor, who lived in Canberra. Norman suggested that he was a better person to talk to about my intended application to the Australian Government for political asylum. Jack had a few connections in Canberra and additionally he spoke French. This would give me a chance to explain everything to him and make perfectly clear my intentions. So it was decided that soon after the Pentathlon competition was over, Norman would organize a get together where I could meet and discuss matters with Jack.

Tuesday 27th November.

Our most feared event, swimming, took place at the new Olympic Pool built on the Eastern bank of the Yarra river. In those days the new pool was a most striking structure, very modern and equipped with the latest technical details. But with the exception of Dumitru who was for a short time a member of a club in Bucharest and could swim competitively, for Victor and myself swimming was a time of intense pain. Both of us started on our own and did not have an efficient technique and by the time we joined the pentathlon, it was too late to learn the correct technique, we didn't have the flexibility in the shoulders to stroke correctly. I had improved considerably in the short time and perhaps with a more dedicated coach, and more training I could have improved by some 20-30 seconds over the three hundred metres race.

As expected the swimming was a most gruelling event and we had to try to do our best times, but as expected we could only finish with mediocre times and placings which gave us a low total score of 2,195 points and placed us in last place. Dumitru was the fastest in our team with a time of 4 min.37 sec., I managed a 4 min.50 sec. whilst "papa" Victor nearly drowned in his epic effort to finish and managed a very low 5 min.14 sec. Probably the only encouraging consequence of our swim was that we managed somehow to retain our 6th place overall in the team event. At least we could all run very well and it was possible to keep our 6th place for the final placing.

We were happy to have finished our worst event and asked permission to go to town and have a chance to see Melbourne at night. Muresanu agreed reluctantly, but he finally relented and let the four of us go. The evening was just right for a stroll along Collins Street which glittered with bright Olympic decorations, blazing lights and happy smiling faces. We hadn't seen much of the city with the exception of the trip to the stadium for the Games' opening, so this was the first time we could actually mingle with the crowd without being watched by our usual "minders". By now we had all learned the name of our allotted official informers who followed us almost constantly and informed our leaders of our movements. We were all having a great time, laughing and talking, smiling at the passing crowd, feeling on top of the world. Ever since we had arrived in Australia we had noticed with interest the great number of tall, attractive girls, who seemed to be the norm out here. Victor, who was older and more experienced with the opposite sex, made the comment which we all had to agree with:

"I would like to know if these girls have any waist?" said Victor with a wicked smile looking at Dumitru, expecting the usual confused reaction from the younger of our team, and winking at us;

"Of course they have waists, all girls have waists don't they ?" retorted Dumitru before we had a chance to stop him taking the bait once again from the old fox.

Victor was already enjoying the huge catch he was about to make, and as usual adopted a concerned tone, talking rather sadly to Dumitru:

"You see my boy, you have problems understanding this English race. They are not like us, they have to grow differently, longer legs, no waist and a pretty face. Don't you understand?" Dimitru became embarrassed as usual when Victor took the micky out of him, and mumbled something about all people being the same, well at least similar?

"Now you see my friend," Victor said, putting his hand paternally around Dumitru's shoulders:

"You see where you are going wrong, you have not learned one single thing from all the lectures I have given you. You should pay more attention or you will embarrass all of us when they ask back home how the girls were here in Australia. By now poor Dumitru was almost beside himself and Viorel and I could hardly control our laughter waiting for Victor to end this farce. Suddenly Victor started to laugh and swiftly, before Dumitru had a chance to escape, applied a head lock on his head and pretended to choke him. Our group stopped for a minute in the middle of Collins Street, and very quickly a small smiling, friendly crowd gathered around us, trying to understand what was going on. There was a small pandemonium for the next few minutes with us all laughing and Dumitru who by now managed to slip Victor's hold, trying to smooth his carefully combed hair.

"So help me, one of these days I am going to kill you, you bastard," Dumitru said, getting a little serious. Viorel and I stepped in and tried to soothe the youngster's ego, whilst Victor pretended to be hurt.

"You see what you get from trying to educate the young ones, they have no gratitude." Finally we got going again with Dumitru still mumbling about "stupid old man", and Victor asking me what he had done wrong, whilst Viorel and I tried very hard to keep a straight face. We were walking once again up Collins when I suddenly had the strange sensation of being followed and I said that to our small group.

"I wonder if my shadow is behind me as usual, watching, taking notes and telling the Minister everything we do. God how I hate these miserable leeches."

We started to regain our composure and kept walking four abreast along the wide footpath. Victor, as usual, didn't allow things to upset him, and he would always change the tone of a discussion by offering an immediate stupid solution or placing a bet on that possible situation.

"Aren't you getting just a little too suspicious, after all this is not Bucharest, this is Melbourne, Australia."

He then slipped into his Shakespearian mode and performed a graceful old French courtier-like salute to a small group of girls who started to laugh and giggle with delight at his melodramatic performance.

"You Victor are a fool. I am sorry to say this "Papa", (mocking name for an older person), but you are starting to forget that we are here only because we are good at pentathlon. But don't forget they are watching us and are going to tell us back home everything we have done."

I knew who my spy was ;An officer in the Romanian Security Forces and one of the Olympic competitors. On the payroll and receiving many benefits for spying on Romanian athletes whilst overseas competing, he was very much hated. He had been trying to be unobtrusive but lacked the necessary finesse and quite often I surprised him listening to our conversation.

"Look Victore," I said, rather tired of trying to convince him. "I bet you 100 lei (equivalent of $1-00 in those days), that just as we are talking now that sneak is just behind us watching every move we make. I bet you . . ."

Victor accepted the bet and we all suddenly stopped and turned around: There, right behind us, no more than three steps away, was "our friend" who immediately tried to hide behind the milling crowd.

He must have been watching us right through the evening and undoubtedly he would tell the Minister the next day about our trip into town. Suddenly we all lost our desire to walk and decided to return to the Olympic Village.

We sat in silence for the rest of the bus trip, each with his thoughts. It was obvious to me that nothing had changed, and that once we were back in Romania, we would have to face the same travesty of truth, asked to pretend and tell the Romanian public of the superior society we lived in, denigrate the corrupt, capitalist Australian society and concede that we were so glad to be back in the Communist Paradise.

I felt so annoyed with my life, so hopeless, with so little chance to do anything. Nothing would change these people, they were beyond logic, they really believed in the power of the new regime, and they would crush anyone who dared say anything to the contrary.

Once again the ugly spectre of my defection started to haunt me; once again I started to spend sleepless nights, torn between the desire to stay in the free world, yet fearful of the consequences. I was still unable to make the final step, to decide once and for all what path I would take. I decided to stop worrying if I could, and finish the last event, the cross-country run which was the next day, and then I would see what was to be done. Actually I had no idea how I would solve my impasse.

RUNNING WITH COURAGE

During the riding event at Oaklands Hunt Club some low individual stole my only Modern Pentathlon Competitor Badge from my jacket which I had left in the changing room.

There were no more badges available to replace the lost or stolen items, so I was quite happy to receive from our minister an amount of fifty Australian pounds which in 1956 was a fairly large amount of money. I decided to replace my lost badge and told Muresanu that I was going into the city to buy some presents for my family. For the first time I was on my own, travelling in the public bus to the city, surrounded by ordinary Australians, watching suburban Melbourne, listening to the English language spoken in the bus. I was at last on my own, free to do what ever I wanted to do, listening and trying to comprehend what was said around me, feeling I had been born into another life.

There were no secret agents watching me or taking notes about what I was doing. It was only a minute taste of what I could sense as being possible yet it was so pleasing, so fulfilling that I felt slightly drunk with happiness, wanting to hug and kiss all these smiling people around me.

Melbourne in those days, by comparison with the war ravaged Bucharest, was a young city pulsating with activity, beautiful shops loaded with tempting wares, and large throngs of people. I spent a few hours looking around, trying to make myself understood by the shop attendants who were only delighted to show me their wares. Very often they would eventually ask two questions: "Where do you come from" and "Do you like Australia"? I tried to give the correct answer but very often I would use the wrong word and finish having a good laugh, parting as good friends. I don't remember meeting anyone who didn't have a big smile on their face or didn't bother with a non-English speaking person, going out of their way to make me feel comfortable.

At first, before coming to Australia, I wanted to go to the US which I considered, from what little information was accessible to us in Romania, to be the most desirable place on earth, but the longer we stayed in this country, the more I liked it.

I started to like this country to the point where I felt that I could live here and not want to go anywhere else, I didn't think that I could find another place where I could feel as secure and accepted as I was here. Norman and his family had accepted me more like a long lost son, and that was another factor which made me even more reluctant to follow to my initial plan and prepare to go to the States. Out of my spending money I managed to buy a beautiful Omega wrist watch, a few things for my parents and from a second hand shop, a business suit and shoes which looked almost new. To my surprise I still had some change left over after all that spending. It had been a liberating experience, something which gave me strength and confidence in my ability to deal with the everyday situations in a new country.

<u>Wednesday, November 28.</u>

The running event was the last event of our pentathlon competition. We had to run over a cross—country terrain, the same one we had travelled with our horses, except that it was a little shorter and we didn't have to jump any obstacles. Muresanu had spent a great deal of time preparing us for this event, and we had all improved greatly, although there was a great difference in time between all of us. Victor, despite the fact that he was the oldest in the team, was the most experienced and the fastest; I was about 30 seconds behind him and Dumitru who was more of a swimmer, some two minutes behind me. There was a much better feeling about this event, we felt confident and from our past experience we could be assured of a good result.

The running event in Pentathlon is designed to emulate the feet of that Swedish officer, who had to travel unaided through unfamiliar and rough terrain, on his own. In the Modern Pentathlon, runners start at one minute intervals with the aim of catching up with as many runners ahead of him as possible, and keeping to the course without being lost. We were allowed to study the map of the actual course but it was important to know the elevation of the terrain to be able to adjust our speed according to the conditions.

It wasn't permitted for the runners or the team official to view the running course before the official start, but as usual Muresanu left the village the night before and walked the unsupervised course in the dark. He told us where the main hills were and discussed the correct speed to be used for various segments of the run, but in reality once the run started all of us knew that we have to give everything, and that we must run faster than we could even imagine, particularly now having almost secured 6th place.

We all did well, in particular Victor who came 9th in the run, with a personal best of
14.08, and Dumitru who finished with a time of 16.34. My run was also a personal best and placed me 17th, with a time of 14.50. Our team achieved a total of 10,613 points, placing the Romanian Team in 6th place, some 360 points behind the Mexican Team.

I finished in 14th place in the individual event, being the first Romanian to break the 4,000 points barrier, whilst Dumitru finished in

20th place and Victor, who did not score in the riding event, finished in 30th place. In the final analysis, our team did everything it was expected to do, and my win in the fencing created a record for the highest number of points ever recorded in the Modern Pentathlon fencing event since its inclusion in the Olympic Games in Stockholm 1912, as well I was the first Romanian to win an Olympic fencing event. My 1,111 points in the fencing event has remained an Olympic record, yet to be surpassed. Perhaps the Sydney 2000 Olympics may see a new champion who will pass the record, but regardless of the outcome, my record would have lasted over a period of 48 yrs. without ever being seriously challenged. Our Team was to be awarded the Diploma of the Olympic Games but due to official inaptitude we never received our just reward for finishing in the first six places. I am in the process of applying to the International Olympic Committee to correct this situation and finally be granted this special award.

DREAM COMPLETED

All of a sudden the pressures of competition, the desperate efforts to be the best, the battle for survival come to an end and made us once again re-join normal life. We didn't have to start the day with a run or complete the usual 3-4 sessions of training in a day, Muresanu was nowhere to be seen and everybody was busy doing something they wanted or planned to do. Victor, who had already been married and divorced before, was busy chasing a pretty Romanian gymnast, Elena Leustean who he intended to marry in the Olympic Village. Viorel had Croatian ancestry, so he made many friends with the large Slavic community in Melbourne, was invited to numerous home parties and was often asked to take gifts or money to relatives back in Romania. Dumitru was hardly seen as he was very much in demand by the young Australian girls who visited the Olympic Village in large numbers.

I had plenty of time at my disposal and I tried to see as much of the remaining events, in particular fencing and athletics. Master Csipler invited me to the women's foil competition to see Olga Orban, our Romanian foil champion fence in the final where she fought brilliantly and finished in second place with a silver medal. In the village, particularly at the evening meal we had a chance of finding out first hand from our various representatives how they had fared in their particular event. Our young rower Leon Rottman who was billeted with our Pentathlon team and slept in the room next to Victor and I, was a totally shy and uncommunicative person, who would just sit at the table, eat his food and not talk to anyone.

All the rowers and canoeists had to travel daily to the regatta course in Ballarat where all the events took place. One evening during meal-time in the dining room we noticed Leon who as usual was eating on his own. We went over to say hello and asked him how he had gone in the 1000 m canoeing event? Did he finish, was he happy with his result?

He mumbled something about the Hungarian Hernek, something about it being a very close event. It was almost impossible to get this fellow to talk as he came from an region of Romania where they literally spend their lives on the water and their only occupation is fishing and rowing their wooden boats. They didn't mix with strangers and distrusted any attempt at communication

"Come on Leon how did you go, are you sure you finished the race?."

He stopped chomping through his huge plate of spaghetti for a moment and quietly pulled something from under his tracksuit jacket. He held it with his left hand whilst resuming his eating with the other hand. We had seen the medals awarded to various competitors, but this one was different, it was a shining gold medal glimmering in the large dinning room. Suddenly it was quiet and everybody stopped talking, looking incredulously at this symbol of supreme success, casually held by this young scruffy athlete, then they all started to applaud warmly.

"Well done Leon, did you expect to win gold?"

"Ah yes, my coach reckoned I could but I didn't." He then slipped the medal around his neck and back under his tracksuit as though nothing had happened and continued his meal.

The next day he won a second medal in the 10,000 m canoe event, and as usual we had to drag it out of him before he told us that he had won. After the Olympics, I heard that he went back to his fishing village to help his father with the daily chores and never competed again.

There was the usual village gossip and there was ever-increasing speculation about what would happen to the Hungarian athletes after the games were over, whether they were going to return to their ravaged country or apply for political asylum in Australia. The Romanian team had a number of athletes with a Hungarian background from the northern region of Transylvannia where there are a large number of Hungarians and Germans. Our Sport Minister was concerned with his own team, trying to find out if any of us had any idea or desire to stay in Australia. Initially I was the prime suspect, and they had every reason to believe that I wanted to remain so I was watched very carefully and interviewed by the officials particularly before my events. Fortunately for me they started to be more concerned about some members of the Romanian water-polo team, all of them being from Transylvania and of Hungarian background. This gave me a chance to talk more often to Norman and make some plans for the future. He told me that shortly there would be a chance his brother Jack would come down to Melbourne from Canberra and talk to me about my plans for future. Jack was to find out what I wanted to do, and then go back to Canberra and make the necessary arrangements.

I was still not totally sure I could go with my plans to defect, but with every day going by I knew that I would never have the same chance again. I would never be allowed to leave Romania, despite my good results in the pentathlon. It was now or never and although I didn't quite know how it would all end, I felt that the time for the big decision had come.

Almost as if by magic things developed and before I knew what had happened, everything started to fall into place.

I was in many ways satisfied that I had fulfilled my obligations to Modern Pentathlon, I did everything that had been asked of me and my coach's efforts had not been wasted. I had fulfilled the responsibility placed on my shoulders by my country, and I helped our young team place its name on the roll of honour.

Apart from that I had nothing to prove or do, I didn't owe anybody anything. The only problem remained my inability to leave my family and perhaps the knowledge that I wouldn't be able to keep my promise and look after my parents as intended.

But gradually there were less threads holding me back, and the thought of not returning to Romania became stronger and harder to resist. As it turned out the final decision was to be made as a result of a totally unexpected event, which normally would have passed without any consequence but in that sequence of events at that moment, was so powerful it erupted with the fury of a cyclone of hatred and anger.

LIGHT FOR A CHAMPION POLE-VAULTER

"We are finally free and we don't have to train . . . is it true 'Papa'? Dumitru said to Victor who was cleaning his riding gear.

"I've told you time and time again I am not your Papa" Victor said, feigning annoyance with the nickname we called him when we wanted to stir him up.

"I can do everything you can do and maybe a few more things you have never heard of Dimitru retorted. Victor finished his tirade, winking at me and Manciu who as usual were the powerless witnesses of the battle of wits which as usual ended in Victor's favour.

"What do you mean by that old man?" Dumitru said, getting slightly red in the face with embarrassment.

"You always start talking in "ghicitori" (riddles) when I get you in a corner."

Victor, who was a frustrated actor suddenly looked sad and spoke in a solemn, prophetic voice:

"The time will come my son when you will regret not listening and learning from someone as wise as me; your chances to become a real man of the world are coming to an end and I have done a lot for you, but you are not making much progress. In fact you are a disappointment to me because I always looked at you as the dear son I never had."

Victor had gradually moved closer to Dumitru, moving his arms eloquently, mesmerizing the young fool who was watching Victor with the awe of a mouse being stalked by a boa constrictor. Suddenly, Victor lunged at Dumitru and embraced him, pretending great affection and empathy and playfully pretending to plant a kiss on his cheek.

"Get out of it, leave me alone you old perve," Dimitru said, fighting like a young colt trying to slip the noose from his neck. Then, when he had finally regained his freedom he called out again to Victor with an attempt at sarcasm.

"Why don't you leave me alone and go and kiss your future "princess", your Elena, or are you not so sure that she still loves you?"

I had to intervene before another battle was ready to erupt. Victor had met and fallen in love with Elena who was years younger than him, but she succumbed to Victor's suave charm for which he was renowned. We were a little envious of his last conquest as Elena was the best gymnast in the country, and had a body worthy of being sculpted by Michelangelo. They decided to get married in the Olympic Village after they had both finished competing.

"Listen you lot, why don't you stop fighting and do something useful" I said, getting off the bed and starting to put my clothes on.

"What else is there to do? "Viorel said with a yawn and a stretch. "Most of the athletic events are over and we even missed seeing Vladimir Kouts run."

Time had gone so quickly and over those last few days I hardly had a chance to see Sandra who had also been very busy competing. In fact I had very little chance to do or see anything else apart from Modern Pentathlon. If I had followed the strict instructions of our beloved leaders I would have missed most of the events. I risked being admonished by our leaders by venturing quite often into the city using the public transport, as our transport officer, made it very clear to us all that we hadn't been brought there for entertainment and he was most unwilling to take us anywhere. I was really getting fed up with the pig of a man so I decided to get permission from Muresanu and go into town to the Main Stadium to watch some athletics. It was Friday, November 30th, and on the program between other events was the last day of the Decathlon, the greatest athletic event; I managed to convince Muresanu that this was my last chance to have a look at the great athletes and in particular I wanted to see my American pole-vaulter friend, Reverend Richards who had already won the pole-vault event with a new Olympic record of 4.56 m. This was his second gold medal as he was the 1952 Olympic Champion in pole vaulting.

Muresanu decided to let me go on the condition that I took Viorel Manciu with me, who he trusted as my personal guardian and calming influence.

By the time we got to the Olympic Stadium the competition was in full swing and we saw some wonderful displays of dazzling skills and performance in events from relay running to the 110 m. hurdles and the women's shot-put final with the great Russian thrower, Galina Zybina who fought valiantly against her compatriot, Tamara Tychkevitch, who won by a mere 6 cm. with a new Olympic record of 16.59 m. It was feast of to be enjoyed by Roman Emperors, a great arena filled with people watching the greatest athletes of the world, witnessing performances which almost without fail ended in new world or Olympic records.

Time went very quickly and I was so engrossed with the magnificent spectacle that I hardly noticed the night approaching. I was waiting for the final of the Decathlon pole-vault event, where my friend Rev. Richards was fighting a tong battle against the eventual second place getter of the Decathlon, Rafer Johnston, and the Russian champion, Vladimir Kouznetsov. By now many of the spectators had left the stadium after a long day of competition and Viorel wanted to go home as well, but I was determined.

"I am not going back until I see who is going to win the pole-vault, even if we have to get back late."

It was getting quite dark and there was no provision for lights in the stadium. I could see Rev. Richards getting ready for his jump in the dim light. He had already won the individual event in pole-vaulting with a new Olympic record, but today it was a different event, a long and arduous test of strength and endurance. I could feel he was trying to draw deep and find the last ounce of energy, but more than anything he wanted to really beat the other decathlletes and maintain his high standard as the best vaulter in the world.

By now the bar had been raised to 4.45 metres, well above the height jumped by his rivals, and Bob Richards was on his own. This had been a long day for all of the decathletes and it was almost impossible to imagine someone who had competed all day, still being able to challenge the thin bar swaying gently up in the semi-darkness. It was magnificently brave and moving, to see this exhausted man not giving up, although he had already won this difficult event. He was determined to have one more jump and get over the bar.

I felt I had to do something to help him, something that would give him the necessary impetus to complete the event. Those were the days when athletes did not look to the crowd and ask them all to start clapping to encourage them in their attempt; The athlete in those days would have been regarded as a real wimp if he had asked for this kind of obvious approbation. But I acted on impulse, I suddenly decided to give him light, to brighten up the evening, to cheer him up. I picked up my program and lit it, I lifted it up and started to wave it backwards and forwards. After a short hesitation Viorel lit his program and start waving it above his head. To our delight, within the next few minutes there were hundreds of burning program flickering all over the stadium, people shouting with delight, applauding, totally caught up in a celebration of joy and freedom. It was a soaring display of exaltation, of unbridled freedom of expression, which was most uplifting.

Strangely enough, not one of the security people tried to stop us, considering the possible threat of fire. Bob Richards looked up to the stands and nodded his head in acknowledgement of this unexpected gift of support, and started pounding down the track, holding the long pole like a cavalier ready to joust, then he swiftly placed the end of the pole in the hole, and his body became airborne, raising like a bird higher and higher until he was just visible over the bar. When he came down and landed on the heavy mat, we all stood up and applauded this great effort, a magnificent display of courage and human determination. He raised his hands in a triumphant gesture and thanked the crowd.

The final effort must have taken too much out of my friend Richards, because he did not take part in the final event of the Decathlon, the 1500 m run. But his efforts in the pole vault event, the delighted spectators and the warm Melbourne night lit by the burning program, more than made his day, and I felt that all of us present in the arena would always remember the indescribable emotions and feelings which embraced us all.

I was rather pleased not to be questioned by Muresanu as to why Viorel and I were so late coming back from town the night before. Fortunately for us Muresanu had other duties to perform. He had been asked to act as host to the numerous Romanian visitors coming to the village, asking questions about relatives left back in Romania. It was the great desire of our Communist leaders to appear as great benefactors and friends to the many expatriates. The big table in the main office of our delegation was often covered with gifts and Romanian souvenirs but in particular there were large carafes of plum whisky, greatly appreciated by most Romanians. What was so annoying for the athletes was the hypocritical attitude of our "leaders" who back home would not even talk to ordinary people, yet here in Australia they tried to show great affection and hospitality to those who had escaped from the Communist regime. But at least we were finally left alone, and even our regular spies were not around. There were no training sessions left, although from sheer habit some of us kept doing the regular morning run. There was less talk about us Romanians and more speculation about our neighbours, the Hungarians, who did not have any desire to return to their home.

BLOOD IN THE POOL AND BURNING MY BRIDGES

When 200,000 Russian troops invaded Budapest to put down one of the major revolts against the Communist regime which had been started by the Hungarian students, it created a great popular reaction against the Russians not only in Hungary but extending also to the rest of the free world. The Hungarian team competing in Melbourne had the opportunity to tell the world about the brutal reprisals used by the Russian troops against their compatriots. During the Games the Hungarian competitors made no secret of their dislike and desire to punish the Russian competitors whom they encountered in competition.

In all fairness, these Russian athletes were not guilty of the events taking place in Hungary; they were in Melbourne for the Games, and had no part of the action taken by the Soviet leaders against the Hungarian students. However by association they were the recipient not only of the fury of the Hungarian competitors but in many ways they were treated differently by the Australian public who regarded the Russian athletes as direct representatives of the Russian regime. This was of course not true, as we Romanian competitors knew from our own experience how little influence ordinary people had over decisions made by the political leaders. Nevertheless these poor Russian athletes were where they could be seen and identified as "aggressors", as "commies" and emotions ran high, particularly when competition brought Russians and Hungarians face to face in direct sporting combat. It was more than a sporting encounter, it was an obvious battle, a desire to hurt the other opponent. Direct contact was possible in a number of sports such as boxing and wrestling, where the referees in charge of the contest had to try very hard not to let the encounter become a bloody fight. Water-polo was introduced to the Olympic Games in 1900 in Paris and after that became one of the sports which was contested in all the subsequent Games. An extremely strenuous game, water-polo involves short swimming sprints and numerous personal contests often penalized by the game umpire.

A lot of the rough stuff takes place under the water so the referee cannot see it and send the responsible player out of the water, but in general, apart from some bruises and the occasional black eye, games are usually completed without any serious complications.

On Thursday, December 6th, the match was scheduled which would bring the Hungarians and the Russians teams face to face in direct combat, and although it wasn't the final game to decide the winner of the gold medal, it was charged with much emotion. This was going to be a blood bath, a vicious body contest, and we all expected to see the Hungarians demolish the Russian team. There was no doubt it was going to be a form of payback, a demonstration of hatred and revenge by an oppressed country against the Communist yoke.

Although we Romanians were not involved directly in this final combat as our team had finished in 8th place, we nevertheless anticipated seeing the Russians being administered some rough treatment by the Hungarians who had their country ruthlessly invaded by the Russian troops. Perhaps now, after the many years that have passed by, I feel how wrong we were, how unfair and unsporting our attitude was, punishing those who perhaps had the least to do with what was happening back home. But in those moments we all hated the Russian more than anybody else, and any form of revenge even if it wasn't fair, was the sweetest thing. We wanted to see anything which had the slightest connection to the Russians being punished, experiencing some of the daily indignities and deprivations which our countries were subjected to for years.

Just after our lunch, we approached our transport official and asked if he could take us to the Olympic Pool in the city to see the water-polo match. We told him that we had finished our chores for the day and that Muresanu had given us permission to go into town for this match. The Romanian team had been given access to a small Volkswaggen. minibus, which was available mostly to our officials and was permanently parked outside the Romanian Headquarters.

This official, as the second in charge with most organization decisions, had the final say and usually decided who could go in the minibus.

It was a pleasant afternoon when our little group of four, Viorel, Victor, Dumitru and I approached the driver and the official, who were near the minibus, and I asked if it would be alright for the four of us to be taken to the Olympic Pool to see the water-polo match.

This unpleasant person, as usual, he was very full of himself, and very abrupt.A man who gained his high position in the sport hierarchy only because he was a communist and related to some high officials. He believed that he was the only one who knew anything about sport, and had very little time to waste on the ordinary competitors.

He was the new breed of leader in Romania, a member of the Communist Party who had served some time in prison as a political objector.

Our conversation went something like this:

"Excuse me tovarase N.Y., would it be possible to take us to the Olympic Pool to see the water-polo match between Hungary and Russia?"

He gave us a short look and then morosely said:

"I don't have enough room in the bus to take you".

I asked him again, saying that there was nobody else in the bus except the driver and that we didn't mind if we were a little short for space.

"We have finished our competition and we haven't seen very much of the Olympics; This would be something we would very much like to see" I said, trying to sound as friendly and polite as possible. Suddenly he stopped pretending to be busy with the bus, turned round so he was facing us fully and started to talk to us in an annoyed voice:

"I've told you before, I haven't got the room but even if I would have enough room in the bus, I wouldn't take you into the city."

He paused for a second and then he started talking again, but this time his voice was full of sarcasm and hatred:

"Just because you've been in the Games, just because you've finished your competition you think that you can do whatever you like, go anywhere, do anything you want, say anything you want . . . Who do you think you are telling me what to do, giving orders like you own the place? Go back to your training, do some work and maybe next time you will do a better swim."

We just stood there frozen, unable to say anything in answer to this verbal barrage, unable to comprehend why he was so annoyed and had reacted so violently. Up until then I had little to do with this character. I somehow felt that he was a very dangerous man, and we had all heard about his occasional fits of uncontrolled temper, when he would literally attack the person he was talking to, if he was in that kind of mood. I felt so dejected and humiliated by this pig of a man who treated us so unfairly, embarrassing all of us for such a small request. He was there representing all the injustice and oppression suffered by all our compatriots for so long, the brutal force used by our Communist enforcers, the lack of freedom, the absolute control that they had over people's lives back home. My heart cried for my father who had been humiliated and imprisoned, for the millions of innocent victims imprisoned, tortured and murdered in the black dungeons of Communist Romania.

I had had enough, I could not continue to be logical, to carefully avoid a confrontation. I needed to tell this bully what I really thought of him and of his Communism. I heard myself starting to talk, at first in a controlled voice and then more passionately, more forcefully, until I was shouting at the top of my voice:

"Who the hell do you think you are, what makes you so great to tell us what we should have done, when you've never done anything outstanding in sport apart from being a communist. You are nothing more than a parasite sucking on our blood, spying on us, cheating and spreading rumours."

I stopped for a second to get my breath whilst a small crowd of Romanian competitors started to gather and listen to our argument. I was really warming up by now so I continued telling him about how much I hated him and the Communist regime:

"You are here only because of us the competitors, you've done nothing to deserve this trip except that you are so good at licking the bosses boots, a real communist crawler, more than that you are a traitor to you country. You and all your Communist mates are nothing but a bunch of low despicable individuals who do not care about Romania, or about its people. You should be ashamed to call yourself Romanian, you are not a leader, you are just a miserable individual without any honour or morals."

Around me I could see faces showing total disbelief, amazed at what I dared say to this high official who back in Romania had the power of life and death over any one of us

"Go on, take your miserable bus and go and watch your Russian friends being beaten, go and do what you do best, kiss their ass, at least you are good at that . . ."

There was a long silence. Nobody moved or said anything and tovarasul N.Y. just stood there in front of me, looking for a moment like a beaten dog with his tail between his legs. I could feel the approval of all those present, their silent pleasure at being finally vindicated, able to hear what every man and woman back home would have loved to say to the Communist leaders. Then N.Y started to talk again but this time in a much quieter voice, yet full of hatred and threat:

"Listen to me Vena, as long as I live, as long as I am involved in the running of the Department of Sport and recreation, I will make sure that you will never get a job as a school teacher, or club coach or member of a National Team. You are finished with sport, you will never get another job, you may as well become a street cleaner. I will make sure that this will go on your record and be reported to the proper authorities and you . . .

By then I had turned my back on N.Y. and told my team to go and watch the match in the main hall.

"Come on boys, let's go and watch the match on TV in the main hall. There's nothing here for us. I knew then that there was no going back to Romania, I had finally" burnt my bridges".

It is 1999 and I am writing these lines early, in the cool of the morning, with the music of Tchaikovsky in the background, and just as I was writing the last few lines, as if by a higher order, the 1812 Overture, the last track on the C.D. accompanied my thoughts and made me weep with a incredible mixture of emotions, of the things long done and thought forgotten, yet everything coming fresh from my deepest corners of my memory, just as powerful as if it had happened only seconds ago. Some things we do because we have to or because we are told to, but the things we should be more aware of are never easy to see or sense; There is the invisible thread already spun by a much stronger hand, which we somehow have to follow, and despite our efforts cannot be avoided. How many of us have real control over our lives, how many of us foolishly believe that what we do is entirely our decision, that we are controlling our destiny, when in reality we are no more than spectators, onlookers, who have very little to do with the final outcome of this great board of human chess, played against the best universal mind.

We can only hope that we are helped and loved by this immense power, and that we will be finally helped to do what we have dreamed of, what we have hoped for.

Following my encounter with N.Y I was called to the main office the next day and told by a very stern looking Minister that I was under suspicion of attempting to defect from the team and that I would be kept under strict watch by our security until further orders. Muresanu was also reprimanded and asked to take better care of our team, as there would be an inquiry when we got back to Romania. I was then asked point-blank by the Minister if I intended staying in Australia. I had to lie and tell them all that I had no such intention, and that my outburst was caused by personal differences between Barany and myself. This statement, although hard to believe, made our leaders a little more comfortable as they all feared a mass exodus of our team, similar to the one which was expected to take place with the Hungarian team. They were told by their leaders that after the Games, due to the situation in Budapest, they would be allowed to decide what to do, to take political asylum in the free world or return home to the Communist yoke. But not our leaders. They continued to preach about the glory of the communist regime and the paradise we were likely to live in . . .

VICTOR IS GETTING MARRIED

Things had gone much better since I had my argument with N.Y and although there was little or no chance of making peace with our leaders, at least I wasn't torn any more between defecting and abandoning my family and staying in Australia. I was extremely fortunate to have the friendship and support of Norman who faithfully and without any question continued to help us all. I told him that I would stay and apply for political asylum in Australia, and that I would like to speak to his brother and arrange for the actual day when I was to leave the village and go into hiding until the Romanian Olympic team had left Australia and returned to Romania.

The opportunity to finalize all these details came sooner than expected. Victor and Elena decided to get married in the village chapel without too much fuss or expense. Norman offered his help, and invited us all to his place after the wedding. He told me also that his brother Jack would arrive on the day and be present at the party. He would be able to speak to me in French and help clarify the fine details involving my departure from the village.

Victor and Elena had become friends and then lovers during the last few months of our stay in Bucharest, getting ready for the Games. It had been a quick and passionate affair, which surprised us all, in particular as there was quite a difference in age ;

But Victor did not look any older than the rest of us and also had in his favour a great sense of humour and maturity; He had been married before but the marriage hadn't worked out and they separated.

Elena was one of the new generation of gymnasts trained by Russian methods, and she had started to show real promise in international competition. She and her team competed with great success in Melbourne and finished 6th in the team event. Elena outclassed her opposition and won a Bronze Medal in the Free Standing Exercise, as well as placing herself in the first 6 places in all of the required events of the Individual Gymnastic Competition. A very talented and pretty girl, she was much admired by all the male members of the Romanian Team who were perhaps a little jealous of "papa's" luck.

The wedding was a success, so different from the usual wedding, being held in the village and attracting many of the athletes who only days ago were in the news and on television. After the wedding we met at Norman's place where we were greeted by his family and other friends. It was more like being home between our own family, surrounded by a lot of love and affection; It was hard to believe that these were people who only a few weeks ago didn't know us, and yet in that short period of time we had become good friends, more like a reunited family. Our dear Norman was at his best, enjoying being the host, introducing us all to his friends, openly praising our results in the Games, recounting events and situations when something funny or different had taken place;

There was no happier person in the room, more like a proud father taking great delight in the achievements of his children. He had been such a good friend that we were greatly affected by his treatment, and forged a life long relationship.

WOULD RATHER DIE THAN GO BACK

It's hard to understand what desperation and hatred can do to a person's attitude, how different one acts and behaves under the negative pressure of living a life devoid of freedom, forced to pretend and lie, to witness injustice, but in particular to have no hope for a better future. This was the most damaging factor which characterized our new Communist regime in Romania, the knowledge that nothing would change in the future, that we were going to remain the "modern slaves", people without any hope for a free life, or any chance to improve our living conditions. With me, it had been like a sickness. This lack of freedom gradually started to suffocate me. I wasn't capable of thinking logically anymore, becoming more and more hateful of a situation which could not be changed, to the point where I turned my fury and dejection inwards, and started to hate myself.

I understand now how one can become suicidal and how under certain conditions life doesn't seem to be worth living . . . Perhaps it sounds now a little melodramatic but in that situation I wasn't myself, I could not control my emotions any longer and the thought of going back to Romania made me decide to end it all rather than go through the whole miserable experience again.

Fortunately for me there was Norman who understood what I was going through, and made sure that he left no stone unturned to facilitate my escape.

I was told that Norman's brother Jack, a doctor, who was instrumental in introducing the compulsory T.B. check in Australia, because of the large number of refugees who were sick at the time of their arrival in Australia, will come to Melbourne.

I could then speak to him in French, as he apparently spoke it fluently.

Jack spoke good French and we had a good talk about what was going on; To avoid the spying eye of Muresanu and few other officials who were invited by Norman to the wedding party in order to get the permission for us to attend, Norman led us to a quiet room at the back of the house, where I was able to tell Jack of my intentions to leave the team and ask for permission to stay in Australia, until I decided what I was to do next. Jack said he had already spoken to few officials in Canberra, and that I would have no problem obtaining a temporary visa until I decided what I was going to do.

"The only thing we have to be very careful of is not to let the Romanian officials realize what you intend to do, because as long as you are in the Romanian quarters in the Village, they can place you under house arrest and that will be it. You will be under their control and we could not get in touch with you."

We talked for a while, trying to find out a method but for the time being none of us could come up with a solution. In the meantime Jack would go back to Canberra and make an immediate application on my behalf to get a temporary visa. He would then contact Norman to let me know what was happening. In the meantime I was to keep a low profile, pretend that I was sorry about happened, and generally look eager to get back home where the press was already hailing me as the new Pentathlon wonder.

We returned to the party where we were greeted by a lot of happy smiling faces, as Norman and his family made sure that the officials were never without a full glass of whiskey in their hand. I joined in and in no time we managed to have everybody dancing a traditional Romanian "hora"(peasant dance), and for the time being I forgot all my worries and enjoyed being with my friends.

NOT READY FOR THE STATES

By now most of the athletes had finished competing, and there were more people in the Village wanting to relax, to finally enjoy their time there without the pressures of competition and training. I was spending more time around the quarters of the American team, which had a large room where people could come and enjoy each other's company; I was welcomed by the Yanks, who were aware of my relationship with L.A.

The manager of the American Modern Pentathlon Team, had found out from her about my plan to defect from the Romanian team and he made a very tempting offer:

"Look Cornel, we would love to have you in the States. You could be our Fencing Master and help us to improve our standard in fencing."

I asked him how would I get to the States as I had no money for travel.

"Don't even think about it. We've got plenty of room in our plane to take you with us, as many of our athletes and officials are going to compete in Europe after the Games and will go from here directly to Europe."

The offer was very tempting and I would have loved to be in charge of the Modern Pentathlon Fencing program for the U.S. team, which had the best facilities in the world at their camp in Port Houston, Texas.

"Thank you, l think about. I tell you." Not wanting to commit myself as yet, particularly as I had become very fond of Australia and its people. I suppose it was only natural to become attached to the people I'd met in Melbourne, but most of all I didn't think I could ever meet another person like "uncle Norman". He, Hilda and Ted had become my new family and I didn't want to lose them.

L.A. and I were getting closer with every minute and our relationship developed to the point where she told me she would like to stay with me after the games had finished in Melbourne. Things were moving a little too fast for me, and I tried to explain to her that it would take another year before I could speak enough English to get back into coaching or school teaching, and that until then I could not support the two of us. She said it was nothing to worry about as she would take a job and provide for the two of us until I was ready to start working again.

In the meantime, although I had been very careful not to raise any more suspicions, I was still under constant surveillance enforced by our minister who wanted to make sure that none of us would defect and stay in Australia. Then, like so many other times in my life, fate decided otherwise, and the events that followed a few days after the finals of the water polo competition changed the situation and once again I was cleared of any wrongdoing. Muresanu called in to my room in the morning and told me to get ready quickly to see the minister.

"What's happening, what am I accused of now?" I said morosely. "I thought they'd got off my back."

But despite my bravado my heart sunk with anxiety, and I was imagining being put under strict house arrest until our departure. Muresanu tried to calm me down.

"No, no for once I don't think it's you except that all the top people are in the conference room waiting for us, so please hurry up and get ready".

I entered the familiar room with its long conference table, with some 10 or 12 people sitting round it. We were asked us to sit down and by the tone of his voice I said to myself that I was already sentenced and next I would be told of my punishment;

"First of all," the minister commenced after clearing his throat. " . . . first of all I would like to extend my apologies for doubting you, and putting you under a lot of pressure. You have performed well and have proved yourself as a future sport leader.

Being without any fault I congratulate you "tovarase" and hope that you will forgive any distrust on our part." He stopped for a minute, looked around as if trying to check the effect of his words. I was totally flabbergasted, not believing what I was hearing. Surely he hadn't changed that much, or perhaps he was setting up a final trap for me, to stop me from wanting to defect.

"To be more exact," he continued, "we were chasing the wrong man when the real traitor or traitors were preparing their filthy escape without any interference from us."

He stopped and once again gave a filthy look to the others sitting at the table, and then he continued:

"We have been here too long and we have become soft and swollen by the evil temptations of the capitalist society, we have forgotten that the enemies of our beloved Communist Party never go to sleep."

In the typical fashion used by the political leaders in Romania, he spoke at length but in actual fact said nothing of substance, nothing to explain why I was called for this special meeting. Just as I was slipping into my usual state of semi-attention, hearing but not registering the usual litany of garbage, he finally told us the only real reason we had been called to his office:

Apparently the night before four members of the Romanian water polo team had left the Olympic Village for a trip into town, and they had not returned.

They had simply disappeared and there was nothing the minister or his secret police could do to trace them. He was furious with his subalterns for not detecting their intentions earlier, for concentrating on my possible departure, and allowing the others to leave without any problem. All of a sudden I was cleared of any wrongdoing and allowed to spend the rest of my stay without any supervision.

(Wouldn't they be supervising everybody after these defections?)

His voice brought me back:

"So once again "Tovarase" Vena I hope that you will enjoy the next few days in Melbourne, and you will forgive the clumsiness of some of our people; I am going to deal with them when we get back home."

Muresanu and I thanked the Minister and quickly left the room, trying to hide our amusement at seeing the worried faces of some of our guards:

"How did you manage that" asked Muresanu whilst walking in his usual fast gait. "I thought they were going to strangle you and put an end to the Modern pentathlon in Romania. I can't believe this is happening, these four boys going away now, particularly when they have done so well here in the Olympic Tournament." He shook his head and then added with a sigh of relief:

"At least you are in the clear now and you don't have to worry anymore". I looked at him, still not able to believe that I had been completely exonerated.

I could not believe Muresanu. As soon as we will land back in Bucharest, the Communist leaders would make my life even more miserable.

ESCAPE PLAN AND TORQUAY BEACH

By then I could only be grateful for the stay of execution, and I was able to prepare my escape without attracting attention. Norman was informed by his brother, Jack, that my application to the Australian government had been approved and that I would be given a 6 month temporary visa to allow me to have a good look around and decide if I wanted permanent residency in Australia.

Alternately, if I wanted to take the fencing coaching position with the U.S. Pentathlon team, I had been told by their Head Coach that I could contact them at any time, and they would arrange for my free air travel to the States. Norman thought that it would be safer if I had some form of documentation, a written statement, which could be used in case I had to leave the village sooner.

I could walk up to the first policeman I saw in the village, hand him the note and asked to be taken to the police station. The note had the following message:

"My name is Cornel Vena, I am a Romanian Olympic competitor and I would like to ask for POLITICAL ASYLUM."

I carried the note with me everywhere just in case I needed it, but as events continue to develop, it was never used.

Aurel Onu was a Romanian immigrant who came to Australia after the WWII and settled in Melbourne together with another Romanians who had spent the last months of the war in various migrant camps in Europe, waiting for the chance to return back home to Romania or migrate to permanently to Canada, the US or to Australia. He fitted very well the type of Romanian who had left his country and quickly tried to assimilate with his new environment, showing excessive knowledge of the customs and habits of the locals, speaking very poor and broken English mixed with a variety of other languages, pretending not to have any financial problems and in general exuding an air of success and confidence. He managed to gain our confidence mainly because of his almost constant presence and his ability to guess with an uncanny ability the smallest wish any one of us had, and attend to it.

His charm and apparent selfless friendliness gained Muresanu's and other official's confidence, and he was gradually allowed to take us into the city for shopping, or to Romanian houses where we were treated to the old traditional Romanian hospitality. After a while he became the indispensable "fait a tout" man in our camp, more like a permanent official who was extremely helpful particularly as he could interpret our language and translate our wishes to the Australians.

In time I started to trust him as well, even if he still looked to me like one of those Las Vegas gamblers. It was actually his partner, Noel, a lovely French woman, who gained my confidence through her kindness and honesty and I reasoned that he must have something to offer to attract this lovely woman. Norman, who I think smelled a rat but as usual never tried to tell me what to do, made some gentle remarks about "Where does Aurel comes from"? or "What actually does he do for living"? We could never extract an answer from Aurel, who spoke about many things but never about what he did in Romania or how he managed to come to Australia. Probably under normal circumstances, I would have had very little trust in him, but these were different trying times, and he must have sensed my inner turmoil and my hatred for the Communists.

Eventually I told Aurel of my intentions and about the suggestion to simply walk to a policeman in the village and ask for political asylum. Aurel jumped to his feet and started to pace furiously in my room where we were talking, showing signs of intense annoyance and disbelief:

"Ce esti nebun mai baiatule, unde crezi ca te gasesti, astia aicea nu stiu nimica despre Communisti, nu o sa te inteleaga. Nu se poate, te rog sa nu faci asa."

(You must be crazy my boy, where do you think you are, these people out here know nothing about the Communists, they won't understand. This is not possible I beg you not to do it.") I tried to explain to him about Norman's letter and his brother's assurance of being protected by the Australian police from the moment I declared my intentions.

"I thought you were an intelligent, well-educated person, but I can see you have no idea about this situation and you are going head first into being returned to Romania and put in prison. We have to talk about this and make a workable plan, or all your friends will have no way to help you."

As I was listening to his outburst of criticism I started to think that maybe he was right as he had experienced the treachery of our Romanian leaders and understood better than me how the Australian authorities worked. I finally agreed to listen to his plan which involved Jack's help in getting my temporary visa, Norman's acceptance by the Romanian officials, and Aurel's contacts and local knowledge. Basically, he suggested that I avoided causing any suspicion and continued to act and do things just like I have done in the past:

"Pretend that you are happy with your results and that you are looking forward to going back to Romania where you have the certainty of a good job as Head Coach of the Army Club." I wasn't convinced that our leaders were that gullible, in particular N.Y, whom I felt was deeply embarrassed by my public insult and would not forget his promise.

Aurel laughed: "You see, it just shows you how little you know about these people. They are not what you think they are, they are greedy and gullible, they will believe anything you tell them as long as you pretend and tell them what great political minds they have. They have believed me already and offered me a good job if I want to go back to Romania. They've even offered a seat in the plane, now that the "traitors" from the water polo Team have left. Can you believe that?."

Indeed it was hard to believe what he was telling me, but the evidence of his success with our leaders, the fact that he was allowed to roam freely around our compound without any supervision, was a clear indication of his acceptance. I decided to listen to what he had to offer and then I would talk to Norman and see what he thought about the alternative plan.

Norman had intended for a long time to take my gymnast friend and I away from Melbourne and show us the rugged beauty of the Victorian coast. There was plenty of free time by then and he easily got Muresanu's permission to take us on a tour of Geelong and further towards Torquay for the day. We started early in the morning when Norman arrived at our quarters with his usual punctuality in his gleaming, freshly washed Jaguar. He had a female friend with him who he introduced as his old and dear friend Helen, who said she had been looking forward to meeting me for some time. We picked up my friend who was waiting for us outside the main gate of the female quarters and after we made ourselves comfortable, we set out on our trip.

It was a lovely sunny day, and we quickly left Melbourne behind and took the road to Geelong where we stopped and filled the tank with petrol. Norman and his inseparable smouldering short pipe was enjoying his drive; He finally had a chance to talk with me without any interruptions and find out what had been happening.

"I am not sure what you want to do Cornel, have you decided yet when you think you going to leave the village, has Aurel come up with another idea?" Norman did not approve of Aurel and his friends but he tolerated them, knowing that they may be able to help. No, I didn't have any idea of when exactly I was going to leave the village, but I would like to attend the Closing Ceremony on the 8th of December 1956 and then make my move. Although I had worked very hard, my English was still very poor and every sentence we exchanged often had to be interpreted ; Norman was quite good at understanding me and often he would instinctively repeat my utterance in a meaningful sentence. I would then sigh with relief and indicate to him that he was right.

The road along the coast was getting very rugged and the scenery of the open ocean and the steep cliffs was a real delight, and after more driving we finally stopped in Anglesea, deciding that it may be better to shorten the trip and have our picnic lunch on the beach. We were having a great time, and after lunch we walked along the beach. My girl had taken her shoes off and was enjoying the sand and the Australian sun. I asked her if she could still do some of her gymnastic stunts, particularly as I never had the chance to see her competing. She decided to give us all a short demonstration of part of her free routine for the floor exercise, and after picking a smooth and firm part of the beach she went through some beautiful strong movements, finishing with a series of perfectly executed flick-flaks. For a second she maintained perfect balance before she broke into laughter and said something about being slightly out of form. We applauded her grace and agility, her ability to do those difficult movements despite the fact that she had a full length uniform and she had just had lunch. The afternoon went very quickly and before long we had to get back to Melbourne.

I told Norman about Aurel's intentions to help and that he had offered to help in any way if we wanted him to do so. Norman agreed that he would get in touch with Aurel and make a final plan for my escape and that I should follow his advice and not attract any attention from N.Y and friends.

As planned, Norman had a talk to Aurel who suggested that it wasn't safe to stay in Melbourne after my departure from the Village, and that he could take me out into the country to someone he knew. I was to remain there until the departure of our team. Finally Norman told me the plan which would guarantee more safety, and would make it impossible for any of the Secret Romanian Agents to stop or to harm me. This was the plan:

After the Closing Ceremony, Norman would organize a big party at his home for the Romanian Pentathlon team as well as inviting few officials to make it more acceptable. During the evening Muresanu and the officials would be encouraged to drink plenty of whisky so that they would not suspect anything out of ordinary. Aurel would also be invited to the party, and late in the evening he and I would quietly slip out of the room, get in his car and drive away. This was a good plan and I had to agree that this was much better than the initial plan which had some faults particularly as the Romanian officials could claim that I had been taken away from the Village against my wishes and that I should be released. Once I was out of Melbourne, nobody would know where to find me, and I would return to Melbourne after the Team's departure on the 12th of December.

CLOSING CEREMONY AND MY FRIEND'S SECRET

The closing ceremony was a beautiful yet sad event which brought us all back to the reality of ordinary life, and we all felt as though we had lost something which we may never experience again.

The Main Stadium was once again filled to capacity by a large crowd, and we the competitors and officials once again marched on the red cinder track and lined up in the middle of the green oval.

Like everything else in life, it was hard to believe that the events of the last couple of weeks had been real, had actually taken place, yet we all had experienced the greatest gamut of human emotions, we had accumulated unforgettable memories which would be with us for the rest of our lives. To know that we had achieved our dream, that we had for a short time touched immortality, was something which would stay with most of us for the rest of our lives, something we knew that nobody could ever deny or take away from us.

The assembled choir sang the tune of Waltzing Matilda, which has become something of an Australian National Anthem, and rendered as a song of farewell:

Homeward, homeward, soon you will be going now;
Momok wonargo ora go-yai,*
Joy of our meeting, pain of our parting,
Shine in our eyes as we bid you good-bye.

Good-bye Olympians; good-bye, Olympians,
Roll up your swags and pack them full of memories,
Fair be the wind as you speed on your way.

* Aboriginal words meaning "Farewell, brother. Bye and bye come back."

There was a lot of gaiety between the various competitors but one could sense the impending finale of this great event, and deep down we all had that sense of despair being close to seeing the beautiful Olympic Flag lowered and the bright Olympic Flame being extinguished. It was hard to accept that even the Olympics were subject to the merciless sickle of time, and would make way for the new venue, for the next Olympic Games in Rome, in 1960. I was feeling the impact of the coming events, not knowing what the future will hold for me, at the point of a dramatic change in the course of my life. I was going to lose all that I had been used to, my family, my career, my friends, and start a new life. Averidge Brundage, the President of the Olympic Committee, stood up on the dais and proclaimed with a sombre voice the closing of the Games:

"I declare the 1956 Olympic Games closed and in accordance with the tradition I call upon the youth of all countries to assemble four years from now at Rome, there to celebrate with us the Games of the XVII Olympiad. May they display cheerfulness and concord so that the Olympic torch will be carried on with ever greater eagerness, courage and honour for the good of humanity throughout the ages."

The Retreat was played by the trumpeters of the Royal Australian Air Force, and I felt tears running down my cheeks; It was all so sad yet so beautiful that my heart was overflowing with incredible emotions and it was very hard not to feel moved. Around me there was a similar reaction and I could see that many others were greatly affected. When the flame was extinguished and the last flickers tried to rise once more from the huge metal bowl, we all felt the temperature in the stadium drop, and a huge sigh was heard from the crowd. It took a few seconds before we all got shaken out of the morbid feeling by the bright, joyful playing of the brass band. We were once again marching out of the stadium, without any order or attempt to stay with our teams; We were suddenly one group, one nation, with no distinction between countries, marching as one team, as proud representatives of the human race. It was then that it become very clear to me how little we all understood the meaning of the words said by the father of the Modern Olympic Games, Baron Pierre de Coubertin of France, who was instrumental in restarting the Modern Olympic Games in 1986:

"The most important thing in life is not to win but the struggle"

Ultimately there is always a winner and a loser but one could not exist without the other or understand its own value. Yet being a winner is only momentary, as we are driven relentlessly by time and very quickly we have to experience a different situation, not being the best and not tasting success. This is then the lesson we all have to learn, to be able to accept that our perfection in any endeavour is only a matter of time and space, and that nothing remains unchanged and that life means a lot of effort and struggle and that the final price is only the knowing that we have tried our best, that our efforts have made us more aware of our worth.

Once the Games were over, the Village become a place where people had time to enjoy their new friends, to celebrate their victories or just being happy to be there and being for a short period of time the best in the world.

There were parties and celebrations and athletes were finally able to have a good time doing all the things they wanted to do, without having to control their desires and concentrate on their training.

I had become very close to my gymnast friend, and we both could not accept the fact that she would have to return to the States shortly and I would be staying in Australia. We talked about different possibilities but there was no easy way out of predicament. One evening we walked down to our favourite spot, a huge gum tree in the middle of a recreation area not far from the little creek meandering on the west side of the village, holding one another, talking about the future. She told me that if I stayed in Australia she would not go back to the States, and she would stay with me and perhaps look for a job and settle here.

"What about your family back home, what would they say"? I asked her.

She shook her shoulders and said that she much rather be here with me than going back home.

We walked for a while in silence then all of a sudden she started to cry. I didn't know what caused it, perhaps I had said something she misunderstood.

"Sorry did I say something wrong?"

"No it's me, I am annoyed with myself for not being honest with you".

I was trying to calm her down, but not sure of what cause her upset. She stopped and grabbed my hands then she told me what was upsetting her.

"I am not single, I am married and I have two beautiful children back home!"

The sudden confession caught me by surprise and I could not believe she was telling me the truth:

"I don't believe you, you're too young to have children."

She laughed and wiped her tears.

"You Europeans are so smooth, thank you for the compliment but it is true, everything I just told you is true; I am married but I don't love my husband, but I adore my children."

We talked for a while about her family life back home, about her children and gradually she started to relax and talked more freely about the things they used to do together, things she looked forward to. As I listened to her I could tell how much she was asking of herself, to sacrifice her young family for the sake of our relationship. I thought about my family and how they were going to be affected by my defection and then I asked myself if I had the right to encourage her to destroy her own young family, and all for the sake of a relationship which was formed under some very special conditions. No, I could not accept this additional sacrifice

"You must not leave your young children without a mother, you must go back to them. Even if you don't love your husband, you have your children to look after, *I don't want to destroy your family as well!*"

She tried to argue, to suggest that maybe after staying here for a while she could bring her children over, but I did not want to listen. I felt that I could not become involved in looking after a family when I didn't have a job or even speak the language. It had been a special relationship but we both had to go different ways and get on with our lives. Perhaps it would have been a different situation if she didn't have children, but I could not be responsible for more lives being affected by our decision. It was too selfish for me as it was to sacrifice my family but there was definitely no need to affect hers as well.

We parted promising to keep in touch and write, but it didn't last long. Eventually she asked me not to write anymore.

TAKE THIS TO MY MOTHER

Norman told Muresanu that he would like to have us all at his place for a farewell party and that he could invite some of the less obnoxious officials. It would be an opportunity to meet some of his family who were coming especially for the occasion from Sydney and Canberra. I had to get ready to leave the Village permanently and pack the few belongings which I had bought with my prize money.

The day selected for the afternoon party was Sunday, December 9th, when we were going to spend the evening at Norman's place. I started packing all my sporting gear issued by the Sport Ministry in Romania, down to my socks. I packed everything in the big suitcase, and then I wrote an inventory of all the items returned, and at the bottom I wrote:

> *"This is the complete inventory which I return;*
> *Please do not charge my family with the cost.*
> *I have returned also my epee, which won the*
> *fencing competition without any faults."*
> Goodbye, Cornel Vena.

It was getting close to the time to leave the village and I had to tell Victor, the only one I could trust, of my intentions. I called him from his room and in a quiet voice I told him what was going to happen that evening:

"I am sorry Victor, I didn't tell you earlier about my intentions, but I didn't want to place you under suspicion as well. I've decided not to go back home, and tonight, after the party, I will run away."

Victor's looked totally stunned, his mouth opened wide. He looked around to make sure that nobody could hear what he was going to say:

"Why didn't tell me about this before, I would have stayed with you; I don't want to go back to those bastards".

He was really excited and was getting red in the face with emotion.

"No; Victor you are now married to Elena and you both have a good future, something to go back to."

Victor was shaking his head in disbelief, not quite sure all this was happening. He had many questions to ask but I had to stop and remind him that there was little time left to change anything and that I told him of my plans because I trusted him, and that I wanted to ask of him a big favour.

"Anything Cornel, I will do anything you ask me to do, you can be sure I will do it for you." He looked very excited and his eyes were full of emotion, we both felt the immensity of this decision, a pause before the big jump into the unknown.

"Can you take the chance to give this letter to my mother and a small gift when you get back, and tell her that I am sorry, that I have no other way that I have to do this or my life in Romania would have no meaning. Tell her that I will try to get in touch with them and perhaps one day I will return to see them all."

I was very upset and was shaking with a mixture of emotions, but perhaps glad to be able to tell Victor what I had wanted to tell him for a long time, but I didn't want to involve him as well, and place him in danger. Victor was deeply moved by my confession and for once he was very serious when he started to talk to me:

"I'm sorry you going to stay here but I understand and I respect your decision; I only regret I cannot stay with you; I wanted for a long time to defect but I didn't have the courage . . . but don't worry, I will go to Turnu-Magurele and explain to your parents what happened, and I will make sure that they get your letter and present. You know that even if Muresanu decided to kick me out of the Team, I've already decided to give Pentathlon away, and will try to get a position as fencing coach with my old club in Bucharest."

I felt much better after his words, realizing that Victor would deliver my message to my parents and that he did not fear the possible repercussions; I was right to trust him, he showed courage and loyalty, and he was ready to take the risk of being branded an accomplice by the Sport authorities.

"Victor you are a true friend and I will always remember your help; I hope some day you and I will meet again under different circumstances, as free people."

We shook hands and embraced; I told him about packing all my belongings in the suitcase and to make sure that were all are returned to the Sport Committee.

There was nothing else to do as I had already said goodbye to my girl the day before, so I got ready for the party and changed into my secondhand blue suit bought from a shop in Melbourne together with my black shoes. I had kept nothing from the Communist Regime, everything I had was mine, including my beautiful Omega wrist watch.

When Norman arrived to pick us up, I took one last look at the small friendly little room which had become a second home to me. On the bed, the big black suitcase looked rather sombre and cold, except for my faithful epee which lay on top, surrounded by the glow of the afternoon sun. It was as if suddenly a sacrifice was to be performed and I was to witness it. I rushed out of the room into the fading light trying to hide my feelings and emotions from the others, and got into the back seat of the Jaguar. Without another word Norman drove out of the village and I saw for the last time the long line of colourful flags of the competing nations lining the entrance to the Village.

LAST PARTY

By the time we arrived at Norman's house, the party was already in full swing with many friends and visitors filling the house and spilling out onto the verandah. We were surrounded immediately by happy faces, people trying to shake hands with us, to congratulate us and tell us how marvellous it had been to have the Olympic Games in Melbourne. There was no question, these Melbournians were the friendliest people we had ever met and it was a great feeling to see that we were accepted and regarded more like members of the family than strangers. The traditional barbecue followed and everybody was drinking large amounts of beer. Muresanu and the other Romanian officials were the centre of a small group of "helpers", who filled their glasses with whisky and kept them occupied.

Norman managed to have a short talk to me and tell me that Aurel would whisk me away around midnight, and drive me out of Melbourne. He didn't tell me where exactly I was going to be taken except that I would be far enough from Melbourne to make it impossible for the Romanian officials to locate me and take me back to Romania.

After that I joined the party and tried to spend as much time with my team mates, talking and reminiscing about our efforts and the events that had taken place in the last two weeks and about plans for the future. Tintea was going to continue with pentathlon but he would take a break from it for at least three months, "If Muresanu lets me," he said and we all joined in laughter which attracted Muresanu who came over and joined our group. Our team was together, a happy and proud group who despite personal differences, had managed to achieve results well above Muresanu's expectations:

"You know," said Muresanu, who wasn't used to drinking and was getting quite drunk, "You know you bastards how much trouble you have caused me, but I have to admit now that you are not a bad bunch after all. No, I think you are actually pretty good. Let's have a drink together and celebrate our success."

We toasted and drank our glasses, my first for the night, and people were applauding and some were taking pictures of our happy group, looking very smart in the official uniforms with the only exception being myself.

"Why are dressed like this?" asked one of the officials who was having difficulty talking, "You are ashamed to be one of us?"

I knew that he was almost paralysed with alcohol but as is the case he had the intuition to sense something wasn't right, and I wasn't doing what I would have normally done. He was right, I wasn't one of them anymore, I had different aspirations and beliefs, and for a long time I had dreamt about this moment when I would regain my freedom and dignity as a human being, when I would cease to be a slave.

"I could explain it to you but it's a long story and let's face it, you are having a good time. For tonight let's enjoy ourselves and forget about rules and regulations.

' Hay sa bem pentru tara noastra scumpa Romania si pentru viitorul ei ca tara libera—" (Let's drink for our dear country, Romania and for it's future as a free country)"

My words must have struck an old chord and he stopped for a second and looked hard into my eyes, trying to understand the full meaning of my words, but the effort must have been too much because suddenly he gave up, lifted his glass high above his head and shouted in a drunken voice:

"Traiasca Romania tara noastra draga" (Long life to Romania, our dear country). Everyone in the room lifted their glasses and although I am sure most of them didn't understand what the toast was about, they drank their glasses.

By now it was almost midnight, and as arranged Aurel told me that was time to go and that I was to meet him outside the house near his big black car. I shook Victor's hand and left the room followed by Norman:

"Don't worry Cornel, you will be safe and they won't know where you are. When your team leaves Melbourne on the 12th of December, I will personally come over and bring you back to Melbourne. Everything is OK and you will have no problems staying here in Australia.

See you soon."

Norman shook my hand vigorously and gave me an encouraging slap on the back.

"Come on, come on" said Aurel who was getting a little impatient, "We've got to get going or they may wake up to what's going on. Let's go."

The huge car lurched into the dark and sped through the familiar streets of Norman's neighbourhood. This was it; it was actually happening just as we had planned it to the last detail. I was finally free and I didn't have to fear being stopped and placed on house arrest by the Romanian Security; I had finally escaped their rapacious claws and I could taste for the first time being once again a free human being, in charge of my destiny. Aurel drove very fast and it didn't take long before we left the city behind us.

I could not tell where we were going as it was a dark night and all that I could see was the long stretch of road in front of us. Finally, after what seemed to be a long time, I asked Aurel where was he taking me.

"We are going to an old friend of mine, an Australian who has a orange orchard near a place called Mildura. He will take care of you for few days until your team leaves Melbourne, then Norman and I will come and bring you back to Melbourne."

He paused for a minute and then continued trying to reassure me

"You don't have to worry anymore about being caught by "our friends". They could never find where you are, and once they return to Romania, you can come out of hiding and stay with me and Noel until you get settled; We will look after you for as long as you need, and you can decide when the time comes what you are going to do."

It was getting lighter and I could see now the endless Australian countryside, and then I witnessed a glorious sunrise, something I had never experienced back home; It was as if the whole horizon was on fire and painted in most brilliant colours and shades of red and orange. Aurel looked at me from the corner of his eye and smiled:

"Great country Cornel, you will get used to it, you will love it. Just give yourself a little time and see what happens."

WHERE AM I?

We arrived at the farm sometime after 9 a.m. where we were greeted by a young man and his wife, who were obviously very much excited about my arrival. Aurel spoke to them in English and then he told me that he would go straight back to Melbourne to avoid any suspicion and that the people I was staying with would look after me; All I had to do was to ask them and they would do the rest. The next few days were a real test for me in that I could not communicate with my hosts, who could not speak French or German, and my English proved to be very shaky.

They made every possible effort to make me comfortable, and they looked after any small wish I indicated, but they were also aware that I was going through a very difficult stage. In the morning, the husband (I cannot remember their actual names at all) would take me with him and we would walk to the orchid filled with small orange trees, laden with sweet and juicy fruit. I should have been happy and enjoyed the new experience but to my surprise I started to doubt my actions and questioned the outcome of this act of rebellion.

Now that the excitement of the competition days and the escape from the village had been accomplished, I started to realize how little I was prepared for normal everyday living in a foreign country, unable to make myself understood with the exception of a very few simple essential things. I could not read the paper and did not understand the radio; I felt as though I'd been suddenly deported to a lonely island where I had no contact with the outside world. But the thing which started to really upset me was the realization of not going back to my family, that I would not see them for what could be a long time or perhaps never. Was I right in sacrificing my family, my sport and my career just to be free, or had I over-reacted and should have tried a little harder to put up with life under the Communists?

Of course I didn't have the answer in those days, I was too much involved, too close to the events to be able to analyze logically the best path to follow and it took a long time before I understood that my actions weren't totally the result of my will, and that somehow life pushed me along a path which probably I wouldn't have had the courage to take on my own.

But I was now physically removed, unable to contact anyone. It would have helped a lot if I could have talked to Norman or Aurel, but there was no phone in the house, so I was getting more anxious with every day closer to the 12th of December, the day when I knew that our Olympic Team would leave Melbourne on their way back home to Bucharest. But there was nothing I could do, I just had to go through a lot of mental anguish on my own, trying to cope with the situation.

Finally the day came when I knew that my team would be leaving in the morning, and I paced for hours inside my room, talking to myself, trying to calm myself down, on the verge of a complete mental collapse. I finally sat down on the bed and my eyes filled with tears of despair and sadness;

There was no going back and I had to say goodbye to everything I knew and loved in Romania.

DELAYED DEPARTURE AND MY NEW COUNTRY

Many years after these events took place, I was able to find out what happened after I left the village, how the Romanian officials tried to find out where I was but without success.

I was told that Muresanu in particular could not accept my defection from the team and was convinced that I was going to come back in time for the scheduled departure of the Romanian team.

In the meantime another two members of the Romanian team had left the village, one was the radio sports commentator Raul Bart, who had relatives in Israel and was planning to bring his mother out of Romania and settle in Jerusalem, the other was the Head Coach of the Romanian Athletic Team and Senior lecturer at the ICF, Ion Nicoara, who I believe had similar reasons to stay back in Australia as I had, total rejection and dislike of the Communists. So a total of seven members of our team defected:

Four water-polo players, one modern pentathlon athlete, one journalist, and a coach. While the Romanian officials tried to prevent at all cost any attempt by team members to escape, the Hungarian officials showed a much greater understanding of the political situation back home, where the Russian tanks had destroyed half of Budapest in a matter of days, and brutally crushed the demand for freedom by Hungarian students. The Hungarian athletes and officials were assembled by their Sport Minister and told that they could choose to stay in the free world or they could return to Hungary, as he was going to do. He understood how they all felt about the Russian domination and gave them a choice without any threat of penalty or repercussions on their families. They had some guts and dignity, unlike the Romanian officials who desperately continued to demand loyalty to a corrupt and vicious regime.

On the day of departure I paced furiously in my room realizing that there was no way back, that I was going to be left behind and that I had to fend for myself in a completely strange environment.

I was having second thoughts on my drastic action and questioned myself for perhaps acting out of uncontrolled hatred rather than logic, that perhaps I could have gone back and waited for another opportunity . . . no, I had to do it now, I reasoned, or I would have missed my last chance to escape to the free world.

I would have been a marked man for as long as I lived in Communist Romania: I had to do it and that was the inescapable reality. From now on I had to keep going right ahead without regrets, and build myself a new life in a new country, and apply to my ordinary life the same determination and attitude as I learned to do in the sport arena.

It was going to be hard, but it was going to be fair and not manipulated by corrupt leaders, I had the opportunity to live my life as a free citizen, to do all the things I only dreamed possible in my old country, I was going to succeed . . .

I left the room and walked out into the bright sun shining over the green orange trees laden with fruit. Everything looked fresh and alive. I was alive . . . had a new country.

I was free.

EPILOGUE

The Romanian Team delayed its departure for 30 minutes at the request of Muresanu, but finally the plane had to leave Essendon airport without any of the defectors returning.

The results achieved by the Romanian Pentathlon Team at their first Olympic attempt were unequalled, and our 6th place in the Team Event remained the highest by a Romanian team in Olympic competition.

Cornel's result in the Fencing event remained the highest score ever achieved in Olympic Competition covering the period of 1912 to year 2,012. It is possibly the longest record in the Olympic Games.

Cornel was not allowed to compete again in the Olympics because the rules of the Games in 1956 prevented men from competing for another country except for their country of origin. Interestingly this rule did not apply to females; They could compete for another country if they married a man who was a citizen of her new country.

In 1957 Cornel competed in the Australian Fencing Championship in Brisbane, and won the title of Australian Epee Champion, after which he decided to start coaching and settled in Melbourne.

1998, 42 years after the Melbourne Games, Cornel after many attempts finally received from the new Romanian Government, his Master of Sport Diploma for his results in Modern Pentathlon and was entered in the Romanian Hall of Champions as the First Romanian Modern Pentathlon Champion, and the first Romanian to win a Fencing event in Olympics Games.

1-06-1999,
Townsville, Australia.

Romanian gift to Melbourne Olympic Games

My first qualification fencing competition . (Bucharest)

Mr. Norman King, with Victor, Dumitru Tintea and Manciu.

Victor and self with the Russian Olympic Team.

UNION INTERNATIONALE DE PENTATHLON MODERNE

President : General Gustav Dyrssen (*Sweden*)
Secretary : Colonel Sven Thofelt (*Sweden*)

ADMINISTRATIVE COUNCIL AND JURY

Lt.-Colonel Hugh T. Paris (*U.S.A.*)
Lt.-Colonel O. Larkas (*Finland*)
G. Benedek (*Hungary*)
Dr. Marcello Garroni (*Italy*)
Colonel Manuel Valle Alvarado (*Mexico*)
Lt.-Colonel O. G. W. White (*Great Britain*)
General A. P. de Castro Filho (*Brazil*)

AMATEUR MODERN PENTATHLON UNION OF AUSTRALIA

President and Member of Jury : J. X. O'Driscoll
Honorary Secretary : W. McB. Williams

ARENA MANAGERS AND ASSISTANTS

W. A. Wheatland	.. *Equestrian*	N. Kayser	.. *Fencing*
C. Simpson	.. *Shooting*	W. Berge Phillips	.. *Swimming*
E. Ryall ..	.. *Running*	J. A. Noseda	.. *Chief Assistant*
E. Delzoppo	.. *Chief Timekeeper*	K. Campbell	.. *Horse Superintendent*
J. E. M. Hall	.. *Starter*	E. W. Best	.. *Course Superintendent*
B. Boskovic	.. *Chief Judge*	I. S. Eager	.. *Assistant Statistician*

Air Vice-Marshal A. M. Charlesworth .. *Chief Statistician*

XVI OLYMPIAD
MELBOURNE 1956

Cornel Adrian VENA,
Romanian Modern Pentathlon Champion,
Olympic representative and winner of the
Modern Pentathlon Fencing in a world record score
of 29 Vic.,1,111 points.
1956 Melbourne Australia.

Romanian Olympic Team marching in the Olympic stadium.

View of the Melbourne Olympic Stadium.

First event. Riding.

CORNEL COMPETING IN THE EQUESTRIAN RIDING EVENT
MELBOURNE 1956 OLYMPICS

Recovered after a fall and doing well.

Vena of Rumania (left) and Malta of Brazil.

Vena (Rumania) was a clear winner in the fencing with twenty-nine victories (1,111 points), from Korhonen (Finland), with twenty-five victories (963 points), and Moldrich (Hungary), with twenty-four victories (925 points). Fourth position was shared by Hall (Sweden), Benedek Hungary), Andre (U.S.A.) and Bódi (Hungary), with twenty-three victories (889 points).

Eight of those who ultimately finished in the first ten in the whole competition were in fact in the first ten in the fencing.

Hungary took first place in the teams' contest with 2,566 points ; U.S.S.R. and Rumania (each with 2,194 points) shared second place and U.S.A. and Finland (each with 2,008 points) shared fourth place. With two events concluded, U.S.A. maintained first place in the aggregate, but U.S.S.R. had moved into second place to lead Finland now by 141 points, while the order of the next five teams remained unchanged.

Second event. Fencing. Olympic Record.

The shooting in progress. From left : Ninrd (illustration). Photo O Rik's Kent (Rossman), at this time, Rosman and...

Third event. Pistol Shooting.

Hall (Sweden) splashes through a
creek on the cross-country course.

Running

The running event over 4,000 metres was held at Oaklands Hunt Club on Wednesday, 28th November, at 11 a.m., all the remaining thirty-six competitors taking part. The course, a testing cross-country run, was laid within the circuit covered in the riding event. Portion of the route lay across ploughed fields, while the runners had to follow the winding course of a small creek, which was crossed and re-crossed on four occasions, there being a difference of almost 50 metres (about 150 feet) in elevation between the lowest and highest points on the course. Comparison of times is difficult due to difference in courses, but it would appear that the performances have improved considerably. The standard time had been set at 15 minutes, for which 1,000 points were given, and for every second better or worse than that time three points were added or subtracted. Nineteen competitors bettered the standard time, while two others were within a few seconds of it. Six finished in 14 minutes or better. The best performance was registered by Cobley (Great Britain and Northern Ireland) who covered the course in 13 mins. 35 secs. ; Haase (Sweden) ran 13 mins. 48 secs. The three Russians, Deriuguine, Novikov, and Tarassov, were next in order, all bettering 14 minutes.

Main interest was centred in the question whether the two Finns, Mannonen and Korhonen, or the American, Lambert, could overtake the 1952 winner Hall. Hall in fact finished in eighth position in front of Korhonen, less than a second behind Mannonen, and within 13 seconds of the first of the Russians, so that his position at the head of the field was assured. Hall thus established the remarkable record of winning the modern pentathlon championship at the Games of two successive Olympiads.

Fifth event. Running.

Training after the games by myself.

INDIVIDUAL

Previous Oly

1912 G. M. Lillienhook .. *Sweden*
1920 G. P. W. Dyrssen .. *Sweden*
1924 B. S. G. Lindman .. *Sweden*
1928 S. A. Thofelt .. *Sweden*

There were 54 entries from 18 nations ;

| Place | Competitor | Country | Riding 23rd November | | | | | Fencing 24th November | | |
			Time	Time Score	Obstacle Faults	Points	Place	Victories	Points	Place
1	HALL, L.-G. I.	Sweden	9·46	1,035		1,035	4	23	889	4
2	MANNONEN, O. A.	Finland	10·01	997·5		997·5	5	21	815	8
3	KORHONEN, V. K.	Finland	9·58	1,005	120	885	9	25	963	2
4	Novikov, I.	U.S.S.R.	10·55	862·5	60	802·5	14	21	815	8
5	Lambert, G. H.	U.S.A.	9·32	1,070		1,070	1	17	667	17
6	Benedek, G.	Hungary	10·56	860		860	11	23	889	4
7	Andre, W. J.	U.S.A.	9·57	1,007·5	120	887·5	8	23	889	4
8	Tarassov, A.	U.S.S.R.	10·44	890	80	810	13	20	778	10
9	Deriuguine, I.	U.S.S.R.	11·02	845		845	12	14	556	26
10	Bódi, J.	Hungary	10·43	892·5	120	772·5	15	23	889	4
11	Riera, L. F.	Argentine	9·39	1,052·5		1,052·5	3	17	667	17
12	Pérez Mier, J.	Mexico	10·25	937·5		937·5	6	18	704	13
13	Daniels, J. T.	U.S.A.	9·35	1,062·5		1,062·5	2	9	371	36
14	Vena, C.	Rumania	13·11	522·5	80	442·5	22	29	1,111	1
15	Facchini, A.	Italy	11·41	747·5	80	667·5	17	17	667	17
16	Katter, B. L.	Finland	10·52	870	240	630	18	15	593	25
17	Haase, B.	Sweden	12·18	655	140	515	20	17	667	17
18	Cortes, G.	Chile	10·47	882·5		882·5	10	14	556	26
19	Sayers, N. M.	Australia	10·30	925		925	7	10	408	35
20	Tintea, D.	Rumania	11·29	777·5	60	717·5	16	17	667	17
21	Moldrich, A.	Hungary	14·10	375	280	95	30	24	926	3
22	Almada Félix, A.	Mexico	13·30	475	80	395	23	18	704	13
23	Cerny, V.	Czechoslovakia	14·27	332·5	200	132·5	29	14	556	26
24	Floody, N.	Chile	10·54	865	280	585	19	18	704	13
25	Cobley, D.	Gt. Britain and N. Ireland	12·02	695	380	315	25	12	482	32
26	Van Greunen, O. J.	South Africa	14·10	375	180	195	27	18	704	13
27	da Costa Lemos, S.	Brazil	13·38	455		455	21	14	556	26
28	Hudson, T.	Gt. Britain and N. Ireland	15·04	240	220	20	31	16	630	24
29	Romero Vargas, D.	Mexico	12·29	627·5	260	367·5	24	14	556	26
30	Teodorescu, V.	Rumania	18·10	0	180	0	33	19	741	11
31	Malta, W.	Brazil	14·31	322·5	860	0	33	19	741	11
32	Coomer, S. M.	Australia	15·46	135		135	-	28	482	32
33	Hamel, J. C.	France	14·49	277·5	80	197·5	26	17	667	17
34	Norman, G. R.	Gt. Britain and N. Ireland	17·16	0		0	33	17	667	17
35	Nicoll, G. T.	Australia	21·39	0	320	0	33	13	519	31
36	Schmidt, H. C.	South Africa	16·04	90	140	0	33	11	445	34
	Ferreira da Silva, N. J.	Brazil	14·49	277·5	260	17·5	32			
	Thofelt, B.	Sweden	18·40	0	140	0	33			
	Carmona, H.	Chile	Abandoned				33			
	du Plessis, M. J.	South Africa	Abandoned				33			

Final results of the Modern Pentathlon, 1956.

mpic Winners

1932	J. G. Oxenstierna	..	*Sweden*
1936	G. Handrick	..	*Germany*
1948	W. Grut	.. ..	*Sweden*
1952	L. Hall	.. ..	*Sweden*

40 participants from 16 nations.

Score After Two Events		Shooting 26th November			Score After Three Events		Swimming 27th November			Score After Four Events		Running 28th November			Final Scores	
Points	Place	Target Score	Points	Place	Points	Place	Time	Points	Place	Points	Place	Time	Points	Place	Points	Place
1,924	1	181	720	24	2,644	4	3·54·2	1,030	2	3,674	1	14·07·4	1,159	8	4,833	1
1,812·5	3	189	880	5	2,692·5	2	4·16·4	920	15	3,612·5	3	14·06·9	1,162	7	4,774·5	2
1,848	2	189	880	5	2,728	1	4·19·5	905	16	3,633	2	14·21	1,117	12	4,750	3
1,617·5	10	191	920	2	2,537·5	7	4·03·6	985	6	3,522·5	6	13·56·3	1,192	4	4,714·5	4
1,737	6	190	900	4	2,637	5	4·05·8	975	7	3,612	3	14·33·2	1,081	15	4,693	5
1,749	5	191	920	2	2,669	3	4·29·8	855	18	3,524	5	14·18·4	1,126	10	4,650	6
1,776·5	4	188	860	8	2,636·5	6	4·26·2	870	17	3,506·5	7	14·19·2	1,123	11	4,629·5	7
1,588	11	189	880	5	2,468	9	4·35	825	21	3,293	9	13·58·1	1,186	5	4,479	8
1,401	15	184	780	16	2,181	14	3·46·7	1,070	1	3,251	12	13·53·8	1,201	3	4,452	9
1,661·5	8	186	820	10	2,481·5	8	4·41·3	795	24	3,276·5	10	14·27·8	1,099	14	4,375·5	10
1,719·5	7	176	620	29	2,339·5	11	4·14·1	930	13	3,269·5	11	15·07	979	21	4,248·5	11
1,641·5	9	185	800	13	2,441·5	10	4·12·4	940	10	3,381·5	8	16·36	712	32	4,093·5	12
1,433·5	14	185	800	13	2,233·5	13	4·13·3	935	11	3,168·5	13	15·30·4	910	25	4,078·5	13
1,552·5	12	182	740	23	2,292·5	12	4·50·9	750	30	3,042·5	15	14·50·3	1,030	17	4,072·5	14
1,334·5	17	186	820	10	2,154·5	16	4·10·3	950	9	3,104·5	14	15·23·8	931	23	4,035·5	15
1,223	20	183	760	19	1,983	21	4·14·5	930	13	2,913	18	14·23·3	1,111	13	4,024	16
1,182	21	180	700	27	1,882	22	4·34·7	830	20	2,712	21	13·48·5	1,216	2	3,928	17
1,438·5	13	176	620	29	2,058·5	19	4·52·3	740	31	2,798·5	19	14·43·8	1,051	16	3,849·5	18
1,333	18	186	820	10	2,153	17	5·32	540	35	2,693	23	14·52·9	1,024	18	3,717	19
1,384·5	16	184	780	16	2,164·5	15	4·37	815	22	2,979·5	17	16·34·6	718	31	3,697·5	20
1,021	23	181	720	24	1,741	24	3·58·3	1,010	4	2,751	20	15·28·6	916	24	3,667	21
1,099	22	193	960	1	2,059	18	4·13·2	935	11	2,994	16	17·06·4	622	35	3,616	22
688·5	31	188	860	8	1,548·5	27	4·08·9	960	8	2,508·5	25	14·56·7	1,012	19	3,520·5	23
1,289	19	183	760	19	2,049	20	5·08·5	660	33	2,709	22	16·09·9	793	27	3,502	24
797	28	173	560	31	1,357	30	4·38·3	810	23	2,167	31	13·35·5	1,255	1	3,422	25
899	26	184	780	16	1,679	26	4·44·1	780	26	2,459	27	15·19·7	943	22	3,402	26
1,011	24	183	760	19	1,771	23	4·43·1	785	25	2,556	24	16·30·4	730	30	3,286	27
650	33	167	440	34	1,090	33	4·02	990	5	2,080	32	14·00·2	1,180	6	3,260	28
923·5	25	185	800	13	1,723·5	25	4·47·1	765	27	2,488·5	26	16·27·6	739	29	3,227·5	29
741	29	177	640	28	1,381	29	5·14·5	630	34	2,011	33	14·08·1	1,156	9	3,167	30
741	29	183	760	19	1,501	28	4·49·8	755	29	2,256	29	15·41·8	877	26	3,133	31
617	34	181	720	24	1,337	32	3·57·4	1,015	3	2,352	28	16·23·2	751	28	3,103	32
864·5	27	169	480	33	1,344·5	31	4·30	850	19	2,194·5	30	16·43·1	691	33	2,885·5	33
667	32	162	340	35	1,007	35	4·48·1	760	28	1,767	34	15·06·7	982	20	2,749	34
519	35	170	500	32	1,019	34	5·07·7	665	32	1,684	35	17·58·1	466	36	2,150	35
445	36	142	0	36	445	36	5·48·9	460	36	905	36	16·53·3	661	34	1,566	36

Final results of the Modern Pentathlon, 1956.

Last night at Mr. King's place before defecting.

Guard of honour for Paula and I in 1957.

Competing in the Veteran Modern Pentathlon.

Olympic Stadium 1986 with my coach, Colonel Ion Muresanu.

Teaching fencing in Melbourne.

Enjoying sport and freedom.

Burning ideals triumph

In 1956 Cornel Vena experienced the exhilaration of entering the Olympic Stadium in Melbourne as part of the Romanian team. He defected and 44 years later still believes in the Olympic ideal

Story by IAN FRAZER

CORNEL Vena still loves his old flame, despite warnings from wowsers who say she's sold her soul.

He survived this week in a state of anticipation, waiting for her to rap back into his life in a cloud of phosphorous and gunpowder, speeches, anthems and advertising.

No jealous lover, he happily shared the experience with 3.7 billion fellow TV viewers when she arrived at Stadium Australia, Sydney, last night.

Now he's ready for two weeks of simple pleasure — watching young athletes striving for excellence as he did 44 years ago at the Melbourne Games.

Cornel, 83, who represented Romania with distinction in the modern pentathlon at the 1956 Games and then defected to Australia, says he will be barracking for both countries.

"I've always felt nationalistic about Romania, but I am now following with interest, if not great interest, Australia," he said this week on his shady Townsville verandah in a home almost devoid of Olympic souvenirs.

Received Olympic Diploma after a long wait.

No. 1697

Congratulations

The Romanian Embassy
congratulates :

Mr Cornel Vena
on official receiving the title of
Master of Sport
(no. 5411 / 17.06.1997)
from the Romanian Government,
Ministry of Sports and Youths

Canberra **Ambassador**
10.09.1997 **Dr. Ioan Gâf-Deac**

Nominated as Master of Sport by Romanian Government.

Major medals won between 1950 and 1990

WORLD'S LONGEST RECORD IN THE MODERN OLYMPIC GAMES.
MELBOURNE 1956 TO LONDON 2012.
1,111 Points obtained by Cornel Vena of ROMANIA
the Fencing event of the MODERN PENTATHLON COMPETITION.

956, Romanian Team of Modern Pentathlon competed for the first time in Melbourne.
Team was made of: Cornel Vena, Victor Teodorescu and Dumitru Tintea with Manciu
:el as the team reserve.
e team has been formed in late 1953, members been selected through a national
thlon Competition held in Bucharest, and won by Cornel Vena.
charge of the team was Captain Ion Muresanu .
:out international competition experience, the Roumanian Team finished on the
place and individually Cornel Vena finished 14th, Dumitru Tintea 20th,. and Victor
dorescu 30th.
:markably ,in the fencing event, Cornel Vena won 29 bouts of the 35 matches and was
rded a total of 1,111 competition points.
result has not been equalled or beaten since 1956 and remains the longest record
ie history of the Modern Olympic Games.

MODERN PENTATHLON OLYMPIC FENCING RESULTS 1956-2012

YEAR	PLACE	WINNER	COUNTRY	No.Competitors	Points
1956	Melbourne	Cornel Vena	ROM	36	1,111
1960	ROME	Imre Nagy	HUN	58	1,000
1964	TOKIO	Ferenk Torok	HUN	37	1,000
1968	MEXICO	Istvan Molna	HUN	47	1,046
1972	Munich	@Ferenk Torok	HUN	47	1,046
		Boris Onischenko	RUS	59	1,076 (rigged epee)
1976	Montreal	Paul Ledniev	RUS	46	1,096
1980	Moscow	Lazlo Horvath	HUN	43	1,052
1984	Los Angeles	Achim Bellmann	GER	52	1,066
1988	Seoul	Fabian Lazlo	HUN	63	1,051
1992	Barcelona	Fabian Lazlo	HUN	66	1,034
1996	Atlanta	Alexandru Parygoin	KAZ	24	1,000
		@Heorny Chymerys	UKR	24	1,000
2000	Sydney	Oliver Clergeau	FRA	32	1,000

Record of the longest Olympic modern penthatlon-fencing results.

My beautiful family: Paula, Hayley, Shari and Christy.

I wished to fly, but I had to learn other things first.